D0891539

Contents

Manufacturing Management

Principles and concepts

P. Gibson

Bond University
Queensland
Australia

G. Greenhalgh

PA Consulting Group
Sydney
Australia

and

R. Kerr

The University of New South Wales
Sydney
Australia

 **CHAPMAN & HALL**

London · Glasgow · Weinheim · New York · Tokyo · Melbourne · Madras

**Published by Chapman & Hall, 2–6 Boundary Row, London
SE1 8HN, UK**

Chapman & Hall, 2–6 Boundary Row, London SE1 8HN, UK

Blackie Academic & Professional, Wester Cleddens Road, Bishopbriggs,
Glasgow G64 2NZ, UK

Chapman & Hall GmbH, Pappelallee 3, 69469 Weinheim, Germany

Chapman & Hall USA, 115 Fifth Avenue, New York, NY 10003, USA

Chapman & Hall Japan, ITP-Japan, Kyowa Building, 3F, 2-2-1
Hirakawacho, Chiyoda-ku, Tokyo 102, Japan

Chapman & Hall Australia, 102 Dodds Street, South Melbourne, Victoria
3205, Australia

Chapman & Hall India, R. Seshadri, 32 Second Main Road, CIT East,
Madras 600 035, India

First edition 1995

© 1995 P. Gibson, G. Greenhalgh and R. Kerr

Typeset in 10/12pt Times by Best-set Typesetter Ltd., Hong Kong
Printed in Great Britain by TJ Press (Padstow) Ltd., Padstow, Cornwall

ISBN 0 412 37370 X

A catalogue record for this book is available from the British Library

♾ Printed on permanent acid-free text paper, manufactured in accordance with ANSI/
NISO Z39.48-1992 and ANSI/NISO Z39.48-1984 (Permanence of Paper).

Preface

This book is intended to provide an overview of the current key issues facing manufacturing managers today. The approach, in line with modern strategies in manufacturing business, has been to integrate the issues with the aim of allowing the reader to obtain a solid grasp of the total business, and understand that the effective and efficient adding of value is the key to business success. It is stressed throughout that the value adding process should be oriented towards the customer, and that the activities associated with the value chain are the links through a manufacturing organization that can be used create a competitive advantage.

There has recently been what might be termed a revolution in fundamental ways of thinking about manufacturing management. This has received its impetus mainly from the Japanese attention to the systematic elimination of all forms of manufacturing activities that do not add value to the product. The use by the Japanese of revolutionary manufacturing management techniques to create competitive advantage in an increasingly global market has forced the Western world to rethink how manufacturing management is both taught and practised.

As an example, one result of this revolution has been the much greater emphasis on the simplification of production set-ups and the smoothing of materials flow through the factory. This is associated with minimal in-process inventories and quality control at source by the systematic elimination of defects in products, production processes and management systems that lead to poor quality. Poor quality must be eliminated not just from the product itself but from all aspects of the organization's activities in so far as these affect its ability to compete effectively. A further trend is towards what has been termed 'time-based competition' in which time to market of new products and rapid delivery of existing products are increasingly important metrics of performance. This requires close collaboration between marketing people, design and production engineers to develop rapidly products which genuinely satisfy customer needs, are easy to manufacture and can be produced with very short cycle times. Customers have come to demand and expect greatly increased degrees of product variety and customized 'specials' and the current challenge is to supply this variety at comparable cost and quality levels to those achievable for high volume products.

The intention of this book is to provide an introduction to the techniques of modern manufacturing management in a pragmatic way that can be easily related to the reality of modern manufacturing environments. However, the book also places strong emphasis on underlying concepts and principles, and how these have been influenced by evolving views of the different operational ways in which a company can meet its strategic objectives. Various 'buzzwords' such as Total Quality Management (TQM), Value Adding Management (VAM), Manufacturing Resources Planning (MRP 2), Just-in-Time Production (JIT) and the Theory of Constraints (TOC) are shown to be special cases of the application of these more general principles, and the internal and external conditions under which each is most relevant are clearly demonstrated. This book is not intended to provide detailed comprehensive training in manufacturing management techniques. Rather it is intended to provide an overview of the underlying principles and issues behind these techniques. Where it has been felt that an understanding of a specific technique is important in the grasping of the principles behind the technique, the technique itself has been presented in a simplified form.

The book is organized into four main sections.

PART ONE CORE CONCEPTS

The first two chapters give a systemic view of the manufacturing organization as it operates within the wider environment, and how the internal operations of the organization need to be managed in a general sense for it to be competitive in this wider environment. The dynamics of competition within different industry groups is examined, as is product differentiation and the basis for achieving competitive advantage within a group. The performance criteria thus established are examined from the point of view of their operational implications, and the concepts of value added, waste and total quality are examined. This first section concludes with a discussion of the simultaneous consideration of product design and process planning to meet market requirements with ease of manufacture, acceptable process variability and rationalized materials flow.

PART TWO THE MAJOR INTERNAL MANUFACTURING MANAGEMENT FUNCTIONS

The next group of chapters (3–8) looks in more detail at the internal manufacturing management functions of ensuring a coordinated flow of materials through the manufacturing plant from the time of their arrival in store to the time of their shipment in the form of finished products. This section starts with an examination of the key issues relating to the dynamics of materials flow through a multi-product, multi-stage manufacturing organization and the practical problems of the coordinated planning and control of this flow to meet a given external demand (including the role of inventory, centralized vs decentralized planning and control, pull vs push systems of production, and the significance of bottlenecks and process variability for materials flow).

The next four chapters take a systematic look at hierarchical production planning techniques, how a long-term aggregate forecast demand is progressively broken down over shorter timescales and greater degrees of detail into the master production schedule for end products, how this master production schedule can be translated into detailed shopfloor production requirements, and how the satisfaction of these requirements can be executed. In particular, the three major production management techniques of MRP 2, synchronous manufacturing and JIT are examined and compared, and we see how a manufacturing company can set about deliberately restructuring its operations to take advantage of JIT techniques. The section concludes with an examination of modern maintenance management techniques to emphasize the increasing importance of what is termed 'total productive maintenance' in ensuring a high velocity of materials flow through the organization.

PART THREE   MANAGING THE LOGISTICS INTERFACES

The third section (Chapters 9–10) looks at the management of the main interfaces as far as materials flow is concerned. The purchasing function, modern approaches to vendor selection and management of quality assurance are all examined. This section also looks at the management of physical distribution and how a systemic view of this is needed in order to integrate it with the other activities of the organization.

PART FOUR   GLOBAL ISSUES

The final chapters (11–13) move away from a detailed consideration of the individual manufacturing management functions back to a more in-depth consideration of some of the global issues that were foreshadowed in the first section and which pervade every aspect of manufacturing management. The subject of total quality management is examined with reference to a number of specific tools and techniques with which it can be implemented across all the functions of a company. The problems associated with developing and implementing an effective manufacturing strategy are examined in the light of the material that has been presented up to this point, and the establishment of manufacturing performance measures that act in such a way as to bring the organization's behaviour in line with stated goals is also discussed.

This book will not enable readers to go out and immediately apply the principles as practising manufacturing managers. It will instead help them to appreciate the common philosophical underpinnings of the techniques and to understand the changes to attitudes and work practices that will be required to generate a climate for the application of such techniques. Further, the book should enable readers to evaluate the techniques themselves on a comparative basis in terms of applicability to the specifics of individual organizations.

PART ONE
Core Concepts

PART ONE

Core Concept

Dynamics of industrial competition

1

1.1 OVERVIEW

This chapter is designed to assist the reader understand the broader context in which manufacturing must exist. Competition determines the success or failure of organizations. Within any given industry the competing firms carry out their strategy which may be explicit or implicit. An explicit strategy is the product of a formal strategic planning process and will usually be in the form of a written document. An implicit strategy is one which has arisen over time through a series of decisions and associated activities. It is not normally formalized into a written document.

Traditionally the designers and managers of systems of production management have paid little attention to the need to ensure that the systems enhance the capability of the business to compete. Today there is continuing debate as to the merits or otherwise of the various approaches to managing manufacturing. Rarely has a broad, business-based view been taken. For example, teaching institutions have tended to present manufacturing systems with a bias towards MRP 2 and have treated JIT, OPT, etc., as emerging technologies. The consulting profession, in the main, have pedalled one particular approach to the exclusion of the others. In short, readers and managers alike have had little guidance as to how to evaluate the available technologies and how to ensure they resolve real business issues.

In this chapter we will be looking at the fundamental factors determining the nature of competition, the three generic competitive strategies and the implications for manufacturing.

Specifically, on completing the chapter readers should be able to:

- use Porter's model to describe an industry of their choice;
- describe, explain and use the value chain concept;
- understand and use the three generic bases for competition;

- understand the problems in pursuing multiple strategies;
- understand and use the concept of oligopoly market structures;
- understand and use the concept of key success factors for a specific industry;
- understand and use the concept of sustainable competitive advantage;
- be able to describe some of the implications of industry dynamics for manufacturing

1.2 CHAPTER STRUCTURE

This first chapter concerning the dynamics of industrial competition is divided into the following sections:

- Porter's model of industry structure;
- the value chain;
- generic competitive strategies;
- pursuit of more than one generic strategy;
- trends in generic strategies;
- market structure and competitive position;
- key success factors;
- sustainable competitive advantage;
- implications for manufacturing.

The chapter starts by describing Porter's model of the forces driving industry competition and the use of the model to determine power relationships and threats to the business. From here we move on to consider Porter's concept of the value chain, a powerful means to describe the firm in terms of its value adding activities and how they may be used to identify sources of competitive advantage.

We then move on to examine the three generic strategies, namely cost leadership, differentiation and focus.

Having described the problems in attempting to pursue multiple strategies we identify an important evolutionary trend displayed by successful companies, led by the Japanese, in moving towards 'time-based' and 'flexibility-based' forms of competition.

Some substructures of oligopolistic competition and their importance in determining a strategy for the firm are then addressed, followed by a description of key success factors and their link with the value chain. An important additional issue is that of the sustainability of a competitive advantage, and how sustainable strategies can differ for cost leadership and differentiation.

The chapter concludes with a description of the relationship between industry structure, business strategy, competitive advantage and manufacturing strategy.

1.3 PORTER'S MODEL OF INDUSTRY STRUCTURE

Michael Porter (1980) has developed a model of the forces driving industry competition. This model is based on the fact that industry in general consists of a **network** of organizations each of which performs a part of the process of converting primary raw materials (e.g. minerals extracted from the ground) into consumer products (e.g. cars or washing machines). The organizations in the network act as customers and suppliers of each other as shown in Fig. 1.1. Different organizations within this network which deal with similar types of product or raw material may be grouped together in **industries**. Within a particular industry there may thus be many competitors for market share. Also, the customer–supplier relationships operating between organizations in different industries means that the activities and performance of any single organization cannot be analysed in isolation but only in the context of the organization's position in this network. In particular, Porter's model asserts that the profitability of a particular industry, and therefore its attractiveness, will be determined as the product of five 'forces' operating on and within that industry, as shown diagrammatically in Fig. 1.2.

The five forces depicted in the model determine the profitability of the industry because together they influence prices, costs and the amount of investment necessary. The relative influence of the five forces depicted above may vary over time.

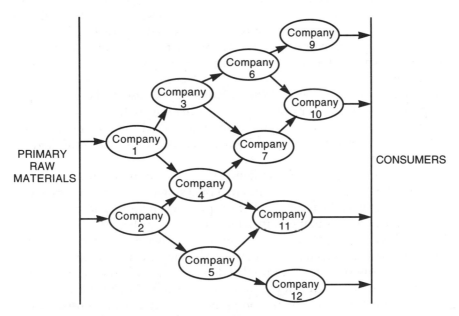

Fig. 1.1 Organizational network.

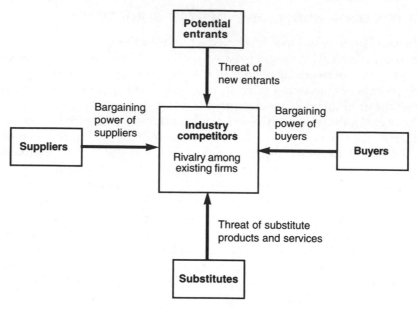

Fig. 1.2 Porter's model.

Buyer power and the threat of substitution both influence the price that firms may charge for goods and services. Strong buyers (e.g. a buyer who dominates the sales of a particular industry, who could easily go elsewhere for its source of supply, or who poses a threat of backward integration by self-manufacturing the product in question) can attempt to force down prices and also play competitors against each other. Powerful buyers may also influence costs and levels of investment through demands for higher service. Threat of substitute products (i.e. other types of product that can perform the same function as the product of the industry, such as plastic liquid containers which can in many cases fulfil the same function as glass bottles) can often only be countered by price-cutting.

The bargaining power of suppliers influences the costs of raw materials. A particular industry that is dominated by a single supplier is particularly vulnerable to price increases by that supplier when no alternative supplier is available. Other situations in which strong supplier power exists are those where the supplier could easily use 'forward integration' to take over the further conversion activities performed by its customers.

The intensity of competitor rivalry determines to a large extent pricing structures as does the threat posed by new entrants. High rivalry between a small number of dominant competitors (as in the car industry) can manifest itself in the form of price wars which can erode profitability.

New entrants to an industry, who may have developed superior technology or may have access to more distribution channels for the product, can also lead to price-cutting which can reduce industry profitability.

An organization often does not have unrestricted choice as to the industry in which it should operate. Most firms, particularly those operating in capital intensive industries (e.g. steelmaking), have a substantial investment in infrastructure both in terms of technology and human expertise which can mean prohibitively high 'switching costs' if they wish to make a short-term change of industry. Although long-term industry changes are possible – and even in many cases essential in order to get out of industries in decline – (e.g. a change from manufacture of records to manufacture of compact discs) – in the shorter term most organizations are 'stuck' within the industry that historical events have determined they should find themselves at that particular point of time, and are therefore consigned to making the best of their situation.

The ability to make the best of one's situation can be enhanced by attempting to understand the nature of the five forces and to manage them to one's advantage rather than merely to be at their mercy. In a sense the forces govern the 'rules' by which organizations may compete and an understanding of their nature for a particular industry will assist in the development of an appropriate strategy for the individual business. In turn this will influence the choice and application of particular systems of production management. The link between the forces in a particular industry and the choice of production management system in a given organization is the **business strategy**. The business strategy describes how the organization will compete given the realities of the market and the forces affecting it. The **manufacturing strategy**, which should be designed to support the business strategy, will then derive the framework on which decisions on production management systems may be based.

The most important implication of Porter's model is that firms should attempt to influence the balance of forces through strategic moves and thereby strengthen the firm's position. An example of this is in the pharmaceutical industry when one manufacturer reduced the power of wholesalers by deciding to distribute direct to many pharmacies – a decision with significant cost, service and production management systems implications. Another approach would be to reposition the firm to defend itself against negative forces. Examples of this include backward and forward integration where the organization acquires key supply or distribution businesses. A further alternative might be to predict or anticipate the significant shifts in the forces and deliberately exploit them in order to gain an advantage. Swiss watchmakers, having suffered a decline with the advent of digital watches, have made a comeback through the introduction of high value added 'dress watches' – a situation made possible because digital watches became so cheap.

It should be pointed out that while Porter's model provides an excellent basis for viewing the dynamics of an industry, it does not include environmental forces external to the industry. This may appear to be an unfair criticism given the seemingly infinite number of possible environmental forces. However, it is possible to simplify the problem by grouping the forces under useful headings. The most commonly used are:

1. **economic**: usually referring to the macro- and microeconomic situation within the particular country concerned;
2. **legal**: this refers to current or future legislation which might impinge on the firm's activities;
3. **technological**: this force is particularly potent because of the possibility of a product being rendered obsolete within a very short time;
4. **social**: this refers to the changes in the way individuals and communities carry out their activities and the values and beliefs they hold;
5. **global**: such forces are of increasing importance due to the rise of international trade and competition.

1.4 THE VALUE CHAIN

Manufacturing is concerned with the process of 'adding value' to raw materials by converting them to finished products which are worth more to customers than the unprocessed materials, and which can therefore be sold at a higher price. The profit to the manufacturer is the revenue from goods sold, less the cost of raw materials and the cost of adding value to these raw materials through the conversion process. Within a given manufacturing company, there will be many different types of activity that add value to the product, either directly or indirectly. These may be represented by a construct known as the **value chain**.

Figures 1.3 and 1.4 are taken from Porter (1985) and represent the generic value chain for a firm and a specific value chain for a copier manufacturer. Every firm is a collection of activities that are performed to design, produce, market, deliver and support its product. These activities can be represented using the value chain – a diagram showing the steps in the value-adding process and how they are linked together. The chain, then, is a diagram of the value-adding activities. Porter draws a distinction between 'primary' and 'support' activities within the value chain. The **primary activities** are the most obvious value-adding activities because they are part of the physical process of converting raw materials into saleable product, the physical logistics of ensuring a flow of materials through the factory and out to customers, and the sales and marketing activities involved in making customers aware of the products the firm is selling. The **support activities**, such as the development of new technol-

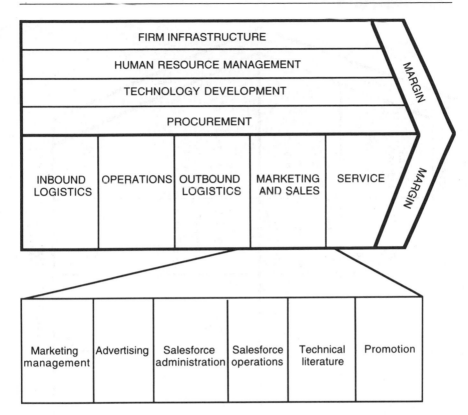

Fig. 1.3 The value chain.

ogies or new information systems, are important because they provide the necessary reinforcement or assistance which allow the primary activities to function smoothly over time and to increase the degree of competitiveness of the organization.

Porter also identifies three activity types that may be present in either primary or support activities. These are:

1. **direct** activities which are directly concerned with adding value to the product (e.g. product design, fabrication, assembly, etc.);
2. **indirect** activities that make it possible to perform direct activities on a continuing basis such as production scheduling, financial administration, etc.;
3. **quality assurance** activities which ensure the quality and conformance to standards of other activities, and may include inspecting, testing or reworking.

These three types of activity are present in both primary and support activities. For example, the physical machining of a part is a direct

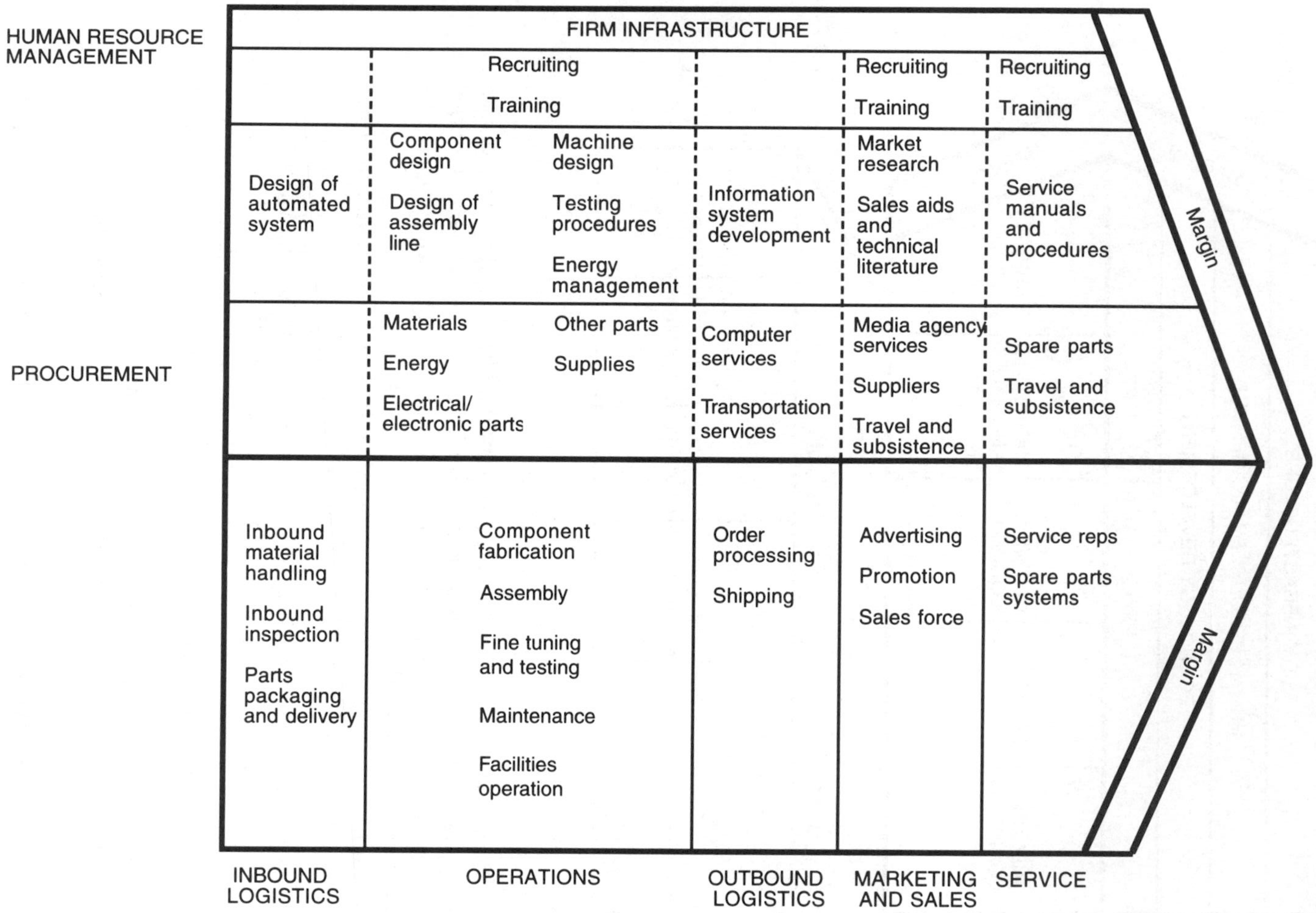

Fig. 1.4 Value chain for a copier manufacturer.

	INBOUND LOGISTICS	OPERATIONS	OUTBOUND LOGISTICS	MARKETING AND SALES	SERVICE
FIRM INFRASTRUCTURE					
HUMAN RESOURCE MANAGEMENT		Recruiting / Training		Recruiting / Training	Recruiting / Training
(Technology development)	Design of automated system	Component design, Design of assembly line, Machine design, Testing procedures, Energy management	Information system development	Market research, Sales aids and technical literature	Service manuals and procedures
PROCUREMENT	Materials, Energy, Electrical/electronic parts	Other parts, Supplies	Computer services, Transportation services	Media agency services, Suppliers, Travel and subsistence	Spare parts, Travel and subsistence
(Primary activities)	Inbound material handling, Inbound inspection, Parts packaging and delivery	Component fabrication, Assembly, Fine tuning and testing, Maintenance, Facilities operation	Order processing, Shipping	Advertising, Promotion, Sales force	Service reps, Spare parts systems

Margin

primary activity as it adds value directly to the product, whereas the setting up of a machine is an indirect primary activity as it does not directly add value. Similarly, product design is a direct support activity which directly adds value to the product, whereas the administration of the design department is an indirect support activity.

The value chain is not a set of independent activities but rather a system of linked, interdependent activities, in which the way in which one activity is performed can affect the cost or efficiency of other activities. For example, purchase of superior raw materials can result in reduced scrap in fabrication. Advertising and promotional campaigns can be timed to coincide with periods of spare capacity, etc. Effective linkages in the value chain can promote good coordination between different activities which can itself be a source of competitive advantage.

Firms within a given industry will have similar value chains but there will be important differences reflecting the individual firm's history, strategy, its approach to implementation, its management style and so on. These differences can represent important sources of competitive advantage, and an analysis of an organization's value chain can assist in identifying sources of competitive advantage. For example, firms placing emphasis on improving the 'service' section of the value chain will be competing differently to those emphasizing the 'operations' section. But competitive advantage depends not only on the value chain of the organization but also on the value chain of its customers. An understanding of the customer's value chain allows the organization to ensure a proper fit with its own value chain and to identify unique customer requirements that will enable the organization to differentiate itself from its competitors. For example, if analysis of a customer value chain indicates that attention is being focused by the customer on on-time delivery to his own customers as his own source of competitive advantage, then reliability of supply to that particular customer would clearly represent a better 'fit' to that customer's value chain than would a lower cost product supplied erratically.

Depending on the nature of the industry any one of the activities may provide an advantage if it can be carried out more cost effectively or in a superior manner compared with competitors. For example, outbound logistics is important in the confectionery industry (product has to be available at as many outlets as possible), less so for mainframe computers.

Support activities are also a potential source of competitive advantage; for example, the software houses such as Microsoft are heavily dependent on the quality of their people – the human resources. Technology in terms of new products is an obvious source of competitive advantage but so are less obvious applications such as the use of information technology for sales order placement on the customer's premises.

Every activity that occurs in a firm should be captured and placed in its appropriate position in the value chain. Questions can then be asked such as 'In what way is this particular activity adding value to the product?' or 'How could this activity be redefined or redesigned in such a way as to become a greater source of competitive advantage?'

1.5 GENERIC COMPETITIVE STRATEGIES

Having determined the dynamics of the industry and examined a firm's value chain, it is necessary to decide what the firm's competitive position will (or should) be in that industry. This strategic positioning governs whether the firm's profitability will be greater or less than the industry average. The correct choice here can provide relatively high financial performance even though the industry itself might be considered unfavourable.

Porter has categorized three generic bases for competition, namely overall cost leadership (being the lowest cost producer and therefore able to offer the lowest prices), differentiation (offering some particular feature such as higher quality or service for which the customer will be prepared to pay extra) and focus (specializing in the particular needs of a specific group of customers). These are shown in Fig. 1.5.

1.5.1 OVERALL COST LEADERSHIP

Cost leadership normally applies to commodity products, since more specialized products and services with a strong differentiation generally have additional operating requirements which add to the total cost. Competing on the basis of being the lowest cost producer usually translates into higher profit margins but it should not imply poor quality or service. The lowest cost producer in any industry must remain within 'striking'

		Source of competitive advantage	
		Unique value as perceived by customer	Lowest cost
Strategic scope	Broad (industry wide)	OVERALL DIFFERENTIATION	OVERALL COST LEADERSHIP
	Narrow (segment only)	FOCUSED DIFFERENTIATION	FOCUSED COST LEADERSHIP

Fig. 1.5 Generic competitive strategies. (After Reimann, 1987.)

distance of the leaders in terms of quality and customer service. Overall cost leadership generally means high stock availability (but not high stock levels) since by definition there is no differentiating factor. When stockouts occur customers are able to go to an alternative producer of the commodity.

A low cost position tends to protect the firm from all five competitive forces. The cost leader has a greater margin and is therefore able better to cope with cost increases from powerful suppliers. The low cost position is a good defence against substitute products and services and where high capital investment is used to achieve low costs it also acts as a barrier to entry by others. Finally customer power is offset to the extent that prices can only be reduced to the level of the most efficient producer. However, a decision to become cost leader means being **the** cost leader. Where more than one firm attempts to be cost leader the result on profitability is usually unfavourable as the firms fight to maintain market share through cuts.

The sources of cost advantage vary somewhat with industry but may include:

- no-frills product;
- product design;
- favourable access to raw material;
- location advantage;
- production process innovation;
- automation;
- proprietary technology.

1.5.2 DIFFERENTIATION

Meaningful differentiation means being visibly superior or significantly different to competitors in some aspect of the business that has value for the customer, who therefore is willing to pay a price premium. A differentiator will achieve above-average performance if its price premium exceeds the additional costs of being unique. For this reason a differentiator cannot ignore its cost position since the positive impact of its premium pricing will be eroded if costs get out of control. The most commonly cited examples include superior product quality and superior service. The important point about differentiation is that it must be something of direct importance to customers. There are of course many other potential forms of differentiation. Some of these are:

- product range variety;
- unique product features;
- product reliability;
- distribution channels;

- flexible response;
- additional services;
- stock availability;
- technical service;
- brand name;
- delivery time.

A differentiation strategy also protects a firm against the five forces of competition, but in a very different way than low cost. Its price premium improves its capability to deal with input cost increases. Customer power is reduced because users lack a comparable alternative, and will therefore be less price sensitive. The customer loyalty and brand preference exacted by a differentiated product act as natural barriers to entry. The threat from substitutes is also greatly reduced by a product that is perceived as unique in some way. A differentiation strategy provides direct protection against competitive rivalry by reducing users' price sensitivity.

Differentiation can also put a cap on a firm's potential market share, since the number of customers valuing certain unique or exclusive attributes may be limited. Often differentiation means a tradeoff with costs, especially if it is achieved by expensive means such as R&D, high-quality inputs, customer service or sophisticated information technology.

1.5.3 FOCUS

Competitive strategies based on cost leadership or differentiation assume that the organization will compete on an industry-wide basis. A strategy based on focus means that the organization has selected a particular segment, that is customer group, a geographic area or perhaps a particular product line, and meets the needs of the relevant customers in a way that is both valuable to the customers and difficult for competitors servicing the entire industry to emulate. A focus strategy has two variants: **cost focus** if the firm pursues cost leadership within its target segment; **differentiation focus** if the firm seeks to be unique in its chosen segment. A focus strategy will only be successful if there are some fundamental differences between segments. The idea of focus strategy is similar to the 'niche' strategy found in textbooks on marketing.

1.6 PURSUIT OF MORE THAN ONE GENERIC STRATEGY

The organizational requirements of the different strategies are not the same. Given this, it is extremely difficult for a single firm to pursue all three generic strategies at the same time. Even if it is possible, a major constraint would be the amount of resources required for implementation. Usually a firm must make a choice or it will become 'stuck in the middle' – and a firm that fails to carry out a specific strategy is often indeed 'stuck in the middle'. This generally is a result of the firm trying to do everything, that is be the lowest cost producer, provide a number of forms of differentiation and at the same time focus on various different market segments. The usual outcome of being stuck in the middle is average financial performance compared with others in the industry.

This does not mean it is impossible to combine one generic strategy with another. Firms that rely on differentiation are often able to drive costs down relative to competitors through the application of, for example, total quality management. These firms may not become **the** lowest cost competitor but they do achieve a low cost position which translates into higher margins. In a similar way the cost leader may develop some forms of differentiation, particularly relative to competitors, that is when the truly differentiated competitors are weak in some aspect of their business. This leads us to Porter's three conditions under which a firm can simultaneously achieve both cost leadership and differentiation:

• when competitors are stuck in the middle;
• when cost is strongly influenced by market share;
• when a firm pioneers a major innovation.

1.7 TRENDS IN GENERIC STRATEGIES

There has been a tendency for the most successful companies to evolve in a rather similar fashion in terms of how they have moved over time from one generic strategy to another. Discernible differences in this trend also, however, exist between Japanese and Western companies. These trends are illustrated in Fig. 1.6.

In the 1960s most companies worldwide were concerned with competing on the basis of cost. As a result, performance measures and improve-

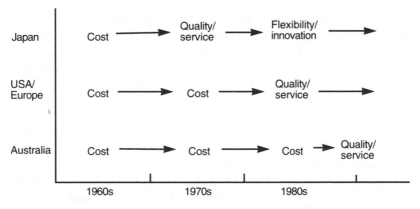

Fig. 1.6 Trends in competitive strategies.

ment programmes were almost all related to achieving efficiencies and cost reductions. However, starting in the 1970s a number of Japanese companies started to target quality as their dominant basis of competitive advantage and this continued with gathered momentum into the 1980s whilst Western companies were still predominantly targeting cost. During the course of the 1980s Western companies realized that the Japanese were starting to produce superior quality products at equal or lower costs, and so started turning the major focus of their attention to quality improvement programmes. In the meantime, however, the Japanese had turned their attention to flexibility and delivery time as their main competitive thrust. In the 1990s, Japanese companies are making increasing progress towards the ideal of 'one-of-a-kind production' (OKP), in which individual, highly customized products are manufactured with little or no cost premium, and time-based competiveness, in which such customized products can be both designed and produced with very short lead times. Thus time-to-market of new products and number of new product introductions per month are becoming increasingly important measures of competitiveness for such companies. The West has only recently started to pursue these concepts as many Western companies are still grappling with quality problems.

1.8 MARKET STRUCTURE AND COMPETITIVE POSITION

A firm's competitive position and the market structure in which it operates is a major determinant of the selected strategy and the results of that strategy. Most industries are **oligopolies**, meaning that the market is controlled by a few large producers with a small portion of market share being accounted for by a larger number of smaller firms. There are a number of substructures of oligopoly which are relevant to competitive strategy.

- **Monopoly dominance** refers to a market structure in which one firm has a very large share of the market, while all other oligopoly firms each have a much smaller share. In this market structure the dominant firm will tend to lead changes in the level of pricing. An example of this dominance is BHP in the Australian steel industry.
- **Joint dominance** or **duopoly** refers to a structure in which two companies jointly dominate a market while all other competitors as a group have a small market share. In this situation the two dominant firms primarily react to each other's strategy. Until deregulation the Australian domestic airline industry was an example of a duopoly.
- **Oligopoly dominance** refers to a structure in which the dominant firm has a much smaller share advantage over its next competitor than is the

case with monopoly dominance. In this case the dominant firm's position is more easily challenged by other oligopolists. The car rental market is an example of this.

- **Equal oligopoly** refers to a market structure in which no firm has clear dominance. In such markets competitive behaviour is difficult to predict.

1.9 KEY SUCCESS FACTORS

In any industry there are certain things which an organization must have or do well in order for it to survive over the longer term. These things are termed **key success factors** for the industry. Key success factors are not necessarily the same as the bases for competing, although they are clearly sources for competitive advantage. The value chain is a useful analytical tool to identify the key success factors for an industry. Some examples of key success factors are:

- economies of scale in manufacturing – shipbuilding, steelmaking;
- economies of scale in distribution – beer industry;
- owning large forests/yields – timber industry;
- control of servicing costs – elevator industry;
- product range/variety – department stores;
- design – aircraft industry;
- raw material sourcing – petroleum;
- salesforce – cars;
- refrigeration capacity – ice cream.

As a general rule there are only a few key success factors for any particular industry. Note that the key success factors impact on different functions for different industries.

1.10 SUSTAINABLE COMPETITIVE ADVANTAGE

A primary aim for organizations is to identify business advantages over competitors that are sustainable, that is which will not be imitated by competitors or eroded by industry changes. To maintain cost leadership, for example, the organization must find or develop sources of cost advantages. Although these sources will vary from industry to industry some tend to be more sustainable than others. Porter (1985) provides some examples:

- **economies of scale** – because the cost of replicating scale is high and because market share must be 'bought';
- **interrelationships across business units** – these can force a competitor

to diversify to match a cost advantage. If entry barriers also exist then sustainability can be very high;

- **linkages** – these are often difficult for competitors to detect because they require coordination across organizational lines;
- **proprietary learning** – although difficult to achieve in practice it is equally difficult for competitors to emulate;
- **proprietary products and processes**.

Clearly the sustainability of cost leadership will be even greater if a number of sources of cost advantage are utilized.

According to Porter the sustainability of differentiation depends on customers continuing to see value and the inability of competitors to emulate the differentiation. Multiple sources of differentiation are very powerful as is a form of differentiation that also provides a cost advantage. Differentiation will be more sustainable under the following conditions:

- the sources of uniqueness involve barriers such as proprietary learning, linkages, interrelationships and advertising;
- the firm has a cost advantage in differentiating;
- the sources of differentiation are multiple;
- a firm creates switching costs at the time it differentiates. Switching costs grow out of the way the product is used by the buyer.

1.11 CONCLUSIONS AND IMPLICATIONS FOR MANUFACTURING

What does all of the above mean for manufacturing and manufacturing systems? The diagram in Fig. 1.7 is a useful way to represent the relationship between industry dynamics and manufacturing. The implications for manufacturing will become clearer as the reader progresses through this book. In general there are five implications which may be summarized as follows.

- The manufacturing strategy must support the business strategy.
- The chosen basis for competing must be translated into meaningful issues for manufacturing to address.
- Where manufacturing is required to 'deliver' the basis for competing (e.g. product quality, delivery service) the manufacturing strategy must develop goals, strategies and implementation plans which provide the organization with a sustainable business advantage over its competitors.
- Where relevant the manufacturing strategy must recognize the key success factors for the industry.
- The manufacturing systems must explicitly recognize and support

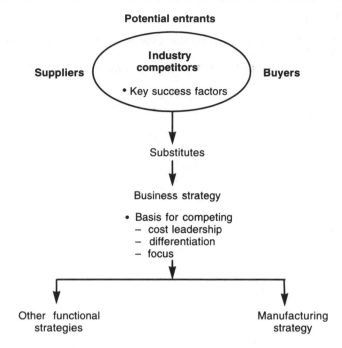

Fig. 1.7 Implications of business strategy for manufacturing strategy.

what the business generally and manufacturing in particular is trying to achieve.

In the past, many manufacturing companies have had a relatively well-defined business strategy, but this has not been translated into any meaningful manufacturing strategy that has had direct implications for what happens at shopfloor level. Factors that discriminate between good and bad performance of the individual functions within the value chain are those which motivate shopfloor activity. These have often tended to be the same (and frequently oriented solely towards cost reduction), regardless of what strategy the company is pursuing. To achieve a 'fit' between the declared strategy and what actually occurs on the shop floor requires careful analysis and consideration of the issues outlined above. These must be adequately reflected in the systems which are designed to plan and control daily shopfloor operations, as will be apparent throughout the remainder of this book.

REFERENCES

Porter, M.E. (1980) *Competitive Strategy*. The Free Press, New York.
Porter, M.E. (1985) *Competitive Advantage*. The Free Press, New York.
Reimann, B.C. (1987) *Managing for Value*. The Planning Forum. Oxford, Ohio.

FURTHER READING

Buffa, E.S. (1984) *Meeting the Competitive Challenge*. Dow Jones-Irwin, Homewood, Illinois.
Ohmae, K. (1982) *The Mind of the Strategist*. Penguin Books, New York.

The concept of
added value

2

2.1 OVERVIEW

Each section of this chapter addresses a basic question related to the generation of profit from manufacturing activity. These questions should provide a guide towards a better understanding of the relationships between adding value, successfully manufacturing a well designed product from the start and the characteristics of a manufacturing system capable of generating profit. At the completion of this chapter the natural links between these areas will become apparent. Chapter 1 on the dynamics of industrial competition has shown how manufacturing industry must survive in a competitive environment. We now develop this idea in relation to a number of key activities within a manufacturing organization. Particular mention is made of the core concept of adding value for the customer. From Chapter 1, it should be appreciated that success in a competitive environment means satisfying (and preferably delighting) the customer. To achieve this, we must be better at adding value to our products or services than our competitors. This chapter considers the way we should think about the underlying philosophy behind the way we manage our value-adding processes and builds on the ideas put forward on the competitive environment previously introduced. Specifically, on completing this chapter, readers should be able to:

- understand the true meaning and importance of value adding in manufacturing industry and how the customer sees this;
- appreciate the role of total quality management and elimination of waste in value-adding processes;
- understand the potential for value analysis to improve product and process design in such a way that customers' perceptions of value can be maximized at minimum cost;
- appreciate the need for quality function deployment and how it can

ensure that customers' perceptions of value are translated to the product specifications and manufacturing processes;
* consider the linkages which are essential to the creation of value in an organization.

2.2 CHAPTER STRUCTURE

This chapter is divided into six main sections:

* the meaning of value added;
* value-adding management;
* waste and total quality;
* product design for manufacture and the market;
* consequences for manufacturing systems design and management;
* design for manufacture.

We first examine what is meant by 'adding value'. Manufacturing and customer service are in a unique position where true wealth can be created. Other business activities which involve no more than 'wheeling and dealing' might appear to add value, but the activities of some prominent entrepreneurs in the late 1980s have clearly demonstrated that wealth is not easily created in this way. Manufacturing and customer service create a product where profit is a direct result of that creative activity. The selling price is greater than the cost of creation of the product because raw materials and other resources have been converted into a commodity which a customer can utilize, often to create more wealth and further economic activity. It can justifiably be asked therefore why many manufacturing organizations are unprofitable when their purpose is to add value and hence create wealth? Clearly, it must be recognized that to be successful, the customer must be offered value. The answer must lie somewhere in the difference between adding value successfully or unsuccessfully. When these questions are investigated further, it will be seen that manufacturing means much more than supplying the customer with what has been specified. It also encompasses the progressive elimination of wasteful activity that does not add value. The difficulty comes in determining what form of value will satisfy the customer. Having concentrated on concepts of value adding that lead to wealth creation, questions can then be asked about the product. In the final analysis, the success of a value-adding activity can only be judged by the performance of the product in the marketplace. Therefore, questions must also be asked about the customer-perceived attributes of a product and how these should be translated into product design to allow efficient value adding. Finally, we examine a very powerful tool which will allow us to transfer product/market characteristics into parameters for the design and management of a manufacturing system. This tool, known as **quality function deployment (QFD)** enables the voice of the customer to be heard at all stages of product or service design and manufacture thus optimizing the value-adding process, customer satisfaction and market success. Throughout this chapter we will be emphasizing that it is the customer who decides whether we add value, not only in a way that satisfies, but also in a way that excites and enthuses. In the long run, value is all a manufacturer or service provider can offer. When customers do not perceive value they might not complain – they just do not come back. Manufacturers are in the business of adding value, and in doing so, must ensure that value is added to the products whilst waste is avoided by maintaining a customer focused management system involving the whole organization, from tender to delivery.

2.3 THE MEANING OF VALUE ADDED

Porter (1985) describes value added as 'selling price less the cost of purchased raw materials'. He goes on to state value added is not a sound basis for cost analysis because it incorrectly distinguishes raw materials from many other purchased inputs used in a firm's activities. Furthermore, value added fails to highlight the linkages between a firm and its suppliers that can reduce cost or enhance differentiation.

In Chapter 1, Porter's concept of the value chain was introduced. This concept is very important in the development of this chapter. Porter implies that traditional ideas on value added are inadequate and suggests that the value chain should be considered instead. The value chain disaggregates a firm into its strategically relevant activities in order to understand the behaviour of costs and the existing and potential sources of differentiation. A firm gains competitive advantage by performing these activities more cheaply or, in other words, by adding customer-perceived value more efficiently than its competitors. Every organization operates a collection of processes that are performed to design, produce, market, deliver and support its product and service. Firms in similar industries may have similar chains of activities, but the value chains of competitors usually differ. For example, a car-hire company which offers the latest models and 'fussy' service is likely to have a very different value chain (and hence different processes) to 'rent-a-wreck'. Significant differences will exist in staff policies, vehicle operations and customer services. Differences in such competitor value chains are the source of competitive advantage, which will be reflected in the customer's perception of value.

2.4 VALUE-ADDING MANAGEMENT

The term **value-adding management (VAM)** has been coined as describing any system of management which aims at a strategy of continual improvement through the progressive identification and elimination of all non-value-adding activities. Many manufacturing companies have attempted to implement VAM in some form or other. VAM consists of a collection of techniques which are aimed at reducing the non-value-adding proportion of a firm's activities. VAM is applicable to any company whose value-adding time is less than approximately 50% of total manufacturing lead time. Typically, a VAM model indicates that value adding (VA) and non-value adding (NVA) are in the ratio of 5% to 95%. Traditionally, emphasis has been given to improving value-adding activities but this may result in a further deterioration of the value-adding to non-value-adding ratio (see Table 2.1).

This clearly implies that the value chain can be considered in terms of value-adding activities and non-value-adding activities. The efficiency of value-adding activities can be improved by improving both value-adding and non-value-adding elements. At this point we will confine attention to value adding as a stand-alone concept (which of course it is not). It must also be appreciated that JIT (just-in-time production) and ABM (activity-based management) and other ideas to be considered in later chapters must be combined with the value-adding equation.

To illustrate simple concepts of value adding, consider the following example:

> In the manufacture of potato crisps, a manufacturer has found that the time from when the potatoes are brought into his warehouse to when a bag of potato crisps ended up on a supermarket shelf is about 28 days. The company has invested heavily in modern, highly productive, automated machinery for slicing, frying, conveying and bagging the crisps. They now find that the proportion of time spent in adding value to the product is around 30 minutes.

This example indicates that the crisp manufacturer's ratio of NVA:VA is much worse than even 95%:5%. In terms of the manufacturing process involved in the manufacture of potato crisps, three value-adding activities might be slicing, frying and bagging. Three non-value-adding activities might be storage, transportation within the plant and inspection. These latter activities clearly occupy a very high proportion of the organization's activities and are targets for improvement.

Table 2.1 Value-adding and non-value-adding activities

Non-valuue adding	Value adding	
95.0%	15.0%	Typical company
97.5%	2.5%	Improved value added performance
50.0%	50.0%	VAM target

In typical manufacturing companies, it is believed that non-value-adding activities are a much larger proportion of what is happening than value-adding activities. In service industries they may be even higher. Investment in high technology (e.g. automated manufacturing processes) tends to concentrate on value-adding activities. The VAM scenario suggests that whilst this is important, there are also numerous opportunities for improvement in non-value-adding activities which tend not to be technologically orientated. There are often opportunities for waste reduction, leading to massive overall efficiency improvements from non-value-adding activities.

A typical VAM strategy may be considered to operate in three main areas:

1. **processes**: understanding that processes must be identified and designed to meet customer requirements;
2. **people involvement**: everyone believing in customer-centred value creation and playing a role in the improvement of it;
3. **quality at source**: getting the job right from the start.

Typical policies which are utilized in these areas are:

- employee involvement – involvement of everyone in the company in continuous improvement;
- quick changeover – better techniques for changing set-ups as set-up time is very wasteful and adds no value to the product or service;
- selection of correct plant and equipment – that is correct technology, not necessarily high technology;
- quality at source – e.g. specifying the right tools and materials to control and improve quality during manufacture;
- operations and systems – use of standardized methods and procedures to minimize variable performance;
- total productive maintenance – optimizing maintenance strategies and maximizing equipment availability;
- supplier relations – cultivating good suppliers by cooperation to reduce the number of problems resulting from poor supplier performance.

2.5 WASTE AND TOTAL QUALITY

2.5.1 TOTAL QUALITY AND VARIATION

The effects of variation rebound throughout organizations in the form of errors, waste of all kinds and disruptive conflict between people, all of which results in poor performance of the enterprise (NIES, 1990). We have seen how non-value-adding activities can have a dramatic effect on the success of a manufacturing organization. In simple terms, to be successful in manufacturing it is necessary to be competitive, or better than anyone else who is attempting to sell their goods or services in the same markets. Non-value-adding activities will have a major influence on an organization's ability to compete, since they consist substantially of waste. In controlling waste, it is clear that overall value-adding performance can be improved, and hopefully a competitive edge developed. **Total quality** is much publicized in many areas of manufacturing and service industry as well as the government sector. This includes many organizations other than manufacturers, such as hospitals and banks. The reason for this lies simply in the fact that any organization has customers who perceive value (or lack thereof). They must be efficient in the control of waste. **Total quality control (TQC)** or **total quality management (TQM)** is seen as a means of achieving this. Total quality really means that quality is controlled throughout a whole organization. Every person, whether they are the managing director or a shopfloor worker, can be considered to have internal customers whom they must satisfy. Clearly, it is not possible to satisfy customers if errors are constantly made, which result in variation in what the customer receives, leading in turn to waste. Waste costs money, lost money means lost profit and hence lost competitiveness, inefficient value-adding and customers who are less satisfied than they should be. This is expressed well in the quotation from NIES (1990):

> An enterprise cannot expect to win the external markets until it has won its internal markets.

Customer perceptions of quality are of major significance because quality is directly related to value. Data collected in international surveys correlates quality performance with financial performance. Organizations which rank highest in quality are often those which yield superior long-term financial performance. Conversely, organizations which exhibit poor quality performance are those who exhibit poor financial performance. However, it should be noted that quality is not excellence in products or services but is customer-perceived value which will satisfy, or preferably 'delight', the customer (NIES, 1990).

2.5.2 QUALITY AS A CUSTOMER/SUPPLIER STRATEGY

Customers' future needs and preferences (and hence perceptions of value) should be the focus of improvement activities within the organization. Manufacturers often find themselves in the very wasteful activity of correcting their suppliers' quality problems after accepting delivery of supplies. Worse still, there are many examples where manufacturers pass on their suppliers' quality problems to customers. In some instances in the motor industry suppliers have been responsible for over 50% of customer complaints. The future potential of the supplier's value chain should be identified so that benefits can be translated into improving the customer's perception of value received. However, none of this can be achieved without the creative involvement of people working within a supplier organization, who must all adopt a customer focus. Clearly this involves a major cultural change in many organizations. People must no longer see their jobs as a stand-alone activity but must see themselves as part of a team whose sole purpose is to offer customer value. The customer must be able to predict the value which will be received. Therefore variation in what the customer receives must be continuously minimized by the team. Offering customer value must be consistently achieved, but the capability of offering value in itself is not sufficient if variation is not closely controlled. For example, motor manufactures must avoid the 'Friday syndrome' as one excuse for variation which causes the 'rogue' vehicle. Value must be offered consistently (without variation) every day. From this, it should be apparent that TQM has its success rooted in behavioural change in people which challenges many of the well established work practices and habits which manufacturing industry has come to accept as the norm over the twentieth century. The problem of variation inevitably leads to waste, whether this is in warranty claims, scrap, rework or customers who do not come back. Changing the attitudes and behaviour of people can avoid this waste.

The question arises as to why Japanese manufacturing industry is considered to be so much more efficient in adding value to its products than Western industry. It is claimed, for example, that some countries (such as Australia) must erect tariff barriers if there is to be any chance of home manufactured products being attractive to customers in the marketplace. Of course, Australia has many other factors to consider in evaluating the success of manufacturing industry, not least of which is a small segmented domestic market. However, many Australian manufacturers realize that there is a great deal of waste in the way they add value to their products. Evidence of this in a survey reported by Gibson and Spragg (1991) showed that 100% of Australian manufacturing companies surveyed were aware of total quality ideas and around 60% had recently adopted some of these ideas. Of course, it is well known that Japanese success in manufacturing is believed to have its roots in total quality but, in the final analysis, only the customer will decide whether one manufactured product offers superior value compared to another. For this reason, total quality must be seen to be directly beneficial to the customer. Voss (1994) points to many organizations (e.g. DuPont, B.F. Goodrich and Xerox) who have found that certain aspects of TQM have been unsuccessful because they were not directly aligned with 'customer satisfaction, response time and cost containment'.

If we consider what makes a customer satisfied, four main areas become apparent, roughly corresponding to Porter's generic competitive strategies: price, delivery, product fitness for purpose (quality), and customer service. Total quality is simply a strategy able to aid waste reduction and encourage continued improvement throughout a manufacturing or service operation.

For success, the implementation of total quality must convince the customer to believe that the product is the best available in the market at the time in relation to the above four areas. This brings us to an inference that total quality is not only a way of improving the product, but also a cost-effective business tool. To understand why this should be, let us consider **quality costs**.

Quality costs fall into four main categories:

- product failure costs – internal to the organization;
- failure costs – external to the organization;
- appraisal costs;
- prevention costs.

The relationships between these cost categories are well documented. In TQM philosophies we would attempt to direct investment towards prevention of variation rather than suffer failure costs caused by variation. A further benefit is that value can be improved by avoiding appraisal costs (e.g. inspection). There is less need to appraise products and services if variation is prevented and the quality of manufacturing processes can be assured. Figure 2.1 illustrates this idea.

Many notable authors in the field of quality present models similar to that shown in Fig. 2.1. Whilst they are widely accepted, there is very little objective evidence to support the view that the manufacturing industry is to the left of the curve (on the side of poor quality). However, Fig. 2.1 does

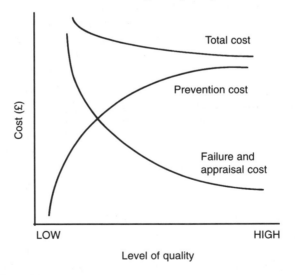

Fig. 2.1 Quality costs.

illustrate that continuous improvement should always result from paying attention to prevention of poor quality – although the total gains will become less evident as we approach higher and higher levels of quality. Three examples to support this view are:

- higher warranty costs in some organizations;
- excessive waste;
- competitive disadvantage.

Taguchi, a well-known Japanese quality practitioner, extended these loss ideas further to the concept of 'loss to society'. For example, consider a truck which must be returned 'under warranty'. The truck owner incurs a loss, as the truck is not available. The manufacturer incurs a loss as something has to be reworked. However, there are also further losses in that whatever the truck delivers will not be available on the market leading to further chain reaction losses throughout society. All of these losses are simply quality-related lack of value. The more variation there is in manufacturing or service, the larger the loss to society.

2.6 PRODUCT DESIGN FOR MANUFACTURE AND THE MARKET

Product design is the root of the value-adding process. A cynical view of engineers suggests that they do not always appreciate this. For example, it is sometimes felt that engineers design a product, attempt to make it, find it cannot be made that way, then remake it and find it cannot be sold in the marketplace. In designing a product, it is important to look first at customers' requirements in terms of economic value, fitness for use, and value of the product esteem. Design and manufacture must then be related to meet these requirements.

2.6.1 THE VALUE ANALYSIS TECHNIQUE

There are a number of techniques which can assist in achieving valued products. One well-established technique is that of **value analysis**. Value analysis is usually applied to existing products but a variation, known as **value engineering** is applied to products at their design stage.

As an example of the results of value analysis, consider the case of a car heater box. Prior to value engineering the various steel sheet sections were pressed out, assembled by welding and using nuts and bolts, and painted, with inspections after every stage. This resulted in a total of six operations, including the inspections, to produce a component that the customer saw as a rattling, rusty box in the vehicle. After value engineering, the box assembly was replaced by two plastic injection mouldings. There was no need to paint or assemble and inspection was not necessary until the product was completed. The customer now experienced a rustproof box that was much less inclined to rattle. This was a much more 'valuable' product to the customer which also cost the manufacturer much less to make.

2.6.2 THE SEVEN STAGES OF VALUE ANALYSIS

Firstly a product or service must be chosen for the application of value analysis. This could be a product where the customer does not perceive good value (for example, a product (or service) where there are excessive complaints or loss of market share).

The analysis process itself consists of the following steps:

(a) Define the product to be analysed

A problem should be sought such as a product which is subject to market resistance.

(b) Collect the facts

For example, customer reactions, sales figures, manufacturing problems, samples and costs should all be collected.

(c) The critical examination

This should be a searching examination of all aspects of the product – the size, shape, finish, materials and customer requirements. A standardized method of examination should be used. For example, the following may be asked:

- Who
- What?
- Where?
- How?
- Why?

in the following categories:

1. Product use:
   - Who uses the product?
   - For what?
   - Where?
   - How?
   - Why?

2. Product materials:
   - What is the material used in its manufacture?
   - Is there more than one?
   - Why?
   - Alternatives to that?
3. Manufacturing processes:
   - What processes are used?
   - How?
   - Where?
   - Why?
4. What type of labour is used?
   - How?
   - Where?
   - Why?
5. How much does the product cost?
   - Why?
   - Is it competitive?
   - Is it profitable?
6. What is its esteem value? (Will the customer buy simply because it is what it is? For example, products like Reebok and Rolls-Royce have high esteem values.) Level of esteem – high, moderate, low, nonexistent, unknown.
   - Why?
7. How do aesthetics contribute to the product?
   - Why?
   - Improvements?

Now each of the categories 1–7 above is rated using the following scale:

1. Essential
2. Important
3. Desirable
4. Optional
5. Unnecessary

(d) Speculation

Using the information assimilated in (c), suggestions for their own sake are made and ideas for improvement are offered.

(e) Analysis and evaluation

Each idea is carefully analysed for feasibility and cost. The points of view of the entire manufacturing team are taken, by including opinions on, for example, manufacturing, marketing, quality control, etc. Explicit consideration should be given to possible linkages in the value chain at this point.

(f) Choosing and recommending

1. Progress is summarized.
2. Favoured suggestions are listed.
3. Costs are considered and final recommendations are made.

(g) Implementation

In a real-life situation, careful consultation with all departments involved and minimized disruption to production would be essential factors to consider. It should be recalled that TQM is basically a team activity which involves changing behaviour to encourage people to view the customer's perception of value. In practice, a multi-disciplinary team should work together, to ensure inclusion of the concepts of 'linkages' and 'totality'. For instance, design, finance, manufacturing and marketing are likely to be in the team. This also applies to value analysis, and is probably the most difficult part of the whole procedure. To be successful, an organization must be able to utilize a cross-disciplinary and cross-departmental commitment to value analysis. In many organizations, this culture may require considerable work before value analysis can be effective.

Value analysis is a very powerful technique. Some of the benefits in improving value adding processes in this way are:

- more customer satisfaction;
- reduction in costs with same or better performance;
- use of less costly manufacturing methods;
- elimination of some operations;
- use of cheaper materials;
- removal of features that serve no function;
- use of standard parts;
- ensuring extra costs are not resulting from too high a specification;
- production of a more aesthetic product.

2.7 CONSEQUENCES FOR MANUFACTURING SYSTEMS DESIGN AND MANAGEMENT

The earlier sections of this chapter have stressed the importance of ensuring the voice of the customer is heard throughout the organization. If this occurs effectively, it will clearly have a critical influence on the design of the manufacturing system and its management. This section examines a powerful technique for 'listening' to the voice of the customer. The concept of linkages and totality is extended by illustrating a technique aimed at ensuring that the manufacturing system is perfectly in tune with the aim of maximizing the customers' perception of value in the organization's products and services.

For success in the 1990s and beyond, a manufacturing system must be innovative. In this context, innovativeness means the ability to renew its product quickly. In order to be innovative, a company must have flexibility in its manufacturing system so that its design and management can be a direct result of customer requirements. One of the major problems in any manufacturing organization is determining these customer requirements and ensuring that they are communicated to the manufacturing system so that this can be designed and managed in a way to allow maximized value-adding efficiency.

Quality function deployment (QFD) is simply a means of communicating the voice of the customer to the manufacturing system. Once the voice is heard, the manufacturing system can react in a way that will allow it to add value with optimum efficiency. Quality function deployment allows this optimization to take place whilst also taking note of similar products manufactured by competitors. In this way, an organization can see how it should be designing and managing its own value-adding manufacturing system so that it can place its business in the best possible competitive position in the market.

2.7.1 QUALITY FUNCTION DEPLOYMENT

The following will guide the reader through an introduction to the basics of QFD. First a product must be chosen to which the quality function deployment technique is to be applied. This could be a product which is known to be uncompetitive.

QFD then consists of the following steps:

Step 1 – Customer requirements

Customer requirements are listed in a table similar to that shown in Table 2.2.

Table 2.2 Customer requirements table

Primary	Secondary	Tertiary
•	•	•
•	•	•
•	•	•

Primary requirements are the very basic customer needs. These are expanded into secondary and tertiary requirements to obtain a more definitive list. For example, if coated steel roofing sheet is taken as the product, primary requirements might be durability and attractiveness. Secondary requirements could be uniformity and tertiary requirements could be coating thickness.

Step 2 – Control characteristics

Final product control characteristics are now listed. This means design requirements that relate directly to the customer requirements. Design requirements must be measurable (this is because the control characteristic must be controlled by comparison with objective targets). For example, in the case of the coated steel roofing sheet, final product control characteristics could be yield strength or profile.

Step 3 – Relationship matrix

A relationship matrix is developed between customer requirements and product control characteristics as shown in Fig. 2.2. Degrees of correlation between customer requirements and product characteristics can be considered by using the symbols in the figure. This will facilitate an understanding of the significance of the relationships.

Step 4 – Market evaluation

A market evaluation is now added to the matrix. This covers customer-expressed importance ratings for the listed requirements and competitive

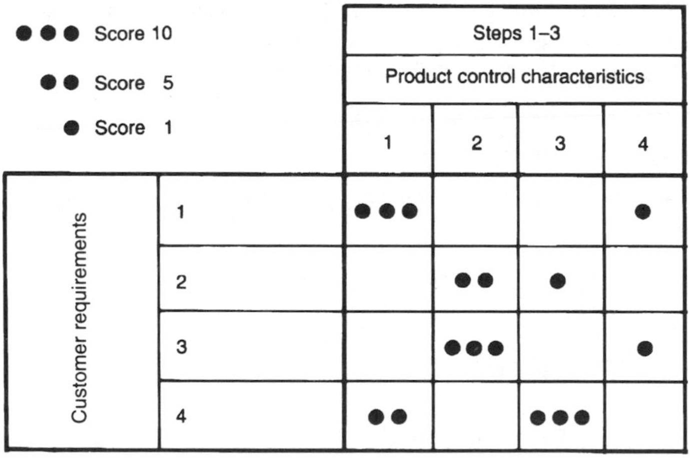

Fig. 2.2 Product control matrix: Steps 1–3.

evaluation data for existing products. The evaluation shows the strengths and weaknesses of the products in the marketplace. The customer importance rating is expressed as a number, usually out of ten, for each of the customer requirements. (See Fig. 2.3.)

Step 5 – Product comparison

Competing products are now compared with the product under investigation for each of the final product control characteristics. The rating for the product under investigation is taken as 100 and then compared with the competing products. (See Fig. 2.4.)

Step 6 – Key selling points

Key selling points are listed for a new product. These selling points are advertisable characteristics to be emphasized in the marketplace. For example, for the case of coated steel roofing sheet, it might be emphasized that the coating resists degradation from sunlight better than any other in its class. The right-hand column in the relationship matrix is completed for each of the customer requirements listed on the left-hand side. (See Fig. 2.4.)

Step 7 – Control characteristic targets

Control characteristic targets must now be developed for each of the final product control characteristics. These targets are determined by considering selling points, customer importance rating and current product strength. For example, if customer importance rating is 10 and the product is lower than competing products in competitive evaluations, then it may be decided to utilize a control characteristic target of 115 or 120. At this stage it may also be found that the product rates considerably higher than competing products, for no particular benefit in the marketplace. This implies that the manufacturing system is controlling that characteristic much more tightly (and probably at greater cost) than is necessary. In this stiuation it might be possible to achieve cost reductions by utilizing a control characteristic target below 100. (See Fig. 2.4.)

Step 8 – Product control characteristics

Product control characteristics that are to be deployed through the remainder of the QFD process are now selected. This selection is based on customer importance, selling points, competitive evaluations and the difficulty involved in achieving the target (an x is placed in the lowest row of the relationship matrix to indicate a selection).

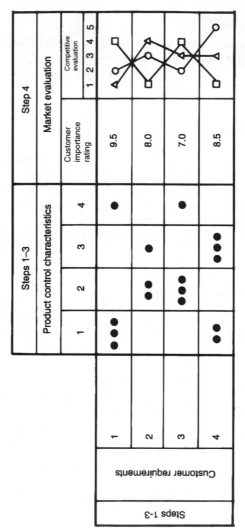

Fig. 2.3 Product control matrix: Step 4.

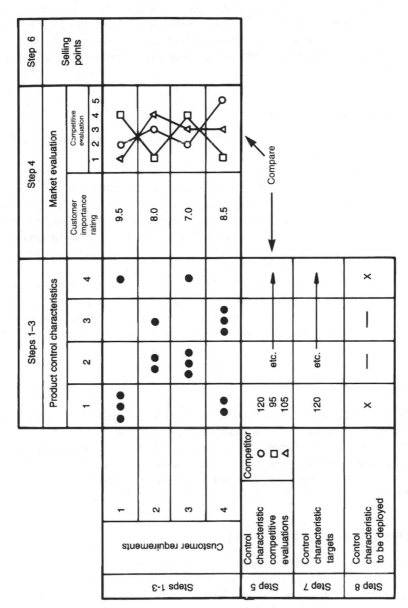

Fig. 2.4 Product control matrix: Steps 5–8.

Step 9 – Component deployment matrix

The component deployment matrix translates the output of the relationship matrix into critical component part characteristics. The result of this stage is that finished component characteristics are defined. It will now be necessary to consider the product as a series of sub-systems (or perhaps sub-assemblies) and then break these down into individual components.

Step 10 – Process planning

The critical component part characteristics are now transferred to the process planning chart.

For example, taking the steel roofing sheet's critical component part characteristic of thickness, the process may be identified as, say, 'cold rolling'. One of the control points could be 'sheet thickness dimension' which would relate to a check point of 'roller gap setting' where the monitoring method could be a control chart which is to be monitored at a frequency of 15 minutes. The aim of this phase is to force the investigators to consider the important control points in the manufacturing system by identifying the need for and methods of controlling manufacturing processes. In so doing, the investigators should be planning, identifying and controlling the most critical value-adding activities in the manufacturing system so that the customer's requirements are translated to the shopfloor manufacturing process.

2.7.2 SUMMARY

Quality function deployment has considerable potential for controlling value adding in an economical way, in line with customer requirements. However, it should be realized that the above is only an introduction to the concept of QFD. Further consideration of the manner in which QFD can be developed and applied is given by Hauser and Clausing (1988).

2.8 DESIGN FOR MANUFACTURE

Hearing the voice of the customer is one of the most important factors in providing value. Manufacturers cannot provide value to the customer unless they are very clear about the way in which the customer perceives value when a product is purchased, and equally importantly, the service which accompanies it. Quality function deployment is a very powerful step in helping the manufacturer hear the voice of the customer. However, there is little point in hearing the voice of the customer and providing the desired value, but at such cost as to threaten the business viability of the enterprise. Value must therefore not only be provided, but also in an extremely efficient manner. Efficient value adding really stems from two main areas:

- the design of the product itself;
- the design of processes and support activities which are required for procurement of the product.

In the past, manufacturers have tended to emphasize the design of the product, and hence innovative design aimed at demonstrating excellence to the customer has been seen as the primary activity. This has resulted in less efficient value-adding processes. In Japan, it could be argued, value is not only seen in the product itself, but also in the processes which create the product.

2.8.1 SHELF ENGINEERING

Sound product design must be closely allied to sound process design. This can be seen in the concept of **shelf engineering**. In the past, for example, where a new car has been designed, it has been designed to provide customer-perceived value by incorporating a number of highly innovative features such as colour-keyed bumpers, voice synthesized instruments, proactive suspension, etc. Unfortunately these types of feature tend to be designed into vehicles without fully understanding that it must be possible to procure them in an economic way which will achieve the quality, cost and reliability (in other words, the value) which the modern consumer now expects. However, some winning motor manufacturers have overcome this problem by concentrating design and development on perfecting the excellence and manufacturability of specific features which are then lifted 'off the shelf' and incorporated into new models. In this way, not only is the customer assured of proven product designs but also the procurement processes in the value chain are assured of being capable of providing the value which will allow the model to achieve a competitive advantage. Not only does the organization then know what to make, but also how to make it in a way which will allow the customer to perceive value in the purchase of a motor vehicle.

In the past, it may have been argued that the shelf engineering approach has led to products which are less innovative than the most advanced designs available in the world at the time. The Japanese, in particular, have been noted for doing relatively little in the way of innovative or new design, but have been charged with making someone else's designs work extremely well and, equally importantly, developing exceptionally efficient value-adding processes. In so doing they are building a reputation for quality in products which do not quite represent the state of the art. At one time, there may have been a little truth in this. In the 1990s, however, it could be argued that the ideas which are now 'on the shelf' in organizations which employ the shelf engineering philosophy do in fact now represent the state of the art. We could extend this argument by suggesting that this is a result of slow, continuous, people-based improvement in the *kaizen* style in contrast to the innovative leaps in product design often attempted by Western manufacturing organizations (see Chapter 11 on total quality management).

A particularly profound example of this can be seen in the highly lucrative, but increasingly competitive, luxury car market which, until recently, has been dominated by European manufacturers. The entrance of the Lexus and Infiniti from Japan has shown that vehicles which do not offer particular esteem value are able to compete and, many would argue, offer superior customer-perceived value in the prestige car market. (Both the Lexus and the Infiniti have won many accolades for being the best currently available prestige vehicles.) There is little doubt that the Lexus and Infiniti are able to offer such excellent value because they have been designed to 'delight' the customer by utilizing 'off-the-shelf' advanced technology and highly developed (but again off-the-shelf) manufacturing organization and techniques which create value in the most efficient manner currently available. Much of this is the result of slow, continuous, people-based improvement in manufacturing enterprise.

It must ultimately be accepted that 'value' is all any manufacturer can compete and prosper on. Therefore, by incorporating esteem value in a design it may in fact be possible for an organization to survive by providing the customer with a product which is inferior to the competition. The prestige motor industry again provides examples of this. Cars which have been seen as the best in the world have in fact, for many years, been unsophisticated, much too expensive and generally very old-fashioned. They were expensive because of outmoded manufacturing techniques, which in reality were difficult to control in creating a consistent product, and were marketed on the strength of esteem value resulting from a romantic image of being 'hand-made'. Manufacturers can only survive on providing this type of value to a limited extent for a limited period of time. Customers may be persuaded by their emotions when they are assessing value but ultimately will realize that value can only be the result of manufacturing techniques which allow the best quality (and hence value) products and services to be procured. This value can only be achieved by paying considerable attention to design wtih manufacture and the customer in mind. Evidence of the effects of customer-perceived value can be found in the dramatic rise of the Japanese motorcycle industry, which should serve as a dire warning to prestige motor manufacturers.

2.8.2 LEAN PRODUCTION

To expand on the need to carefully consider design for manufacture, we can examine the importance of the design function in the concept of **lean production** which is expanding rapidly around the world. In simplified terms, lean production (a concept popularized by Womack, Jones and Roos (1990)) means doing much more with much less. Otherwise expressed, value-adding processes must be designed to prosper on less space, less inventory, less people, less investment and less and ever-decreasing waste in general. Much of this book is in fact aimed at suggesting ways in which value adding can be improved to achieve exactly that. However, there is a common misconception of the word 'lean', especially in the popular press. A lean organization is often characterized by one which is 'cut to the bone' where the manufacturing system is doing more or less what it has always done but there is a much greater degree of stress applied to it. In fact, lean production involves becoming lean by a planned and systematic approach to the elimination of waste. Manufacturing systems have always been characterized by slack or buffers designed into the system to counteract their conceived inevitable variation in performance. Lean production challenges this view adopting the philosophy that there is always a better way to add value. It is also pertinent to note that waste can be eliminated in two ways:

- by improving the existing manufacturing system;
- by utilizing conceptually leaner technology.

Clearly, the design process must underpin all of this. We can summarize this view by reciting a rather cynical appraisal of the situation often found in typical manufacturing enterprises: It is not manufacturing that creates waste and scrap, but design that makes manufacturing create waste and scrap! (In this context 'design' refers to both products and processes.)

Let us now take a look at the concepts of 'lean design' and 'manufacturability' in the areas of (a) product design and (b) manufacturing technology.

Womack, Jones and Roos (1990) outline the notion of product manufacturability in the motor industry. Motor manufacturers are in the habit of taking each others' products and doing a 'tear down' to assess how manufacturable they see their competitors' products. Table 2.3 illustrates some results of this.

Component-by-component comparisons are carried out to determine which manufacturers have designed their products so that they can be manufactured in a way which maximizes the efficiency of the value-adding process. This may, for example, include comparisons of the

Table 2.3 Manufacturability of products in the assembly plant: car producers ranked by other producers (after 'tear down' of each other's products)

Producer	Average rank
Toyota	2.2
Honda	3.9
Mazda	4.8
Fiat	5.3
Nissan	5.4
Ford	5.6
Volkswagen	6.4
Mitsubishi	6.6
Suzuki	8.7
General Motors	10.2
Hyundai	11.3
Renault	12.7
Chrysler	13.5
BMW	13.9
Volvo	13.9
PSA	14.0
Saab	16.4
Daimler-Benz	16.6
Jaguar	18.6

Adapted from Womack, Jones and Roos (1990).

number of parts in a bumper panel assembly. A lean design may have, say, only two parts but a less manufacturable assembly at the foot of the manufacturability table may have, say, 20 or 30 parts. In terms of customer-perceived value there is probably no difference in the two assemblies. However, the organization manufacturing the two-part assembly will clearly possess a major competitive advantage and this is typical of the type of reasons put forward for the Lexus and Infiniti being so competitive in the prestige car market. These products are simply much more 'manufacturable' than those offered by their older-established competitors.

In terms of lean manufacturing technology we can look at another example. Motor vehicles involve a large number of cast metal components. In setting up a casting facility for certain types of these, it is essential to utilize the most efficient value-adding process. Traditionally, a green-sand moulding process has been used and fairly sophisticated, relatively automated plants of this type have become the norm in the motor industry. A typical plant may cost, say, £16 million to set up and require 18 workers to operate it. By contrast, a manufacturer setting up a lean plant would not accept this without question. Several motor manufacturers have decided to invest in the alternative technology of lost-foam casting. This involves a simpler process (where many steps, for example the inclusion of cores, have been eliminated). A typical lost-foam plant could cost £8 million and require only seven workers to operate it and is capable of a similar output. There will be a clear competitive advantage for the manufacturer who decided to add value by utilizing this technology.

To be fair, it must be acknowledged that the above is a gross oversimplification of the situation. For example, lost-foam casting is at a much earlier stage of development than its well-established competitor. It must be recognized that although lean technology does offer potential improvements in the efficiency of the value-adding process, there are often risks attached to designing it into manufacturing systems. However, it is likely that the organizations with a long-term view who are prepared to shelf engineer such processes will ultimately achieve a competitive advantage.

2.8.3 DESIGN FOR MANUFACTURE – A COMPROMISE?

There has been a great deal of debate centred around the importance of taking account of value-adding manufacturing systems at the product design stage. There is a widely held view that generally there is a need to compromise between what the designer would prefer and what is practical in manufacturing terms. A typical example of this was in the way wings were designed for a popular light aircraft. The designer would have preferred a tapered design because such a configuration performs most efficiently. However, manufacturing engineers specified a parallel design because it was thought that varying the chord of a wing leads to a much more difficult and expensive manufacturing process. In reality, power and politics take their toll in most organizations, as they did in this case, and the manufacturing people won. The aircraft initially sold well with parallel wings but was soon outsold by a rival with a much more efficient tapered wing which gave the aircraft superior speed and economy of operation. Customers were clearly perceiving greater value from the aircraft with more difficult to manufacture, but more efficient, wings. On closer examination, however, it was found that the competitor's wings were in fact parallel for the majority of their length but the tips of the wings were tapered. The competitor had found a more economical way of designing and manufacturing wings which suffered a minimal performance penalty and hence added greater value to the product and, as a result, obtained a competitive advantage.

What this example serves to illustrate is the need for cooperation between the marketing, design and manufacturing functions. Situations where competition exists between the three with one or other ultimately winning their way are unlikely to lead to the best possible customer perceived value. Design and manufacture are both essential links in the value chain which serve to further illustrate the importance of 'linkages' in gaining competitive advantage.

Walsh et al. (1992) further develop the economic importance of design for manufacture. They state that Rolls-Royce estimate that 80% of the final product cost is determined by design decisions, and Ford estimate that design decisions are ten times as effective as production planning decisions and one hundred times as effective as production changes in reducing costs and improving quality. Walsh et al. (1992) make several suggestions for making sure that design and manufacturing establish strong value-chain linkages. These include awareness by designers of production facilities/skills, the involvement of production staff in the product development team, a committee of senior managers to oversee product development, production staff to be part of both the brief/concept stage in design (i.e. not just included at the prototype stage) and prototype evaluation, and alliance with component suppliers (many crucial design for manufacture decisions are made by suppliers).

In conclusion, we can see that the design for manufacture concept is extremely important in managing manufacturing systems. However, it is simplistic to suggest that design people must be made to understand manufacturing and vice versa. There is only one way to assess success in design for manufacture and that is customer-perceived value. The need for cooperation to achieve this rather than what is prudent for one interest or another must be at the forefront of the minds of all parties involved in design and all other activities that go to create the value chain. This is true whether the subject of design is a product, service or the methods and resources utilized.

2.9 CONCLUSION

In this chapter we have covered:

- the value chain;
- value-adding management;
- waste and total quality;
- value analysis and quality function deployment;
- design for manufacture.

Our study of the value chain has shown that efficient value adding is essential to be competitive. To achieve competitiveness we have seen that manufacturing activities can be analysed into categories of value adding and non-value adding. Consideration of non-value-adding activities brings to the fore the need to control waste in manufacturing activities. Also, total quality and involvement of the total organization is essential to efficient value adding. This reinforces the concept of linkages in the value chain and leads to the idea of the whole manufacturing organization aiming to meet customer requirements. From here, we change emphasis to the product. Value analysis shows that there are often design changes (in product and process) which can be made to the product to allow improved customer satisfaction and more efficient value adding. Design is the start of the value-adding process. It should be remembered when adding value that 'the manufacturing department doesn't make scrap and waste but that the design makes manufacturing make scrap and waste'. We then turn to QFD, the ultimate technique for ensuring that the manufacturing system is in tune with customer requirements. We showed that customer requirements can be translated into design and manufacturing parameters which should percolate through the whole of the manufacturing system.

In concluding that meeting customer requirements in the most efficient way possible is the key to successful value adding, we should consider how customer requirements are defined. Deming, in his definitive book *Out of the Crisis*, states:

> The producer is in a far better position than the consumer to invent new designs and new service. (Deming, 1986)

Deming goes on to point out that pneumatic tyres might never have been invented if it was not for the producer realizing the customer's need. QFD is a technique which should help us come to grips with such issues.

In the following chapter we begin to examine more specific aspects of value-adding activities. In considering the flow of materials through a manufacturing facility, we build on the core concept of adding value to products with the aim of satisfying customers and hence generating profit. It will be shown that there are differences in the way the dynamics of materials flow should be analysed according to the types of manufacturing processes and organizations we are considering. However, in moving on to Chapter 3, it must be remembered that whatever the variations in the ways materials flow is considered, we will always have one basic aim, i.e. efficient value adding by the elimination of waste throughout the total manufacturing activity, or throughout whatever system the material flows through. Much of what is covered in Chapter 3 has been considered to be non-value adding. It must not be forgotten that much of the value the customer perceives can be generated from improvements in activities of this type.

REFERENCES

Deming, W.E. (1986) *Out of the Crisis*. Cambridge University Press, Cambridge, Mass. p. 167.
Gibson, P.R. and Spragg, R.C. (1991) Cost-effectiveness of quantity systems.

Proceedings of the 5th Asia-Pacific Organization for Quality Control Conference, Vol. 3, pp. 22–8. Asia-Pacific Quality Control Association.

Hauser, J.R. and Clausing, D. (1988) The house of quality. *Harvard Business Review*, May–June, pp. 63–73.

NIES (National Industry Extension Service) (1990) *How to Approach TQM – Guide to Concepts, Principles and Imperatives*. Australian Federal Government, Department of Industry, Technology and Commerce, pp. 9–20.

Porter, M.E. (1985) *Competitive Advantage*. The Free Press, New York.

Voss, B. (1994) Quality's second coming. *Journal of Business Strategy*, Vol. 15, No. 2, pp. 42–5.

Walsh, V. *et al.* (1992) *Winning by Design: Technology, Product Design and International Competitiveness*. Blackwell Business, Oxford.

Womack, J.P., Jones, D.T. and Roos, D. (1990) *The Machine that Changed the World*. McGraw-Hill, New York.

PART TWO
The Major Internal Manufacturing Management Functions

Dynamics of materials flow

3

3.1 OVERVIEW

In the last chapter we examined amongst other things the important concepts of adding value and eliminating waste in manufacturing activities. One of the ways in which value can be more effectively added to a product, and waste more effectively eliminated, is by ensuring a coordinated flow of materials through the organization from purchasing through production to customer delivery. Coordinated materials flow reduces inventory (itself a form of waste) and reduces lost sales through late deliveries. An understanding of the dynamics of how materials flow in manufacturing organizations is a prerequisite to understanding how this flow can be coordinated. The objectives of this chapter are to explain the basic dynamics of materials flow in manufacturing organizations, and some important related issues that must be addressed by any system intended to regulate this flow to achieve the best possible degree of coordination between supply and demand.

The chapter introduces a number of concepts including:

- the way manufacturing organizations can be classified into distinct types according to their materials flow characteristics;
- the role of inventory in controlling production and maintaining smooth materials flow;
- the distinction between push and pull systems and centralized and decentralized methods of production control;
- the significance of production bottlenecks and the effect of process variability on materials flow.

3.2 CHAPTER STRUCTURE

This chapter is divided into the following sections:

- classification of manufacturing industry by materials flow patterns;

- representation of materials flow the manufacturing network;
- regulating materials flow;
- push vs pull systems of production control;
- centralized and decentralized systems of production control;
- manufacturing classification revisited;
- bottlenecks;
- V, A and T plants;
- effect of process variability on materials flow.

In the first section we examine the Harvard Industries Classification Scheme which classifies manufacturing companies as either continuous flow, repetitive, large batch, small batch or jobbing production.

From here we move on to discuss how the materials flow through a manufacturing company can be represented and analysed in terms of repetitions of a basic building block consisting of a production/inventory/demand module with the input to one module constituting the demand on the previous module. At this point, we examine some terms and definitions which are frequently used in the analysis of materials flow in manufacturing systems.

The role of inventory in ensuring an uninterrupted flow of materials through the plant by acting as a cushion between demand and production is examined. The notion of establishing reorder points as levels of inventory at which orders for the production or purchase of replenishment batches of an item is examined critically. Another means of classifying manufacturing companies, in terms of the extent to which production is to firm customer order or to stock, will determine the principle positioning of inventory in the company.

Inventory can be reduced by better coordination between demand and production, and the superiority of pull rather than push systems of production are examined in this regard. The contrast between centralized and decentralized systems of production control and their relationships to push and pull systems are examined.

Nearly all manufacturing plants have some form of production bottleneck which will determine the maximum output of the plant. We discover how the presence of a bottleneck will have an effect on the utilization of the surrounding resources, and how particular attention needs to be paid to keeping the bottleneck resource running. We also look at why the location of the bottleneck can be sensitive to batch sizing policies.

A very recent method of classification, based on the shape of the organization's manufacturing network, is discussed. V, A and T plants are so called because of the similarity of the manufacturing network in each case to the letters V, A or T. The importance of this classification is that it assists us in finding the bottleneck resource.

Process variability can also be an important limiting factor on the output of a manufacturing plant. An elementary mathematical analysis, in terms of queuing theory, can be used to show the effects of process variability on materials flow. The analysis shows how high process variability, together with operating near the limits of production capacity, can lead to long throughput times and high levels of work in progress.

3.3 CLASSIFICATION OF MANUFACTURING INDUSTRY BY MATERIALS FLOW PATTERNS

There are a number of different ways of classifying manufacturing industry as far as materials flow is concerned. One such classification is known as the **Harvard Industries Classification Scheme** (Fig. 3.1) and divides manufacturing plants according to the size of separately identifiable batches that flow through the plant. The individual classes run from continuous flow (in which batches of what may be regarded as 'infinite' size are continuously made of just one product) through large batch and small batch to jobbing plants which produce one-off products to individual customer order.

Obviously these classes do not have sharp boundaries, but should be regarded as forming a continuous spectrum, from pure continuous flow manufacturing of single products at one extreme, to pure jobbing production of one-off products at the other. This spectrum can be represented diagrammatically as shown in Fig. 3.2. From this diagram, you will see that as we move from pure flow to pure jobbing production, not only does the time interval between the production of successive units increase, but also the number of sub-parts in the product increases.

3.4 REPRESENTATION OF MATERIALS FLOW: THE MANUFACTURING NETWORK

The fundamental activity in manufacturing consists of the conversion of materials from one form to another. This can be represented diagrammatically as shown in Fig. 3.3.

The conversion process, represented by the rectangular block in Fig. 3.3, has an input in the form of raw materials, and produces an output in the

Continuous flow	Repetitive	Large batch	Small batch	Jobbing

Fig. 3.1 Harvard Industries Classification Scheme.

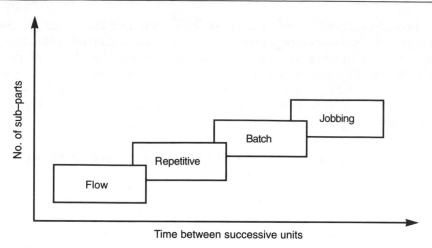

Fig. 3.2 Time/complexity relationships in manufacturing. (Reproduced from Vollman, Berry and Whybark, 1988.)

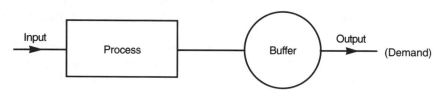

Fig. 3.3 The manufacturing conversion process.

form of converted materials which feeds some form of demand. Frequently, the output of the process does not feed the demand directly but goes first into a buffer stock with the demand drawing material from this buffer stock as required.

The basic conversion process with its inputs and outputs can be regarded as the fundamental building block for the representation of materials flow in a manufacturing company. We can consider this conversion process at varying levels of aggregation. At the highest aggregation level, the conversion process may be the aggregate of all the operations performed in the factory. The input may be raw materials which are purchased from suppliers, and the output may be the finished products which are shipped to customers. At a much lower level of aggregation the process may be an individual machining or assembly operation, in which case the input may be unfinished or unassembled components arriving from the previous process, and the output may be the machined components or completed sub-assemblies which may in turn feed a demand exerted by a further machining or assembly process.

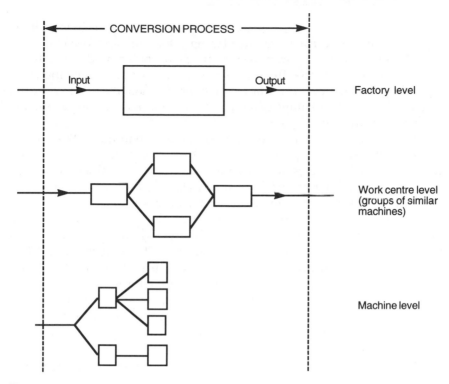

Fig. 3.4 Detailed hierarchies in the conversion process.

If we look at Fig. 3.4 it will be seen that we can break the overall factory operation down into any level of detail we like, and that the operations on each level can always be represented diagrammatically as a series of repetitions of the basic input–conversion–output building block, with the outputs of one block feeding the inputs to another. Thus a particular block will have **upstream** blocks (on the supply side) that feed it with input materials, and **downstream** blocks (on the customer side) to which it feeds its output materials.

The various levels of Fig. 3.4 can be viewed as examples of **manufacturing flow diagrams** or **manufacturing networks** at different levels of aggregation.

We can obviously have variations of the basic building block. For example, a process may have several inputs and one output, one input and several outputs, or several inputs and several outputs. Also the processes themselves are usually performed by some type of physical production resource such as a machine or a production-line worker which we may also want to represent on a manufacturing flow diagram.

In general, materials flow patterns are simplest in continuous flow, repetitive and large batch manufacturing situations and become more complicated as we move through small batch to jobbing production. In the continuous flow and repetitive cases we usually have a simple unidirectional flow of material along a single main production line that may be fed by subsidiary lines. All units generally pass through the same production resources in the same sequence.

Thus in a car assembly line we may have a continuous flow of car bodies that have been pressed out of sheet metal and which are fed through subsidiary lines with various additional sub-assemblies such as door panels, windscreens, side windows, etc. Most of the processes involved in this type of plant are assembly processes (Fig. 3.5).

In an oil refinery, crude oil flows down the main production line through a refining process from which different grades of refined oil are piped off down branch lines to be shipped as different types of finished product. The main processes here are **disassembly processes** (Fig. 3.6).

In a batch manufacturing situation, manufacturing flow diagrams become more complex. There may be no fixed sequence of production resources on which processing occurs, and flow tends to follow a network-like pattern. In the conventional manufacturing plant in which resources are divided by **function**, that is similar resources are grouped together in the form of work centres, a batch can traverse a very long and

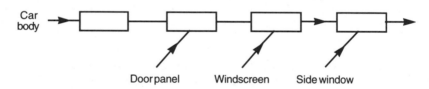

Fig. 3.5 An assembly process.

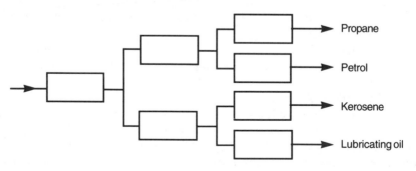

Fig. 3.6 A 'disassembly' process.

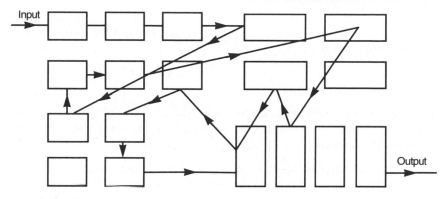

Fig. 3.7 Materials flow in a functionally grouped plant.

complicated route between different work centres before all the required operations have been performed (Fig. 3.7). The greatest complexity of flow is usually in a job shop situation in which a very large number of small batches may each take a completely different route through the plant.

3.5 REGULATING MATERIALS FLOW

A manufacturing flow diagram or network represents a static picture of the paths which materials take when flowing through the various individual conversion processes performed in a manufacturing company. An animated version of the diagram (which can in fact be produced using modern visual interactive factory simulation packages) would show how, when material does start to flow through these paths, various queues, materials shortages, build-ups of material in buffers, etc., occur on a dynamic and ever-changing basis.

A fundamental task of manufacturing management is to regulate the flow of materials through the network so that it is as smooth and coordinated as possible, particularly with regard to:

- maximizing the rate of flow of materials through the network – this basically means minimizing the amount of time material spends in queues or buffers waiting for the next process, i.e. maximizing the ratio of processing time to waiting time;
- minimizing the build-up of inventory in buffers – since inventory buffers are usually associated with queues, increases in the rate of flow of materials through the plant by reduction in the queue time will invariably tend to reduce the size of inventory buffers.

We shall now examine some of the ways in which this regulation may be achieved. Although we have already mentioned inventory as something which should be minimized, a limited amount of inventory can play an important role in regulating materials flow, and we shall examine this in the next section.

3.5.1 THE ROLE OF INVENTORY

Although excess inventory is undesirable, the presence of some inventory is usually essential in the smooth running of a manufacturing company. Inventory basically plays three important roles.

1. It acts as a buffer between supply and demand and insulates each of them from either predictable or unpredictable variability in the other.
2. It can compensate for differences in process batch sizes between consecutive operations.
3. Inventory levels, if monitored, can act as triggers to production to produce more of an item whose inventory has become depleted to below a certain point; thus inventory levels can be used to control production.

Whilst the presence of just sufficient inventory to fulfil these roles is essential in most manufacturing companies, the presence of too much inventory can become very costly. In particular:

- inventory requires storage space which costs money to provide;
- inventory must be insured against such things as fire and theft, which again costs money;
- inventory assumes that a continuing demand for the product will exist. If demand suddenly ceases, inventory will become obsolete and money will be lost;
- inventory ties up capital that might be better used elsewhere. At the very least, the capital tied up in inventory could be invested at bank rate interest (typically 5–15%), and in reality, other forms of investment such as new plant and equipment, or R&D, might bring a considerably higher rate of return.

Common practice is to add an additional component of the basic bank interest rate to represent other costs such as storage, insurance, etc., and to arrive at a somewhat arbitrary percentage (typically 20–30%) of average inventory value, which represents the cost to the company of carrying that inventory over the year. These costs in real terms can be quite high. According to the results of a recent Australian survey, a not uncommon situation is to find companies with three to six months' supply of finished products, components and raw materials in their stores (one might say that the company had two to four 'stock turns' per year). An average small manufacturing company with 50 employees and an annual turnover of £10 m might have a total value of inventory at any one time of between

£2.5m and £5m. At an inventory carrying rate of 25%, the annual inventory carrying costs would be between £0.75m and £1.25m, which could be nearly half the annual wages bill of the entire company. Traditional accounting principles have not in the past made inventory carrying costs explicit, and it is only in recent years, in response to Japanese competition (capable of achieving 50–100 stock turns per year), that manufacturing companies are waking up to the enormous hidden costs associated with large inventories, and the importance of inventory reduction to stay competitive in world markets. Although some inventory is essential, too much inventory is a significant source of waste. Value-adding management suggests that we should pay attention to carrying only just sufficient inventory to fulfil the functions mentioned above and no more.

3.5.2 INVENTORY AS A BUFFER BETWEEN PRODUCTION AND DEMAND

Consider the simple one-stage production/demand situation shown in Fig. 3.8.

We shall assume that the demand exists in the external environment and is not subject to any control by the production system. If the demand were completely known and predictable, and if the production rate were controllable, completely reliable and instantaneously responsive to changes in demand, it would be theoretically possible to match the production rate precisely to the demand rate and avoid the build-up of any intermediate inventory whatsoever. In the real world, however, these conditions do not generally hold. Demands tend to fluctuate, and the magnitude of these fluctuations can often not be well predicted. Production is not always completely reliable, with machine breakdowns, materials shortages, etc., resulting in periods when no production is possible. It is also usually more convenient to produce a given product more rapidly than the demand rate, so that the same production facilities can be used for other products.

The problems associated with this 'mismatch' between demand and production can be largely eliminated by deliberately interposing a 'buffer'

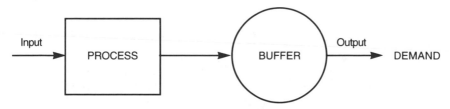

Fig. 3.8 One-stage production/inventory/demand.

stock between the demand and the production process, which serves to absorb or 'cushion out' the irregularities in each. The effect of this inventory is to act as a decoupling agent, which allows production to proceed largely independently of the short-term fluctuations in demand on the one hand, and allows demand to be instantly satisfied regardless of irregularities of production on the other. The only major constraint is that total production should equal total demand over some time period long enough to smooth out the fluctuations.

In manufacturing companies, the presence of such decoupling inventories greatly simplifies the problems of the production manager, since he can attempt to schedule the activities of his department to achieve maximum production at minimum cost without being concerned with short-term demand fluctuations. Also, in any series production line situation, buffer stocks between different workstations on the line (as shown in Fig. 3.9) can allow the production line as a whole to continue running, even in the event of breakdowns of the individual workstations, since the workstation downstream of the one that has stopped is not directly fed by the latter but by the buffer. Provided the buffer level is kept up, the downstream workstation can continue to operate.

A second characteristic of the cushioning role of inventory is connected with the fact that the rate of production of a particular product is often greater than the rate of demand. This implies that in order to match long-term production with long-term demand, it will be necessary to produce intermittently in batches, in order to avoid rapid build-up of unsold stock. The size of the decoupling inventory will obviously be affected by the size and frequency of the production batches that are produced. If large batches of product are made infrequently, the average amount of inventory held will be greater than in the case where small batches are made more frequently. This is illustrated in Fig. 3.10, where graphs of inventory against time are shown for two cases.

Inventory is at a peak just after a production batch has been made, and gradually depletes as it is drawn on by the demand, until the next batch comes in. Since fixed costs such as machine set-up costs, ordering costs, etc., are usually associated with either the production of a batch of products or the ordering of a batch of raw materials, these costs being independent of batch size, the most economical course of action would appear

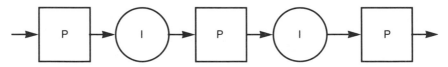

ᴣ. 3.9 Production line with buffers.

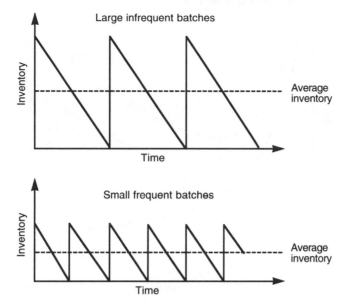

Fig. 3.10 Inventory–time graphs for large and small batches.

to be to produce or order infrequently, in large batches, thereby minimiz-ing the frequency of occurrence of these fixed costs. This must, however, be balanced against the costs associated with carrying inventory. This can be done using the so-called **Economic batch size** formula which is derived as follows.

If we assume a cost C_s is associated with setting up to produce or order a batch of a particular item (and this is independent of the size of the batch) and C_i is the cost of carrying inventory per unit item per unit time, then as the batch size increases, the set-up cost per unit time will be related to batch size Q according to:

$$\text{Set-up cost per unit time} = Q/C_s$$

and the inventory carrying cost per unit time will be related to the batch size by:

$$\text{Inventory cost per unit time} = QC_i/2$$

(where we are assuming that the average inventory held per unit time is one half of the batch size – refer to Fig. 3.10 to verify that this is true for a uniform demand situation).

Thus as batch size increases, the set-up cost per unit time will decrease and the inventory carrying cost per unit time will increase as shown in Fig. 3.11.

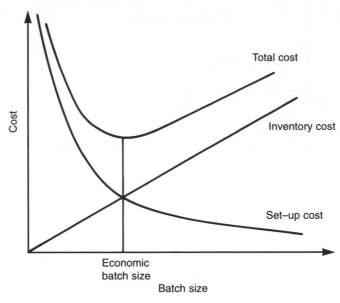

Fig. 3.11 The economic batch quantity.

The batch size giving the minimum cost is at the intersection of these two cost curves, and can be shown by the application of simple differential calculus to be given by:

$$\text{Minimum cost batch } Q^* = \sqrt{2DC_s / C_i}$$

where D is the demand rate (assumed constant).

With set-up and inventory carrying cost coefficients as given, this would be the batch size that would be optimal with respect to simultaneously minimizing both these costs.

Thus for an item for which the demand is 100 units per week, if the set-up cost to produce the item is £50, and the inventory carrying cost is £5 per item per week, then the economic batch size is $\sqrt{2 \times 100 \times 50/5} = 44.7$ units.

Fortunately the sum of the inventory and set-up costs is relatively insensitive to the exact batch size in the region of the minimum cost (it can be seen that the total cost curve is fairly flat at its minimum value) so we can afford some considerable variation in batch size around the optimum value before we see any appreciable increase in cost.

There has been a considerable amount of discussion about the economic batch size formula, and several mathematical extensions have been developed for cases more complex than the one given above. However, focus in recent years has moved away from the formula itself to the fact that

although inventory carrying costs may be relatively fixed an[d]
set-up costs can often be reduced over time. Thus rather t[han]
the cost coefficients in the formula as 'givens' and developin[g]
complex extensions to the formula for increasingly compl[ex]
tion is being paid to reducing inventory by reducing se[t-up]
costs to their lowest possible value, using the basic version of the formula
to obtain a rough idea of the economic batch size in the minimum set-
up situation, but allowing considerable flexibility in the actual batch size
to fit in with other considerations such as production capacity or known
variation in demand.

3.5.3 USE OF INVENTORY TO CONTROL PRODUCTION

Inventory can serve another very important purpose in addition to its
decoupling effect. In batch (as opposed to continuous) production industries, it can also act as the control variable through which the intermittent
production of an item can be triggered. This can be seen with reference
to Fig. 3.12 which shows the inventory against time graph of an item
produced in intermittent batches.

As inventory is depleted, the level is monitored, and when it reaches
what is termed the 'reorder level' a request is made (or an order launched)
for production of a replenishment batch. This reorder level is set
according to the amount of time (called the **lead time**) it will take for the
item to be produced and physically enter stock from the time the order

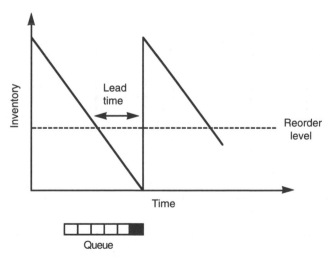

Fig. 3.12 A reorder level system.

as launched. Thus in the presence of a uniform demand, the inventory level will be timed to reach zero just as the new order arrives.

We thus have the simple result that:

Reorder level (ROL) = Demand during the lead time

The size of the replenishment batch would normally be close to the economic batch quantity as computed by the formula given above.

The allowed lead time of an item is generally considerably longer than its physical production time, to allow for the fact that when the order is launched, the production resources required to make it are unlikely to be able to start immediately since there will be a backlog of other items waiting to be produced. Thus the order will join a 'queue' of orders waiting for the resource to become available (as shown in Fig. 3.12). The lead time thus consists of the physical production time together with the time spent waiting in the queue (which can be up to ten times the production time). The sequence of orders in the queue can, however, be manipulated to selectively control lead times, as will be described in the next section.

In cases where the demand is not uniform but fluctuating, the inventory against time graph may appear as in Fig. 3.13.

In this situation, to guard against stockouts caused by unexpectedly high demand, we would carry a certain amount of 'safety stock' as shown

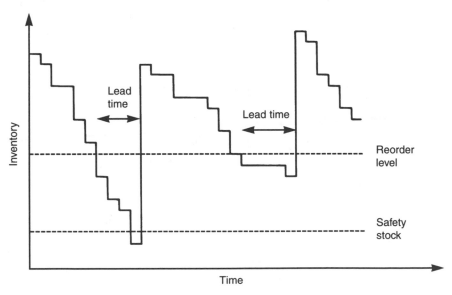

Fig. 3.13 Reorder level with fluctuating demand.

in the diagram. Thus in the first demand period when demand is higher than average, we can still meet it by using up safety stock, whereas in the second period when demand is lower than average, we will have a certain amount of excess stock when the replenishment batch arrives. If we know the statistical distribution of the demand variability, we can compute the amount of safety stock required to give us a certain assurance level of not being out of stock at the end of any particular demand period.

Thus if we assume the demand during the lead time is normally distributed with mean value D and standard deviation s, then in order to give an assurance level (known as the 'service level') that any particular lead time demand can be met from stock, our safety stock would be given by:

$$\text{Safety stock (SS)} = ks$$

where k is a factor that indicates the area under the normal distribution curve corresponding to the required assurance level, and is obtained from a table of areas under the normal curve.

Introduction of safety stock has the effect of increasing the reorder level to:

$$\text{ROL} = \text{Demand over lead time} + \text{Safety stock}$$

Thus for an item having a demand over the lead time of 100 units and a standard deviation of 50 (assumed normally distributed), to obtain a 90% chance of meeting the demand over the lead time, the safety stock would need to be set at 64, and for a 99% chance it would need to be set at 116.

In the above system of triggering production (known as a **simple reorder point system**), we have a simple feedback loop from inventory to production as shown in Fig. 3.14. Inventory is the 'state' variable of the system which is monitored, and feedback of the values of this state variable is used to influence the decision variable (quantity and timing of production).

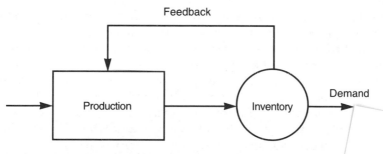

Fig. 3.14 Inventory–production feedback loop.

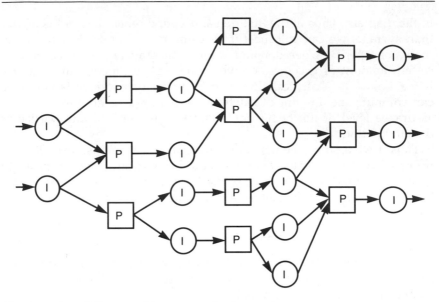

Fig. 3.15 A multi-item, multi-stage production system.

This can be extended to the multi-item, multi-stage situation shown in Fig. 3.15 in which each of the individual production resources have production triggered for the appropriate item at the appropriate time merely by monitoring the inventory levels.

3.6 PUSH VS PULL SYSTEMS OF PRODUCTION CONTROL

In the past, many manufacturing companies have used what has been termed a **push** system of production. In the push system, production is not governed so much by market demand as by the supposed need to keep the stock of all items produced up to certain predetermined levels, regardless of the actual demand for them. This contrasts with so-called **pull** systems of production in which items are only produced when there is an actual demand.

To illustrate the push system of production, consider a production resource which produces batches of different items to meet a demand generated by a customer (either a downstream production resource or a customer external to the organization) with an inventory against time graph as shown in Fig. 3.16. In the push system of production, an order is placed for a batch on the assumption that no knowledge exists about the timing or quantity of any future demand for that item. Thus we see that in Fig. 3.16, although an order for a batch is placed when the stock has run down to the reorder point at time t_1 and this arrives in stock one lead time later at time t_2, there is in actual fact no further demand for this item until

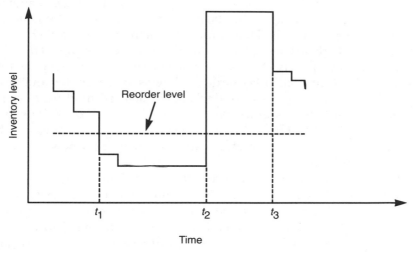

Fig. 3.16 Inventory–time graph for a 'push' system of production.

some considerable time later at t_3, and stock is carried needlessly between times t_2 and t_3. If the timing of the next demand for the item had been predictable, production of the batch could have been delayed so that it only arrived in stock at time t_3.

A factor that encourages the push system of production is the lack of lateral information flow that characterizes many manufacturing companies. We have already mentioned how one of the purposes of inventory is to decouple sequential stages of the manufacturing process from each other so that they can proceed more or less independently. When this is put into effect in a literal sense, with no communication between demand and supply other than through the inventory buffer, then once an order is launched by inventory dropping to its reorder point, no adjustment will be made to the size or requirement date of the order during the course of the lead time to reflect even predictable variations of demand from what is expected. Orders are fed into the system on a 'push and forget' basis. Once this has happened, then with no subsequent coordination between demand and supply, needlessly high stocks may alternate with needless stockouts, both of which could have been avoided.

In a pull system of production, much closer coordination is maintained between demand and supply, even up to the point where production only occurs in response to a firm (rather than forecast) demand. A much greater degree of real-time information flow occurs between demand and production as to how much of what to produce when. In some types of pull system, namely closed loop MRP (material requirements planning), which will be discussed in Chapter 5, the lead time of an item is manipulated by changing its position in the queue in front of the resource that produces it. Thus, orders for items for which there is an unexpectedly high demand after the order is placed can be pulled through production more quickly to meet the demand merely by moving them to the top of the queue (Fig. 3.17). Orders for items for which demand turns out to be less than expected are deliberately delayed until they are required. Obviously this assumes that the average demand over all items is roughly constant, so that for every item that jumps the queue to be produced in less than the average lead time, there must be some other item that can be delayed due to a less than expected demand. Also it requires attention to be paid to actually closing the feedback loop, and ensuring that relevant information is transmitted and appropriate action is taken either to slow down or speed up individual orders as dictated by requirements. This is often difficult to achieve, with many MRP users failing to properly close the control loop. MRP systems in general are thus frequently associated with push rather than pull systems.

More effective pull systems are usually associated with the Japanese system of **just-in-time (JIT)** production, in which both batch sizes and lead times are deliberately reduced (by techniques that will be discussed in subsequent chapters), to the point where all production is in response to an actual firm demand by the customer or the downstream production resource. This will often be because sequential processes are physically located so close together that a system of visual signals can be used for communication to the upstream resource that a production batch is required, with minimal buffer stocks being maintained between the two production resources so that the downstream resource can continue to be fed with materials.

Typical push systems of production are to be found today in large batch manufacturing companies such as oil and steel, where run set-up costs are so high that production, once started, must continue for a set period, regardless of short-term demand, to be economically stable. Pull systems

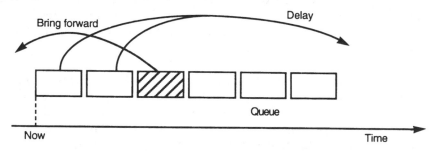

Fig. 3.17 Hedging against uncertainty using queue manipulation.

of production, on the other hand, can be found in manual assembly industries such as light electronics, in which the assembly line can be rapidly changed to accommodate changes in demand.

3.7 CENTRALIZED AND DECENTRALIZED SYSTEMS OF PRODUCTION CONTROL

The reorder point method of production control is basically a decentralized method in that decisions to produce or purchase a particular item are based purely on the local inventory level of that item without reference to any form of global production plan. Thus in Fig. 3.15 each production/inventory/demand block makes decisions about how much of what to produce at what time on an autonomous basis.

Other methods of production control can, however, be used which are based on a more centralized form of decision-making regarding how much of what needs to be produced when. If we look again at Fig. 3.15 we will see that requirements for purchase of raw materials and production of intermediate items such as components and sub-assemblies are in fact not all independent, but are driven by the demand for the end products of which these components and sub-assemblies form a part. If a decision can be made as regards a master schedule for the production of end products, which fixes in advance the quantities and timings of production batches of these products, then this in turn will fix the required quantities and timings of all the sub-assemblies, components and raw materials required to support this schedule. If requirements are transmitted to the individual production resources responsible for producing each item, then these resources can base their production on a schedule that is directly linked to the master schedule for end products rather than being determined merely on the basis of the periodic replenishment of local buffer stocks.

Centralized production control, in which production of individual items is driven by a master schedule for end products, is the basis for the system of production management known as **materials requirements planning (MRP)**. MRP operates by a computer-generated explosion of the master production schedule for end products into the implied set of time-phased requirements for individual components and raw materials. This is performed by referring to stored bills of materials to obtain the identities and quantities of the constituent material items needed to produce the product. A netting and time-phasing calculation is then performed in which, after making allowance for current inventory levels and the average manufacturing lead time required to produce each item, net production quantities and timings of constituent items required to meet the end product master production schedule are computed. This is repeated on a level-by-level basis until, at the lowest level, the computation finishes with the generation of purchasing requirements for bought-in raw materials.

3.8 MANUFACTURING CLASSIFICATION REVISITED

We have stressed in this chapter the essential role played by a limited amount of inventory in the management of manufacturing operations. However, different types of manufacturing companies often vary in the stage of the manufacturing process in which inventory will require to be positioned. This will depend in practice on where the majority of the uncertainty is concentrated. Different types of company will have different concentrations of uncertainty depending on whether they manufacture to stock or to order.

We can in fact distinguish the following classes of company from this point of view:

- make to stock;
- assemble to order;
- make to order.

In make to stock companies, standardized products are made to a forecast demand rather than to a firm customer order. Consumer products such as televisions, washing machines, personal computers, etc. (the type of products customers would expect to buy off the shelf) fall into this category, with the operations of the company focused on a limited range of products. In this type of company, to minimize the customer response time and to hedge against the uncertainty in what the actual demand for the product will turn out to be, inventory is concentrated at the finished product end (this is termed **forward positioning** of inventory). Since a firm master schedule can be decided on to maintain a given stock level of end products, this will generate predictable requirements of sub-assemblies, components, raw materials etc., so stocks of these latter items can be kept low.

In assemble to order companies, end products consisting of optional combinations of basic modules (which would normally be major sub-assemblies) are assembled in a short lead time to produce specific end products ordered by particular customers.

Examples are the automotive industry where individual cars are customized in terms of engine size, transmission type, body colour, trim, optional extras, etc. The uncertainty here is on the demand that will exist for the basic modules which are assembled into the finished car (for example engines, transmissions, body panels, air conditioning units, radios, etc.), so rather than attempting to maintain stocks of finished products representing each possible combination of options, stocks are maintained of the basic modules.

In a make to order company, the operations of the company are normally focused on a particular process rather than a particular set of products. The company will use its process capability to produce individual products to customer order, normally from a fairly standard range of purchased raw materials. Here, since everything is produced to firm customer order, we cannot stock finished products. Inventory is positioned backwards towards the purchased items end, in order to reduce response times at the same time as retaining product flexibility.

3.9 BOTTLENECKS

In very few manufacturing plants are production resources all utilized to the same extent. It is usually found that a relatively small number of resources are invariably much more heavily utilized than the remainder, either because their processing times are long in relation to those of other resources or because they are unreliable, or, as in the case of batch or job shops, they perform some common process through which all manufactured units must pass. Bottleneck resources are very significant because it is these resources in particular which limit the total output of a production plant.

To illustrate this, consider the simple situation in Fig. 3.18 in which we have a flow of production units which are sequentially processed on five resources having the maximum processing rates indicated. It will be seen that each resource can produce a maximum of 10 units per hour except Machine 3 which can only produce five units per hour. Machine 3 will obviously be the bottleneck of this particular production line, because although the machines on either side can produce 10 units per hour, the output of the line as a whole is limited to the output of five units per hour of Machine 3. This means in turn that if the line is working to produce its maximum output, the machines on either side of the bottleneck will only be working at half capacity.

It might be assumed from the foregoing illustration that the bottleneck resource in situations like the one shown is the machine with the smallest capacity or processing speed. However, whether a resource is actually a

Fig. 3.18 Production line with bottleneck.

bottleneck or not at any particular time depends not just on its processing speed or capacity, but also on the loading of the production line as a whole. If a bottleneck were identifiable merely as the minimum capacity resource, then it would be Machine 3 as before. However, if the total required output of the line was four units per hour (that is all machines had excess production capacity), then there would be no bottleneck, with all machines spending some of their time idle. Machine 3 is here the potential bottleneck but it only becomes a real bottleneck when the demand on it reaches its capacity.

In manufacturing situations in which a clear bottleneck exists, and in which the majority of production units flow through the bottleneck resource at some stage of the manufacturing process as shown in Fig. 3.19, the non-bottleneck resources can be usefully divided into two types, those upstream of the bottleneck (pre-bottleneck resources) and those downstream of the bottleneck (post-bottleneck resources).

In a push system of production, if the pre-bottleneck resources continue to produce at full capacity regardless of the rate at which units can subsequently be processed by the bottleneck, then inventory will simply build up in front of the bottleneck resource. The post-bottleneck resources will, however, never be able to run at full capacity because they will be starved of input by the limited production rate of the bottleneck resource. In the pull system, pre-bottleneck resources will only be activated to produce sufficient to feed the bottleneck. Again, this emphasizes the superiority of pull over push systems of production.

This also implies a very important difference between bottleneck and non-bottleneck resources in terms of minimum batch sizes. It is clearly very important to minimize non-productive time in the form of set-ups on bottleneck resources because any time spent on setting up the bottleneck will reduce the total output of the plant. On the other hand, set-up times

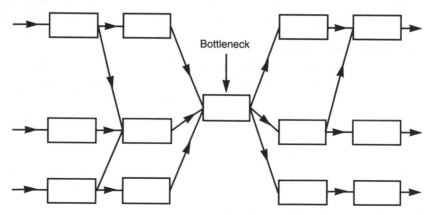

Fig. 3.19 Plant with bottleneck.

for non-bottleneck resources should not have any effect on total output as these must in any case spend a proportion of their time idle to match the throughput of the bottleneck. This in turn means that we can generally tolerate considerably smaller production batch sizes on non-bottleneck resources than we can on bottleneck resources. This has some interesting consequences for production planning and scheduling which we shall look at in more detail in Chapter 6.

Plants which have an obvious and pronounced bottleneck can make effective use of the differences between bottleneck and non-bottleneck resources to simplify their production and scheduling by focusing attention on the bottleneck resource. Since the bottleneck resource alone will determine the overall performance of the manufacturing system, production on the bottleneck must be planned and scheduled very carefully. Its productive time must obviously be maximized by producing in large batches to minimize set-ups, maintaining buffer stocks in front of the bottleneck to ensure it is never starved of work, and ensuring adequate preventative maintenance to minimize breakdowns. The non-bottleneck resources can, by contrast, get by with much less attention.

On the other hand, in plants in which the bottleneck is less pronounced, this approach can lead to problems. Assiduous attention to what was assumed to be the bottleneck resource can quickly result in it being the bottleneck no longer. Under these circumstances we get what is called the **wandering bottleneck** phenomenon, and the type of simplification we have been talking about breaks down. We shall examine what can be done in these circumstances in later chapters.

The conclusions of this simple analysis of the nature of bottlenecks may be summarized as follows.

- The bottleneck resource alone will govern the total throughput of the manufacturing system; performance of the plant can therefore be maximized if most attention is paid to the bottleneck resource.
- Non-bottleneck resources should never be used at 100% capacity, as they might be in a push system.
- Utilization of non-bottleneck resources will not be determined by their own capacity but by the capacity of the bottleneck.
- In plants without a pronounced bottleneck, a focus of attention on the presumed bottleneck can result in the wandering bottleneck phenomenon.

3.10 V, A AND T PLANTS

A different and quite recent way of classifying manufacturing plants is related to the particular symptoms which reveal the location of the bottleneck. This classification is based on the shape of manufacturing network that can be drawn to show how materials flow through the plant. The shape of a manufacturing network will have a close correlation with the shape of the bills of materials of the products the company manufactures. A bill of materials is a representation of the structure of a product in terms of all the sub-assemblies, components and raw materials of which it is composed. For the purposes of differentiating between different types of material flow, it is convenient to represent bills of materials graphically in the form of a tree structure as shown in Fig. 3.20.

You will observe that the tree shown in Fig. 3.20 has the shape of a pyramid, implying that the end product is composed of several sub-assemblies, and possibly of sub-sub-assemblies, each of which consists of several components which are fabricated from raw materials. As we go down the tree from end product to raw materials, the number of individual items increases. If all products manufactured by the company were roughly similar in terms of the shape of their bills of materials, and if common components were used in a reasonable proportion of products, then if all the bills of materials were placed as tree structures on the same diagram the resulting shape would be that of a truncated pyramid as shown on Fig. 3.20.

The topology of the typical Bills of Materials of a given company will usually take one of three distinct types of shape similar to the letters V, A or T (Fig. 3.21). A **V plant** is characterized by the use of a very limited number of different raw materials which may be converted into a proliferation of end products as they go through an increasing number of processes. The bill of materials topology will be in the form of an inverted pyramid (a V shape) which is complex at the end product level and simple at the raw materials level. Typical V plants include plants that produce integrated circuits, steel mills or oil refineries.

An **A plant** is a plant that makes a relatively small number of end products from a relatively large number of components and raw materials, resulting in the bill of materials topology having a pyramid

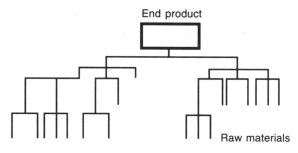

Fig. 3.20 Topology of typical bill of materials.

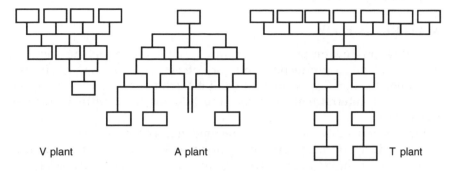

Fig. 3.21 V, A and T plants.

shape. Typical A plants would be plants producing heavy or specialized equipment such as machine tools, generators, etc.

A **T plant** is a plant in which large numbers of end products (generally to individual customer order) are made from a relatively small number of sub-assemblies or components which can be put together in many different ways. Thus car manufacturers produce a large number of product variants based on the combination of a relatively small number of optional extras (for example power steering, sunroof, automatic gearbox, central locking, electric windows, air conditioning) in a large number of different ways. Bill of materials topology in a T plant may have a pyramid appearance in the lower section topped by a rapid outward explosion of complexity at the end product due to the many different combinations of the basic modules that can be assembled. The basic modules themselves are represented by the neck (the narrowest part) of the structure.

The V, A and T classification has been developed as an aid to locating the bottleneck resources in the plant. Empirical evidence suggests that bottleneck resources can be identified by different symptoms in different types of plant as follows:

- in V plants the bottleneck resources will be those with the largest inventory buffers;
- in A plants the bottleneck resources will be those with the most chronic shortages of input materials;
- in T plants the bottleneck resources will be those which make the largest contribution to late shipments.

Since, as we have seen, it is of critical importance to separate the bottleneck and non-bottleneck resources in a plant so that they can be planned and scheduled in different ways, a classification which assists in the bottleneck identification process is obviously of value. However, as with the Harvard Industries Classification Scheme described earlier, many plants will show characteristics of more than one type.

3.11 EFFECT OF PROCESS VARIABILITY ON MATERIALS FLOW

In reality, production process times are rarely constant and predictable, even for identical production units or batches. In most plants, processing times for identical units will exhibit fluctuations about some mean value, and intermittent machine breakdowns will further increase variability.

Process variability has some interesting effects on materials flow which can be deduced from a branch of applied mathematics known as **queuing theory**. In a simple queuing system, units arrive at intervals to be processed by a server, which can process units at a particular rate. Having been served, units leave the system. This is shown diagrammatically in Fig. 3.22.

If the arrival rate is less than the service rate, arrivals occur at precisely regular intervals, and the service rate is constant, then there would never be any build-up of units in front of the server. However, if either arrivals occur at random intervals, or if the service rate is variable, then there will from time to time be a build-up of units in front of the server in the form of a queue. For example, we may get three successive arrivals in a very short space of time followed by a long period with no arrivals, in which case we should alternately have a queue of units in front of the server, followed by a period in which the server was idle, as shown in Fig. 3.23. It is in fact the presence of variability in the arrival or service rates that leads to the formation of queues.

One simple but important result from queuing theory is that if the mean arrival rate is λ and the mean service rate is μ, then if any random fluctuations exist either in individual arrivals or in individual services, for situations in which $\lambda = \mu$ (that is the mean arrival rate is equal to the mean processing rate), the queue in front of the server will gradually build up to infinite length. This can be understood intuitively from the fact that if the processing rate is just equal to the arrival rate, the server must be busy for 100% of the time in order to process all the arrivals. However, if arrivals or services are irregular, the server will sometimes experience enforced idle time due to a particularly long interval between arrivals or to a particularly fast service, and this idle time can never be made up.

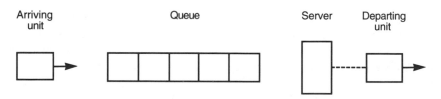

Fig. 3.22 A queuing system.

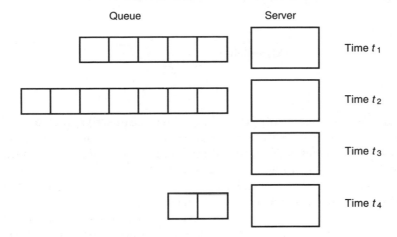

Fig. 3.23 Snapshot of a queue at different times.

The server will be working at less than 100% capacity because of occasional starvation of work, and so by definition will be unable to match the rate at which work arrives, resulting in a progressive build-up of work.

For queuing situations in which $\mu > \lambda$ (that is the processing rate is greater than the arrival rate), a queue will exist of a fluctuating but constant average length. Some arriving units will be processed immediately, whereas others will have to queue. When units arrive for service at a constant average rate λ but with individual arrivals randomly spread such that an arrival is equally likely to occur in any randomly chosen small time interval we have what are termed **Poisson distributed** arrivals. In cases where both arrivals and service completions are Poisson distributed, the following results can be derived:

$$\text{Average number of units in queue} = \frac{\lambda^2}{\mu(\mu - \lambda)}$$

$$\text{Average waiting time in queue} = \frac{\lambda}{\mu(\mu - \lambda)}$$

It can be seen that as the ratio λ/μ (sometimes termed the **traffic intensity**) approaches 1 (that is $\lambda = \mu$), both the mean queue length and the mean waiting time increase to infinity as the denominator of both expressions becomes zero.

If service times are distributed according to an arbitrary distribution such that the mean service time is t and the variance is s^2, then it can be shown that the mean length of the queue in this case is given by:

$$\text{Mean length } = \frac{\lambda^2 s^2 + \left(\dfrac{\lambda}{\mu}\right)^2}{2\left(1 - \dfrac{\lambda}{\mu}\right)}$$

We can see from this result that for any given mean arrival rate and mean service time, the mean length of the queue increases as the variance of the service time increases. The minimum length queue arises in situations where the variance of the service time is zero.

Clearly, we can interpret the individual units in a queuing situation as production units flowing through a factory, a server as a production resource in a factory, the service rate as the rate at which the production resource processes units, and the queue as a build-up of work in process inventory in front of the production resource. The traffic intensity (the ratio) is the degree of loading or utilization of that production resource.

The important consequences of queuing theory when applied to a simple production situation are as follows.

- The greater the irregularity of arrivals of jobs at a production resource, or the greater the variability of the processing time, then the greater will be both the average build-up of inventory in front of the resource and the average throughput time.
- The greater the utilization of a production resource in the presence of arrival and process variability, the larger will be the inventory build-up and throughput time. Thus, in order to reduce inventory and throughput time, we should:
  - reduce variability in both arrivals and process times;
  - ensure that production resources are not trying to operate at 100% capacity.

Let us now extend this analysis from a simple queuing system to a network of queues as shown in Fig. 3.24 which might represent a production line in which items are sequentially processed on different production resources.

Let us assume that the capacities of all the resources are identical, in the sense that they all have the same processing rate and that no inter-process inventory is kept other than that arising from queues of items forming in front of resources. If the arrivals at the first resource are completely

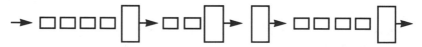

Fig. 3.24 A network of queues.

regular, it will be capable of an output equal to its processing rate, since it will never have any enforced idle time when it is starved of work. However, any process variability in the first resource will result in an irregular flow of units to the second resource (that is the second resource will experience irregular arrivals). Even if the processing rate of the second resource is equal to the first, the second resource will be unable to process all the output of the first because it will never be able to make up the occasional enforced idle time when it is starved of work because of delays between arrivals. The output rate of the second resource will thus be less than its theoretical maximum processing rate.

If we are processing individual parts on a continuous basis, the only means by which we can arrange for the output of the second production resource to equal the input to the first production resource is by deliberately interposing a buffer stock between the two resources. The second resource can then draw on this buffer stock in situations where an unusually long process time of a unit on the first resource would otherwise mean it was starved of work.

We thus conclude that:

A way of maximizing the flow of individually processed items through sequential production resources in the presence of process variability is to maintain buffer stocks between processes above those implied by the normal queue in front of each process.

Let us now consider what happens if we are processing batches rather than individual items. For example, if the first resource processes items in batches of 12 units with associated variability in the batch processing time, then if we move all 12 units from the first to the second resource as one batch (that is we wait until all 12 have been processed before we transfer any), then we will have the same problem as before. The occasional processing delays at the first resource will starve the second resource of work which it will never be able to catch up. However, if we transfer units from the first to the second resource in batches smaller than the process batch size (for example, if we only need to wait until, say, three units have been processed before transferring them to the second resource), then we are much less likely ever to starve the second resource of work due to an abnormally long batch processing time on the first resource. We are essentially increasing the arrival rate at the second resource by splitting the processing batch on the first resource into smaller transfer batches.

This leads us to conclude that:

A way of maximizing the flow of batches through sequential production resources in the presence of process variability is to transfer units from one resource to the next in batches which are smaller than the process batch.

This has become an important concept in modern production management theory. In traditional production planning and control based on **economic batch quantity**, emphasis was placed on maintaining the identity of a single production batch as it moved through the plant from process to process. Although batches might occasionally be split for greater processing flexibility and combined for greater economy, this was normally done on an informal basis. However, it has since been pointed out by Goldrat (1980) that not only can greater efficiency be achieved if transfer batches are allowed to be smaller than the process batch, but also the size of the process batch should often be allowed to change from one operation to the next (for example due to varying set-up costs). This could of course be achieved by regarding the transfer batch as the basic indivisible batch quantity, and combining different numbers of transfer batches at different workstations to give the appropriate processing batch for that work centre.

The mathematical analysis of these types of situation is beyond the scope of this book. However, a knowledge of the basic qualitative characteristics of sequential queuing processes is really all that is required for the management of most practical situations, with the mathematical analysis being mostly of academic interest only. A simplified mathematical treatment of materials flow is given by Baudin (1990).

3.12 CONCLUSION

The detailed dynamics of how material flows through a manufacturing plant, how inventory can build up at various points of the system, and how and why bottlenecks occur, are complex and can be affected by many factors. However, it is very important to understand and to be able to control this dynamics, in order to achieve a coordinated flow of materials which minimizes inventory build-up, and which ensures the arrival of the right materials in the right place at the right time in the required quantity. The concepts and principles we have developed in this chapter will be used in the following four chapters in which we examine the ways in which coordinated materials flow can be achieved in practice.

REFERENCES

Baudin, M. (1990) *Manufacturing Systems Analysis with Applications to Production Scheduling.* Yourdon/Prentice Hall, Englewood Cliffs, NJ.

Goldrat, E. (1980) Optimized production timetables: a revolutionary program for industry. *APICS 23rd International Conference Proceedings*, pp. 172–6.

Vollman, T.E., Berry, W.L. and Whybark, D.C. (1988) *Manufacturing Planning and Control Systems.* Dow Jones-Irwin/APICS, Homewood, Illinois.

Planning hierarchies and timescales – the master production schedule

4

4.1 OVERVIEW

This and the following three chapters are closely interlinked, and deal with the topic of production planning and control. Coordination of materials flow through a manufacturing organization requires adequate planning of the overall levels of production required to meet market demand, and adequate detailed control of precise timings and quantities of individual items to be produced. In these chapters we examine some techniques for the planning of production requirements, and some alternative ways of controlling these activities at a detailed level.

This chapter introduces a hierarchical framework within which planning can take place. Within this framework, aggregate plans for overall production levels over the long term can be progressively broken down into more specific and detailed plans which can actually be executed on the shop floor. Some techniques for planning at various levels of the hierarchy will be examined.

Chapter 5 then goes on to introduce the manufacturing resources planning (MRP 2) approach to translating long-term aggregate plans into detailed operational requirements. Chapter 6 then introduces an alternative paradigm for developing detailed operational production plans that can actually be executed on the shop floor, namely the 'synchronous manufacturing' approach (which has been marketed under the proprietary name of 'optimized production technology' or OPT for short). The final of the four chapters examines the just-in-time approach to production planning and control and its relationship to the broader manufacturing philosophy of waste elimination and value-adding management. In Chapter 7 we shall also examine the relationship between these different approaches, their suitability for different types of manufacturing situation, and how companies can 'evolve' towards approaches that best suit their competitive strategy.

4.2 CHAPTER STRUCTURE

This chapter is divided into the following sections:

- the planning hierarchy;
- planning timescales;
- demand forecasting;
- long-term production planning;
- the master production schedule;
- what items to include in the MPS.

The chapter starts by presenting a framework for hierarchical production planning, discusses the typical timescales over which plans should be developed and how these can be determined, and then considers the forecasting techniques available to anticipate trends in demand.

The different levels of planning are then discussed in more detail. At the top level, long-term plans are developed in terms of aggregate units of production for which common production facilities are needed. These plans are used to anticipate any required long lead time changes to plant capacity. At a more detailed level, a master production schedule for the production of individual end products is developed over a timescale varying from several weeks to several months. The precise items that are scheduled in this way (finished products made for stock or basic modules made for assembly to individual customer order) are determined by the general shape of the bills of materials of the products the company makes.

4.3 THE PLANNING HIERARCHY

In order to ensure that it maintains a competitive position in the market-place, a manufacturing organization must have some form of coordinated plan with regard to its future activities. Although a manufacturing company must engage in many types of planning much of which stems from its chosen manufacturing strategy, the basic activity of a manufacturing organization is of course production, and the planning of production is an essential part of manufacturing management.

Production planning is concerned with decisions about how much of what types of product to produce at what time to meet market demand. Good planning will ensure that timings and quantities are such as to ensure the organization competes effectively in its chosen posture. In this chapter we shall be examining the nature of production plans.

Most organizations employ some form of hierarchical production planning. The schema of a hierarchical planning system for a typical manufacturing organization is shown in Fig. 4.1. You will see that the plan is divided into a number of distinct levels, with each higher level of planning being at a more aggregate level and covering a longer time horizon.

At the top level is the long-term plan. This will be an aggregate plan that will be made for a complete manufacturing plant over a period of a year or more. The aggregate plan is generally concerned with setting production levels for the plant as a whole, or for groups of products that use common facilities.

The long-range plan is refined at the next level into a tactical plan which establishes what is commonly called a **master production schedule (MPS)**, for individual types of finished product (in terms of timings and quantities to be produced) over a one month to one year timescale.

At the lowest level we have the operational plan which is concerned with the actual daily execution of the tactical plan, including the monitoring of shopfloor activities to ensure that production is on target, and taking appropriate corrective action if problems occur.

4.4 PLANNING TIMESCALES

The timescales given in the planning framework in Fig. 4.1 are only provided for illustration, and may deviate significantly from these values. The timescale over which planning needs to occur is determined by how quickly the organization can react to the type of changes which occur in its environment, coupled to the extent to which these changes can be confidently forecast. Alternatively, we can say that the planning horizon should be determined by the lead time required to implement the types of decisions that are likely to be made at each particular planning level.

Fig. 4.1 Planning hierarchies and timescales.

Thus in capital intensive industries such as aircraft or steel production, any major increase in plant capacity may take a number of years to implement. Long-range plans must therefore be developed for a commensurate distance ahead so that actions to increase capacity can be initiated in time to accommodate any expected major increase in market demand that may occur over this timescale. On the other hand, for a given level of productive capacity, it might be possible to make an adjustment to the product mix very quickly, and so it would only be necessary to plan such changes a few days ahead.

No one can predict the future with 100% accuracy. Plans are made on the basis of forecasts, and the further ahead we need to forecast the more likely we are to get it wrong, particularly if we are attempting to forecast to any degree of detail. Thus the steel company would only attempt to make a forecast of aggregate production requirements over the long term and not try to predict sales of individual products. Obviously the further ahead we need to plan because of long lead times or slow response times for initiating changes required by the plan, and as our plans are based only on forecasts, the more likely we are to commit ourselves to a course of action that turns out to be inappropriate.

It is therefore important for a manufacturing company not to develop and commit itself to production plans for too far ahead if the organization is sufficiently responsive that it would be able to accommodate any expected changes in the market at very short notice. A fast-food outlet will not develop a long-range production plan for more than a day or so ahead, and it would be futile for it to attempt to do otherwise. Raw materials can be obtained at short notice and production capacity increased by hiring temporary staff.

Because of the unreliability of forecasts, companies should deliberately try to remove the necessity for planning far ahead by adopting as responsive a posture as possible. In the context of production planning, this means attempting to reduce production lead times as much as possible (for example by using local rather than overseas suppliers) and maintaining flexibility to vary production mixes and volumes at short notice.

4.5 DEMAND FORECASTING

All phases of the hierarchical planning approach require some form of demand forecasting. There are three types of forecast classified by the time horizon over which the forecast is made.

1. **Long-term or 'economic' forecast**. This looks ahead over a period as long as five years and is used for planning new facilities, plant extensions, machines, new ranges of products and a company's general economic future.

2. **Intermediate forecast**. This is a forecast of total demand for the company's products over the next 12 to 18 months and represents the major input to the aggregate production plan described in the next section. It is used for setting overall inventory and production programmes and financial budgets.
3. **Short-term forecast**. This is usually from one to three months duration only and involves predicting the demand for individual product items. It is used as the basis of a firm production schedule for the coming month, a tentative production schedule for the month after, and an even more tentative schedule for the third month.

Sources of information for sales forecasting can come from both inside and outside the company. From inside the company, past sales records can be used to assess trends or make projections. Reports from sales representatives who keep an 'ear to the ground' can be a valuable source of information. Any special advertising, promotional or price-cutting activities will also have an effect.

From outside the company, the general economic condition of the community expressed in terms of certain standard economic indicators can provide advance warning of possible trends in demand, as can activities of competitors or new legislation by governments. A fall in the foreign exchange rate can stimulate demand for home-produced products and vice versa. Trends are often apparent for the particular market sector in which a company is operating, and recent statistics for that particular market sector (e.g. building approvals for the building products industry) can often be useful in developing a sales forecast. It should be remembered, however, that for such statistics to be useful to a sales forecast, they should be the types of statistic that 'lead' trends in demand. For example, if an upward trend in the unemployment ratio is usually associated with an increase in beer consumption, then for the unemployment ratio to be useful to the brewing companies in a predictive sense, changes in the ratio should always precede changes in beer consumption, otherwise the ratio is not providing information that would not anyway be evident from directly observing the increased demand for beer. Estimates of the total market, combined with estimates of the company's market share, are often useful for forecasting, since this provides a quantitative means of estimating the effects of changes in a general market indicator on the demand for products of a particular company.

Much of the above information can only be used qualitatively and judgementally in preparing a sales forecast. Certain types of forecast – mainly short-term forecasts – can, however, be put on a quantitative basis.

We can distinguish four classes of quantitative forecasting technique:

1. regression analysis of demand against a market indicator;

2. regression analysis of demand against time;
3. moving average;
4. exponentially weighted (or auto-regressive) moving average.

4.5.1 REGRESSION ANALYSIS OF DEMAND AGAINST A MARKET INDICATOR

This involves investigating the statistical correlation between the demand and the market indicator concerned (e.g. unemployment ratio, inflation rate, etc.) and attempting to use any correlations found in a predictive sense. The simplest form of this is to plot demand against the indicator concerned and, provided reasonable correlation exists, to use a least squares fit to draw the regression line. The expected change in demand resulting from a given change in the economic indicator is obtained from the slope of the regression line.

Econometrics is the term given to the extensive use of this type of technique, and it is most commonly used for longer-term aggregate forecasts and predictions which are more relevant to government departments and very large companies than to the small or medium sized firm.

The remaining techniques all involve taking demand data from the immediate past and attempting to make the best projection or extrapolation of this data into the immediate future.

4.5.2 REGRESSION ANALYSIS AGAINST TIME

This involves plotting demand data against time and estimating the least squares fit line as in the previous case. An example is shown in Fig. 4.2 where the regression line gives a simple extrapolation of past demand data into the future.

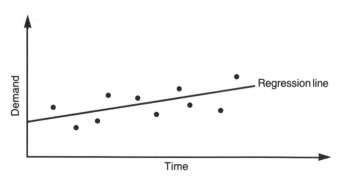

Fig. 4.2 Regression of demand against time.

4.5.3 SIMPLE MOVING AVERAGE

This is a less complex technique that involves considerably less computation than regression on time (which can be a significant factor if forecasts are to be made for thousands of products). The principle is to use the average of the last n periods' demand observations as the best prediction of the next period's demand. When the current period's demand is known, the oldest demand observation is dropped from the average, and the current period's demand is substituted. The sample of demand periods over which the average is taken thus 'moves' as we move forward in time, and we are only considering the most recent data in the average.

Mathematically this is expressed as:

$$\bar{x}_{n+1} = \sum_{i=n-a}^{a} x_i / a$$

where: x_i = demand observation for period i;
$\bar{x}_i$ = demand forecast for period i;
a = number of periods averaged.

The purpose of averaging is to smooth out random fluctuations in demand, and to get an estimate of its mean level and any trends in that level. Averaging over a large number of demand points will be effective at smoothing out random fluctuations, but any change in the level of demand will take some time to be reflected in the average, since the latter will be 'weighed down' by the historical observations for some time after the actual level has changed. Trends in the moving average will thus lag trends in the actual demand and the larger the number of observations, the greater will be the lag. This is shown in Fig. 4.3 in which two moving average forecasts are plotted for averages taken over the last three observations ($a = 3$) and the last six observations ($a = 6$). It can be seen how the $a = 3$ forecast follows the demand fluctuations considerably more closely than the $a = 6$ forecast (or conversely, it is less successful in smoothing them out).

4.5.4 EXPONENTIALLY WEIGHTED (OR AUTO-REGRESSIVE) MOVING AVERAGE

This problem can be partially overcome by a popular extension to the moving average approach called the method of **exponentially weighted (or auto-regressive) moving averages**. Instead of taking a simple average of a number of previous demand observations, a weighted average can be taken with most weight being given to the most recent observations.

Thus if we define a weighting factor a where $0 < a < 1$, we can express a weighted moving average of all demand observations up to and including the nth:

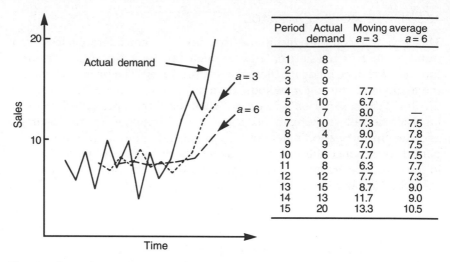

Fig. 4.3 A moving average forecast.

$$\bar{x}_{n+1} = ax_n + a(1-a)x_{n-1} + a(1-a)^2 x_{n-2} + \ldots + (1-a)^n x_0$$

For values of a less than 1, the terms in this geometric series decrease as we go backwards in time. Over an extended period backwards they will obviously approach zero, so historical demand in the distant past will have very little effect on the weighted average.

It can easily be verified that the above expression can be rearranged as the recursive relation:

$$\bar{x}_{n+1} = ax_n + (1-a)x_n$$

i.e.   Forecast next period = a (demand this period)
                     $+ (1-a)$ (forecast this period)

The parameter a is referred to as the **smoothing constant**. A value of a close to 1 will give greater weight to the most recent demand observations, and will respond quickly to changes in demand level, but will not be very effective at smoothing out random fluctuations (or **noise**) in the demand. A value of a close to 0 will give much less weight to the most recent observations, and will smooth out the 'noise' but will only respond slowly to changes in demand. Thus we need to choose a value of a which makes the desired trade-off between smoothing of random fluctuations and response to changes in the absolute level of demand. Exponentially weighted moving averages for values of the smoothing constant of 0.2 and 0.6 are shown in Fig. 4.4 for the same set of data as the simple moving average, showing how a smoothing constant of 0.3 smooths the fluctuations better than a smoothing constant of 0.6, but is less responsive to major changes.

An advantage of the exponentially weighted over the simple moving average approach is that only the current demand x_n is needed to forecast the following period, whereas in the simple moving average approach, knowledge of each individual demand over the number of periods averaged is required. Since most forecasting systems tend to be computerized, this can save a considerable amount of storage, particularly in cases where several thousand products are being forecast with a single forecasting system.

Forecasting seasonal products is a fairly common occurrence. This is best performed by 'de-seasonalizing' the historical demand data using a 'base series' for each of the twelve months of the year, which represents the average proportion of total annual sales which have occurred in each particular month over the last several years. Such a series for two-stroke lawn mowers might be as follows:

Month	Average % of total Annual sales in month	Base series
Jan.	9	0.09
Feb.	9	0.09
Mar.	7	0.07
Apr.	4	0.04
May	1	0.01
Jun.	3	0.03
Jul.	3	0.03
Aug.	9	0.09
Sep.	12	0.12
Oct.	14	0.14
Nov.	15	0.15
Dec.	14	0.14
	—	100 %

If the actual March sales were 1100 units, the 'de-seasonalized' value would be $100/(0.07 \times 12) = 1310$ units.

If we had a de-seasonalized forecast of 1400 units for March, the expected annual sales would be $1400 \times 12 \times 0.07 = 1180$ units.

Once the seasonal effect has been removed in this way, we can use simple or exponential moving average to forecast the next month's demand, or a regression on time to make a projection further out into the future. The forecast must then of course be 're-seasonalized' to give the actual expected demand.

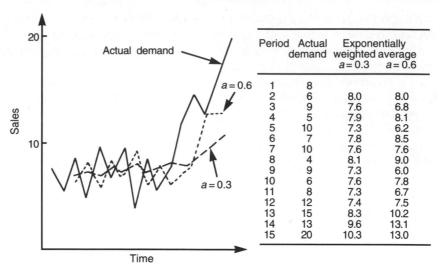

Period	Actual demand	Exponentially weighted average	
		$a = 0.3$	$a = 0.6$
1	8		
2	6	8.0	8.0
3	9	7.6	6.8
4	5	7.9	8.1
5	10	7.3	6.2
6	7	7.8	8.5
7	10	7.6	7.6
8	4	8.1	9.0
9	9	7.3	6.0
10	6	7.6	7.8
11	8	7.3	6.7
12	12	7.4	7.5
13	15	8.3	10.2
14	13	9.6	13.1
15	20	10.3	13.0

Fig. 4.4 An exponentially weighted moving average forecast.

We must remember that all of these quantitative techniques represent attempts to project known demand patterns from the past into the future. Very often, however, a completely different set of conditions apply in the future, such as the entry of a new competitor into the field, changes in the economy, etc., which may cause step changes in the demand pattern that cannot be predicted from past trends. Great care must therefore be exercised if any of these quantitative techniques are to be used for making predictions more than a month or so into the future, since much can happen to the market over this period. Judgement must be used to integrate qualitative information on factors it is known will have an effect on the market together with any quantitative projection of past demand patterns.

4.6 LONG-TERM PRODUCTION PLANNING

The long-term production plan frequently takes the form of a rough-cut capacity plan to determine the expected level of production of the manufacturing plant as a whole, on a month-by-month basis over the following twelve-month period. This is derived from an aggregate sales forecast (relating to demand over all products rather than demand for specific products) and from the monthly production capacity of the plant. Companies that make products to order tend to use the aggregate production plan as the basis for planning labour force requirements and purchasing long lead time materials which they are confident will be required, although the details of what products will be made will not of course be known until later. The make-for-stock batch production company can also use this plan for deciding how best to adjust overall production level to meet demand. Thus if the product range tends to show a seasonal variation in demand, a decision must be made whether to reduce production levels at times of low demand and increase it during the peak periods, or whether to produce at a steady rate throughout the year, meeting the peak of the demand from stock.

Production levels must be expressed in a common unit (such as a unit of labour) that is not tied to an individual product but which represents the productive capacity of the plant as a whole. Since the production level of most plants is traditionally changed by varying the number of shifts or hiring or firing labour (with total machine capacity determining the upper limit of production), the number of planned direct labour hours per month has tended to be used in the past to measure the planned production level. Decisions concerning changes to the production level in order to match changes in demand are thus equivalent to decisions on working additional shifts or changing the size of the workforce. The latter is of course contradictory to the Japanese principle of continuous employment in which the multi-skilled labour force would perform plant maintenance etc. during times of reduced production. This particular issue, together with the issue of whether direct labour hours should be used at all as a basis for planning and control, will be examined in more detail in later chapters.

Having determined a rough-cut capacity plan on a month-by-month basis, this plan can now be disaggregated into groups of products sharing common production facilities or tooling. It is within these groups of products competing for common facilities that bottlenecks start to occur with particular groups of resources becoming more heavily loaded than others at certain times. Bottlenecks can be detected by developing an aggregate cumulative loading profile for each resource group. This is generally on a month-by-month basis in terms of the cumulative hours work generated for a resource group in that month by the decision to produce a certain volume of a particular product group within that month. One of the purposes of aggregate planning is to assist in predicting where the production bottlenecks are likely to be so that any necessary action to increase capacity in those areas can be initiated well in advance.

To perform aggregate planning we must decide what our product and resource groups are and create a **bill of resources**. An example is shown in Fig. 4.5, which associates one unit of production of each product family or group with the number of production hours that will be required on each group of resources needed to produce that unit. Since we are only planning at an aggregate level we would generally be concerned only with notional products that require a representative number of hours on each production resource assigned to the group, even in cases where no actual product in fact uses all the resources. Resources will generally be labour or machine groups and perhaps cash (in terms of

	M/c cell A	M/c cell B	Labour	Capital
Product group A	0.046	0.02	0.263	£20
Product group B	0.027	0.02	0.246	£20
Product group C	0.042	0.017	0.304	£30
Product group D	0.055	0.048	0.412	£33

Fig. 4.5 A bill of resources.

the implications a unit of production has for tying up cash in inventory investment).

It is next necessary to make some form of aggregate demand forecast for each product group over the time horizon for which the plan is being established (typically a year). This would normally be developed by the marketing department. This forecast is then used as the basis of a time-phased projection of the production volume of each product group, on a period-by-period basis, required to meet the forecast demand. Since in a make-to-stock company some of the forecast demand may be met from inventory rather than from production, it is necessary to maintain a projection of the expected on-hand inventory balance from period to period. In order to see how this approach would work, Fig. 4.6 shows aggregate forecasts that have been developed for the two major product groups A and B of a manufacturing organization and how two different rough-cut production plans to meet this demand could be tested in terms of their effect on critical resources.

The simple period-by-period projection shown, in which we subtract the demand in each period from the on-hand inventory at the start of the period in order to assess any net requirements for the period and the starting on-hand inventory for the next period, is called a **requirements record.**

The workload implied by this plan on different resource groups can then be accumulated against each resource group for each time period and compared with the capacity limit on that resource. If the capacity limit were exceeded in a particular period then either some of the production would have to be transferred to another period or the capacity would need to be increased in some way. The bill of resources for the two product groups is that given earlier in Fig. 4.5.

The resource groups are assumed to be Machine cells A and B (level of

	M/c 1	M/c 2	M/c 3	M/c 4	M/c 5	M/c 6
Group A	1000	1500	2000	1500	1500	1500
Group B	2500	2500	3200	3500	3000	3000

Plan 1

		M/c 1	M/c 2	M/c 3	M/c 4	M/c 5	M/c 6
Group A (on hand = 500)	Sales forecast	1000	1500	2000	1500	1500	1500
	Production	1500	1500	1500	1500	1500	1500
	On hand	1000	1000	500	500	500	500
Group B (on hand = 500)	Sales forecast	2500	2500	3200	3500	3000	3000
	Production	3000	3000	3000	3000	3000	3000
	On hand	1000	1500	1300	800	800	800
M/c cell A (hrs)		130	130	130	130	130	130
M/c cell B (hrs)		100	100	100	100	100	100
Labour (hrs)		1100	1100	1100	1100	1100	1100
Capital (£ x 1000)		40	50	36	26	26	26

Plan 2

		M/c 1	M/c 2	M/c 3	M/c 4	M/c 5	M/c 6
Group A (on hand = 500)	Sales forecast	1000	1500	2000	1500	1500	1500
	Production	700	1400	2000	1500	1500	1500
	On hand	200	100	100	100	100	100
Group B (on hand = 500)	Sales forecast	2500	2500	3200	3500	3000	3000
	Production	2300	2900	3200	3500	3000	3000
	On hand	300	700	700	700	700	700
M/c cell A (hrs)		78	124	156	139	129	129
M/c cell B (hrs)		65	96	118	110	100	100
Labour (hrs)		750	1080	1313	1255	1132	1132
Capital (£ x 1000)		10	16	16	16	16	16

Fig. 4.6 An aggregate plan.

resource utilization measured in machine hours), labour (measured in labour hours), and capital utilization (amount of capital in thousands of pounds tied up in inventory). We could also have introduced storage space as a critical resource, although this has not been done here.

The first plan (Plan 1) concentrates on a steady production level of each product group of 1500 items per month for group A and 3000 items per month for group B. This results in on-hand balances at the end of each month as shown in the 'On hand' row, and an even load on resources apart from capital investment.

The second plan has a variable production rate with production peaks in months 3 and 4 to meet the demand peaks. This results in lower inventory but a higher load on all production resources in months 3 and 4. A **safety stock** corresponding to £16 000 worth of inventory is maintained in this plan.

If we assume that the machine hours in each month for both plans is within the available capacity, but that capacity limit on labour hours is 1250, then management would know that in order to implement Plan 2, additional labour would have to be hired in months 3 and 4. Alternatively, since only a few additional labour hours are required in month 4, some of the production in month 4 might be moved to month 3 to avoid having to employ additional labour in month 4. The decision would have to be made with consideration given to the additional capital investment this would involve in month 3. If capital were short, hiring of extra labour for both months might be the best course of action.

The effect of the rough-cut aggregate plan is to set overall capacity constraints within which lower level tactical plans may be made. If Plan 2 were adopted in the above example, then the outcome of the plan would be the fact that total production would have to occur within labour capacity of 1150 hours per month in months 1, 2, 5 and 6, and within a labour capacity of 1350 hours per month in months 3 and 4.

This type of process lends itself very well to a spreadsheet modelling, since the number of product and resource groups is deliberately small (this is one of the purposes of aggregation). Relationships between different columns and rows are very simple, and a spreadsheet allows the rapid performance of 'what if' types of analysis. The spreadsheet model would generally be used in a joint planning session of marketing, production and finance departments to test out various types of aggregate production plan, and to try and reach agreement on a plan acceptable to all. Levels of production and stock maintained can be controlled by specifying a **production order quantity** and a **safety stock**.

4.7 THE MASTER PRODUCTION SCHEDULE

At the tactical planning level it is common to develop what is called a **master production schedule (MPS)** which is basically a statement of how much of each end item is to be produced in any particular time period. The master production schedule is responsible for driving the entire production system. This schedule forms the basis for all capacity and critical resource planning in all types of manufacturing companies, and in medium to large batch production industries serves to control job priorities in order to answer the question: 'Which job does this production resource work on next?'

The master production schedule is a statement of how the expected demand for individual end items will be met from production within the overall resource capacity constraints developed from the rough-cut aggregate production plan. In make-to-stock companies it is important to realize that the master production schedule for each product is not necessarily the same as the forecast for each product. The MPS, although based on the forecast, generally represents a firm commitment to produce a specific number of items of a specific type in each planning period which will only be changed on approval of the production controller. The MPS is thus effectively absorbing much of the uncertainty in the demand forecasts, because as soon as a firm decision is made as to which end products are to be made and in which time periods, this has the effect of fixing requirements for both materials and production resource capacity, although to a level of detail and over a planning horizon that will depend on the specifics of the company concerned and what type of production management system it is using.

For what time horizon should the master production schedule be developed? The answer is found by examining item lead times to discover the longest cumulative lead time of all the end items produced. Figure 4.7 shows a bill of materials (BOM) for an end product A, in which the lead time required to produce or procure each sub-assembly or component has been laid out on a horizontal time axis. We observe that end product A is

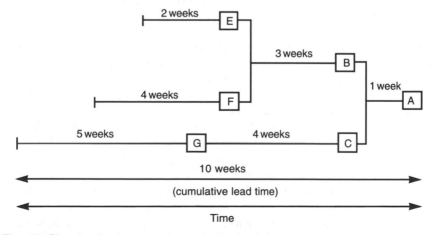

Fig. 4.7 Planning horizons and cumulative lead times.

assembled from sub-assembly B and component C with a lead time of one week being allowed. B is assembled from E and F with a lead time of three weeks, and the purchase lead time for these materials is two weeks and four weeks respectively. C is machined from G with a lead time of four weeks and G is purchased with a lead time of five weeks. If A were the only product made, the MPS would need to extend at least 10 weeks into the future to ensure the timely purchasing of raw materials. If an additional item were made with a cumulative lead time of 12 weeks, the MPS would need to extend at least 12 weeks into the future. In practice. the MPS generally extends over a somewhat longer horizon than the maximum cumulative lead time to allow some forward visibility on purchasing actions, and to try and anticipate problems well before they occur.

The MPS may need to be changed from time to time for a number of reasons which will be discussed later. The important point is, however, that changes to the MPS should be as few as possible, particularly within the time horizon corresponding to the cumulative lead time of the longest lead time product. This will be examined in more detail in a later section.

As with long-term aggregate planning, there is no point in extending a master production schedule for too far into the future. The further into the future we try to predict, the less accurate our forecasts become and the more likely we are to produce a schedule that will subsequently have to be modified. Planning of the more distant future should generally only be done at the aggregate level, as we can normally make better longer-term forecasts for aggregated groups of items than for one end item in particular.

The difficulty of making accurate longer-term forecasts for individual end items, coupled with the fact that the minimum planning horizon is determined by the longest cumulative lead time, provides a strong motivation to reduce lead times. Shorter lead times in general will reduce the length of the period over which the schedule will need to be developed, which in turn means forecasts are likely to be more accurate. This is simply repeating that manufacturing companies should try to be as responsive as possible. In this way they do not need to plan so far ahead, and can hence reduce the associated uncertainty.

There tend to be many types of company in which production lead times for items produced within the company can be very short (a matter of hours or days) but purchase lead times on raw materials or purchased components are long (a matter of weeks or months), for example because of the necessity for shipping these materials in from overseas. In these cases the master production schedule would need to extend sufficiently far into the future to allow adequate planning for the ordering of these raw materials, and hence some form of forecast would need to be developed over this timescale at a sufficiently detailed level to enable raw material requirements to be predicted. This is easiest in companies which use relatively few different types of raw material, in which case forecasting and master scheduling over the timescale required by the purchasing lead times can be in terms not of individual end products, but in terms of total volumes of product groups that require common raw materials. Inventory in such companies would be held mainly at the purchased materials end (backwards positioning of inventory) and we most frequently find this situation in make to order companies.

Demand forecasting may be performed using any of the techniques described in section 4.5. The necessity to estimate demand on a weekly basis over a period several months into the future means that in many cases we will be able to do little more than extrapolate a trend, perhaps using seasonal factors, although as much **market intelligence** as possible should be added to the extrapolation. If the customer is a wholesaler, or one of one's own distribution centres which themselves maintain high stock levels and rely on periodic discrete shipments, then knowledge of their current stock levels would facilitate forecasting demand on the production plant.

When preparing the master production schedule, it will be found that in many companies, much of the demand over the immediate future is already fixed through firm customer orders. The further into the future we extend, the greater the proportion of our demand that is only forecast as opposed to firm customer order. This effect is shown is Fig 4.8.

We can generate a requirements record from the forecast demand for each end item which will serve two purposes.

- It will enable us to plan the actual MPS from the forecast demand.
- It will enable us to track in advance the extent to which actual customer orders, as they come in, remain within the sales forecast, and how many additional orders we can promise to deliver during the time until the next production batch is due.

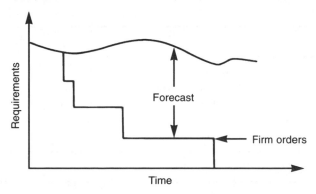

Fig. 4.8 Firm and forecast orders.

A typical MPS requirements record for end item A3 with a current on-hand balance of 40 units is shown in Fig. 4.9.

For week 1, we had a demand of 50 forecast but we already have 55 firm orders (more than the forecast). The arrival of 150 in stock from production in week 1, together with 40 on hand, will leave us with 135 on hand after the booked orders have been satisfied. Stock is progressively reduced by the forecast demand until week 4 when in the absence of any production we should run out. We therefore schedule 200 units to be ready in week 4. The planned production represents the firm master production schedule for this item which, having been set, should be adhered to as much as possible. This can be facilitated by carrying a certain amount of end item safety stock. By stabilizing the MPS, this should reduce the amount of safety stock of lower level items required.

Of the 135 on hand at the end of week 1, we have firm orders for 22 units between now and the arrival of the next batch. This indicates that of the 135 on hand at the time the batch of 150 arrives, 113 are available to promise. Where the batch of 200 arrives in week 4, no firm orders are yet booked, and so all 200 of this batch are available to promise. If a customer makes an order and is indifferent as to whether it should arrive in week 3 or week 4, it should be promised out of the week 4 batch. If a more demanding customer then makes an order, he can be satisfied out of the week 1 batch. This approach allows us to maintain the shortest possible lead times for marketing.

4.8 WHAT ITEMS TO INCLUDE IN THE MPS

Many systems of production planning (of which MRP is the best known example) use 'bills of materials' of end products as a basis for planning the quantities and timings of the materials that will be required to produce the product. A bill of materials is simply a structured description, stored on

	Wk 1	Wk 2	Wk 3	Wk 4	Wk 5	Wk 6
Forecast	50	55	50	60	60	60
Firm orders	55	20	2	0	0	0
Planned production	150	0	0	200	0	0
On–hand 40	135	80	30	170	110	50
Available to promise	113			200		

Fig. 4.9 MPS requirements record.

computer, of the identity and quantity of each material item that comprises the product. A bill of materials is arranged hierarchically in a number of levels, with the end product at the top level, the purchased raw materials at the bottom level and sub-assemblies and components in between. Part of a bill of materials for a pump is shown in Fig. 4.10, the quantity of the item required at any level for assembly into the next level above being indicated in brackets.

When we are developing a master production schedule, we might at first think the obvious items for which to develop the MPS would be the end product items (i.e. the top or 'level 0' items in the bill of materials). The bill of materials itself can then be used to compute the quantities of lower level items (in the pump example, brackets, motors, rotors, shafts, etc.) to support a given master production schedule. However, serious problems can arise here in cases where a product has a large number of optional features. Consider again the example of a pump. A particular model of pump may have a number of optional features as shown in Fig. 4.11 in which the numbers in brackets now represent the number of alternatives of each item that exist.

As can be seen, a particular model of pump can be assembled from four different types of body, eight different types of motor, five different types of bracket, three different types of seal kit, three different types of rotor/shaft sub-assembly and one type of bearing. Each of these items will consist of components, raw materials, etc., in the sense that it will also have its own bill of materials structure. We assume that the customer can specify the type of optional combination he requires to suit his particular

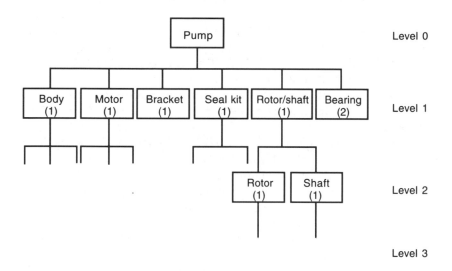

Fig. 4.10 Bill of materials for pump.

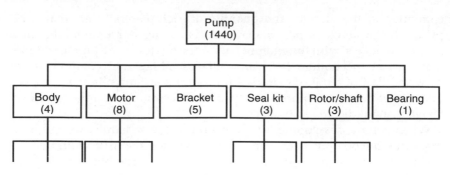

Fig. 4.11 Pump options.

application. Any combination of the allowed body, bracket, etc., would be represented by the same pump model number. The customer order and resulting production requisition would specify the model number of the pump followed by a list of which of the allowable optional features were required.

How would we treat this situation as far as master production scheduling was concerned? We might assume that a separate and unique bill of materials needs to be specified for each pump model option (since these are the 'end' products, and it is the end products which normally appear in the master production schedule to generate lower level requirements). In this case, since there are $4 \times 8 \times 5 \times 3 \times 3 = 1440$ different possible model options that can be assembled from the allowable bodies, motors, brackets, etc., we would require 1440 separate bills of materials to cover all the options possible. This would in turn imply developing a master production schedule for 1440 separate end products associated with this model alone, many of which might be obscure optional combinations that were hardly ever ordered. Note that if two types of bearing were available rather than only one, the number of possible combinations would double to 2880. This is a very common situation in manufacturing companies and has been termed the problem of the **upwards explosion of complexity**.

So far, in discussing bills of materials, we have assumed almost implicitly that the hierarchical structure of the bill of materials, like the hierarchical structure of the manufacturing organization itself, takes the form of a pyramid with the end product as the apex, and an increasing 'explosion' of complexity in terms of the different sub-assemblies, components and raw materials required as we move downwards from the end product to the lower levels. Thus if we grouped the bills of materials for all the products manufactured side by side, the topology of the resulting schema would be as shown in Fig. 4.12, with a relatively small number of finished products 'exploding' downwards into a complexity of sub-assemblies, components and raw materials. This corresponds to the 'A plant' described in Chapter 3.

If, however, the relatively small number of end items in Fig. 4.12 do not represent finished products which go to the customer, but are instead basic 'modules' which can be combined together in a large number of different ways (as in the above example) to give a potentially enormous number of finished products representing optional combinations of these modules, then we also have an upward 'explosion' of complexity as shown in Fig. 4.13. This roughly corresponds to the 'T plant' described in Chapter 3.

In a topological sense we can define the 'neck' of this particular structure (the part with the least complexity) as being at the level of the bills of materials which describe the basic modules of which the optional combinations are composed. In the pump example, the 'neck' is at the level at which body, bracket, motor, etc. (the individual modules) are described. Each module can be 'exploded' downwards into the various components of which the module is composed, and upwards into the many optional

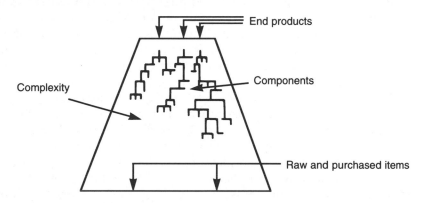

Fig. 4.12 Downwards complexity explosion in BOM.

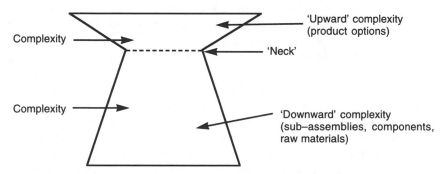

Fig. 4.13 The 'neck' in the BOM.

combinations of modules that will form the end products sold to the customer. Thus at the level in the bill of materials of these basic modules our pump model can be described by $4 + 8 + 5 + 3 + 3 = 23$ items. At the higher level (the level of final end product) our pump model needs 1440 optional combinations to describe it giving an order of magnitude increase in complexity. At the lower levels, we require all the raw materials and components of these modules to describe the pump, which will again be more complex.

It is clear that in the case of the pump example the smallest number of end items in which to describe the different pump options would be at the level of the basic modules of body, motor, bracket, etc. It would be much more sensible to develop a master production schedule based on forecasts for the numbers of each type of body required, the numbers of each type of motor required, the numbers of each type of bracket required, etc., rather than trying to forecast each option separately. These modules, if forecast and produced in approximately the right numbers based on past records of usage, could then be assembled together at the last minute in the particular combination actually required by the customer. We thus need to make forecasts and develop forward production requirements only for the 23 modules from which the pump is put together, rather than for the 1440 different end products that can be formed from the different combinations of these modules. The modules will represent the end item (or finished product) in the bill of materials as far as our system is concerned, and we will not have a unique planning identifier for the particular pump sold other than its generic model number. The precondition for this is of course that the modules can be assembled together in different combinations sufficiently quickly and easily that it is not necessary to perform any long term forward planning on the final assembly process. (Note that the lack of forward planning capability on final assembly is a simple consequence of the omission of final assemblies from the bill of materials in its new status as a planning document.)

Many companies who offer products of optional specification and have not structured their bills of materials for effective master production scheduling may well have formal bills of materials specified for some of the more common options and will handle the remainder by adding, deleting or substituting the optional components using the most similar existing bill as the basis. This is not satisfactory as a basis for master production scheduling because it fails to provide to correct historical data for option forecasting purposes. We are thus often confronted with the task of restructuring bills of materials in a modular form from a limited existing number of end product bills in which all the basic modules are represented, but which do not cover all possible optional combinations of finished products that can be assembled. There are a number of systematic steps for doing this which can best be represented by a simple example.

Consider a simplified version of the pump example and assume the options are restricted to the motor and the seal kit and that two possible motors and two possible seal kits are available. This gives us a total of four optional combinations. Let us assume that bills of materials have been specified for these combinations and are shown in Fig. 4.14(a). The optional combinations are the end items (at level 0) and are designated M1S1, M1S2, etc. The motor and seal kit have not been explicitly represented. The individual items R1, J4, etc., are the components required at the next level down which are assembled together to form the motor and seal kit, and we assume that some of these can in turn be 'exploded' into sub-components and so on. Thus level 1 on the bill gives the individual items which are the daughter items of the alternative motors and seal kits.

To restructure these bills of materials in modular form, we must analyse the component items at level 1 and group them according to their use. If we take the bill of materials for product option M1S1, as shown in Fig. 4.14(b), we see that items R1 and R2 are common to all product options, item J4 is common to those options with motor 1, items P1, Z4 and E1 are common to those options with seal kit 1 and item H4 is unique to this particular motor/seal kit combination. Analysis of the bills of materials for the other product options would reveal those items common to motor 2, seal kit 2 and the items unique to the other combinations of motor and seal kit (i.e. to the other individual product options).

We thus arrive at a grouping of the components that are unique to motor 1, seal kit 1, etc. In general, these components will be just those components of which motor 1, seal kit 1, etc., are composed. Hence the parent item of the group of items we have identified as common to motor 1 will be motor 1 itself. The same will apply to motor 2 and seal kits 1 and 2. We thus have a systematic method of identifying the various modules that we should regard as the end items in the revised bill of materials structure by analysing the commonality of the items at the level below that at which we expect our modules to be eventually identified. Forecasting and master production scheduling on the basis of these modules is a far more practical proposition than forecasting each option individually (though this is not brought out in this example in which the number of modules (2 + 2) is equal to the number of combinations (2 × 2).

There are two points worth noting here. Firstly we have a problems when we identify items that are unique to a particular product option, such as item H4 in the example. How can we plan the requirements for these items without forecasting the requirements for each option individually (something we are trying to avoid)? One method of solving this problem is to break items H4 etc. into their individual sub-components, and try and find commonality of assignment at this level. An example of this is shown in Fig. 4.15, in which we have broken the 'unique' items H4, K2, I3 and Q1 into their individual components. In this case all the sub-

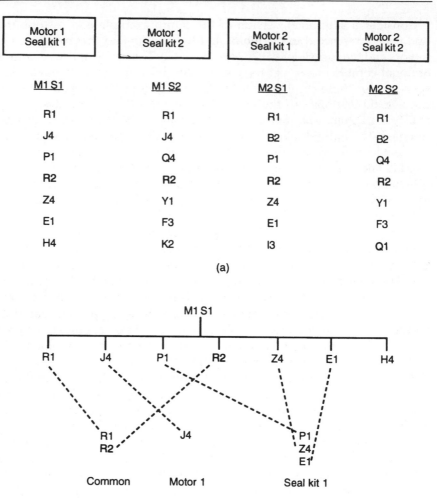

Fig. 4.14 Looking for commonality in the BOM.

components of the items that were previously unique to particular product options can now be assigned to a group or 'module'.

If commonality still cannot be found, or if these items are indivisible components which cannot be broken down further, then consideration should be given to a change in product design in such a way that a 'standard' component could be used in a wider range of product options, thereby simplifying the production planning process. If on the other hand the item is of very low cost, it would often be sufficient to 'overplan' the item by keeping stock levels up and not subjecting it to strict control.

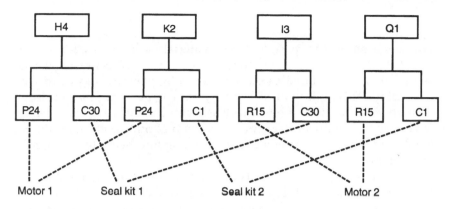

Fig. 4.15 Breaking down items to find commonality.

A second point to note is that the 'modules' identified by this technique do not have to be associated with modules in the physical sense. Although we identified a number of modules such as 'motor 1', 'seal kit 2', there were also a number of items common to all options which we labelled 'common'. Although these are assigned to the same group, they are not assembled together to form a complete physical unit as are the items comprising a motor or a seal kit. However, the 'common' items can themselves represent a form of 'module', represented by a bill of materials, whose planned production is simply generated by the planned production of the group the items are common to. In other words we can allow an end item in a bill of materials to be an entity that will not have an engineering part number assigned to it (i.e. it has no existence as a physical part) but which can still be meaningfully used for planning lower level items. We are now elevating to end item status a number of basic modules most of which will correspond to physical entities but some of which (e.g. the 'common' group) will not. Thus, in this example, at the level of forecasting and master production scheduling we should be concerned with developing individual forecasts and schedules for:

- the group as a whole ('common' module);
- all items with motor 1 ('motor 1' module);
- all items with motor 2 ('motor 2' module);
- all items with seal kit 1 ('seal kit 1' module);
- all items with seal kit 2 ('seal kit 2' module).

These requirements will lead to lower level requirements being generated for the items which are members of the respective modules.

Bills of materials based on assignment of items to groups or 'modules', some of which may not correspond to items which are actually assembled as a unit and hence carry no engineering part number, are called **'pseudo'**

bills of materials or **'S'-bills**. These bills are developed strictly for planning purposes.

Another example of a 'pseudo' bill of materials is where one level in the product structure has a large number of loose parts such as nuts, bolts and fasteners which may be of too low value to be planned and controlled individually. This collection of logically similar parts can be put in an imaginary bag and treated effectively as a sub-assembly to which a non-engineering part number is assigned. Individual nuts, bolts, etc., are not treated individually, the fundamental planning unit being the imaginary 'bag' of items.

In developing our 'pseudo' bills of materials, we must remember that when, for example, we break down the items such as H4, K2, etc., that were unique to a particular product option in order to try to assign their sub-components to groups, the resulting 'pseudo' bill of materials will contain no reference to items H4, K2, etc. For planning requirements based on the master production schedule, this is as it should be. We have deliberately removed explicit reference to these items to avoid having to forecast each product option individually. When, however, the time comes for the customer to specify his precise requirements, items H4, K2, etc., must still be assembled (again this is assumed to be a sufficiently rapid process as not to require forward planning). In order to be able to explicitly refer to these items, to enable us to issue instructions for their assembly (to specific customer order), and for costing, we must set up a separate bill of materials file just for items such as this, called the **'M-bill' file**. Bills of materials for these items are called 'M-bills' ('manufacturing' bills) to distinguish them from the 'S-bills' which are used purely for requirements planning and control purposes. M-bills are used only for the purpose of assembling components planned from the MPS into items having only very short-term visibility in terms of their future requirements because of their being tied to specific short-term customer orders.

In practice, this has different implications for master production scheduling in different types of company. In make-to-stock companies (often corresponding to 'A plants') the master production schedule would normally be stated in terms of the end products that are actually stocked and shipped to the customer, as indicated in Fig. 4.16. The time horizon of the MPS is determined by the typical cumulative lead time (from raw materials ordering to final shipment) of these end products.

In assemble-to-order companies (often corresponding to 'T plants') we may have two types of master production schedule, as shown in Fig. 4.17. One schedule (the long-term schedule that we will term MPS1) is not stated in terms of end products (i.e. that are actually shipped to the customer) but in terms of entities such as major sub-assemblies, kits of items, etc., that are often one level below the end product in a bill of

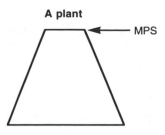

Fig. 4.16 MPS for an A plant.

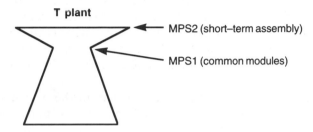

Fig. 4.17 MPS for a T plant.

materials description and are common to a whole range of products. Since the demand for these common items is usually more predictable over a longer term than the ways in which the items can be combined in different product configurations, and the components and raw materials may need some time to procure or manufacture, MPS1 is often extended for weeks or months into the future. The other schedule (the short-term schedule which we shall term MPS2) is a schedule for the assembly of these common entities into end products for which firm orders exist. It is important to remember that MPS2 is generated from firm orders and not from forecasts. Generally lead time for assembly of the end product as a specifically requested configuration of common component entities would be short (a matter of hours, days or weeks) resulting in a short time horizon for MPS2.

In make-to-order companies (often corresponding to 'V plants') we might again have two master production schedules, as shown in Fig. 4.18. The long-term schedule (MPS1) might be for long lead time common raw materials that might constitute the standard inputs to the process on which the company was focused (for example, in a foundry, or paper in a document reproduction business). This would be stated in notional production units such as standard imaginary products containing a representative proportion of all the purchased materials normally used. The short-term schedule (MPS2) would again be developed only to firm

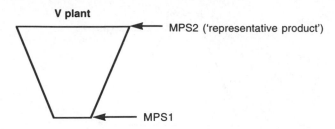

Fig. 4.18 MPS for a V plant.

customer order over a time horizon that was determined by typical lead times quoted to customers, and would be for specific customer-specified products for which bills of materials would be drawn up and production or shop orders launched on the assumption that the long lead time purchased raw materials would be available, having been ordered on the basis of MPS1.

We generally refer to an item that appears in the master production schedule MPS1 as an **end item**. An end item is to be distinguished from an **end product** which is actually shipped to the customer since, as we have seen above, we frequently include non-end products in MPS1. MPS1 end items can generally be represented by a conventional bill of materials structure as previously described. However, the representation of the final end product (for developing MPS2), which may possess a combinatorially explosive number of different optional specifications, is considerably more difficult. What are termed **generative** bill of material processing systems have been proposed in which generic Bills of Materials are defined in which production variants or optional features are defined in terms of parameters. The assignment of allowed values to these parameters in allowable combinations then defines the precise specification of the product variant. Further details of these types of system may be found in van Veen and Wortman (1992).

4.9 CONCLUSION

Whichever production management system is used to control the detailed priorities and movements of individual orders across the shop floor, it is essential for any company to produce some form of master production schedule of end items to be produced in each time period (for continuous production, this can be expressed as a rate), so that this can be translated into a more detailed plan for individual movements of materials on a day-to-day basis. Different types of company using different types of production management system may have very different techniques for the actual realization of this MPS, and three important and contrasting techniques will be examined in the following three chapters.

REFERENCE

Van Veen, E.A. and Wortmann, J.C. (1992) Generative bill of material processing systems. *Production Planning and Control*, Vol. 3, No. 3, pp. 314–26.

FURTHER READING

Higgins, P. and Browne, J. (1992) Master Production Scheduling: a concurrent planning approach. *Production Planning and Control*, Vol. 3, No. 1, pp. 2–18.

Fundamentals of manufacturing resources planning

5

5.1 OVERVIEW

This chapter is concerned with the detailed logic of one method which is commonly used for translating the master production schedule into detailed material and production capacity requirements, particularly in batch manufacturing companies – the **manufacturing resources planning approach (MRP)**. This performs a time-phased explosion to estimate the timings and quantities of all production and purchase orders for the material items that will be required to perform the master production schedule. The MRP approach also allows a trial loading of production orders on production resources to be carried out to check for production overload situations at the individual work centre and machine levels.

There are a number of serious criticisms of the MRP approach which are discussed towards the end of the chapter. These lead into a consideration in the following two chapters of alternative approaches that are available.

5.2 CHAPTER STRUCTURE

This chapter is divided into the following sections:

- the context of MRP;
- the components of MRP;
- the MRP explosion process;
- capacity requirements planning;
- lot sizing in MRP;
- MRP and safety stock;
- MRP and purchasing;
- MRP and inventory control;
- regenerative and net change systems;

- time-bucketed and bucketless systems;
- MRP in practice.

After a general description of the MRP explosion process and the components of an MRP system, the detailed steps of both material and capacity requirements planning are described using requirements records and resource loading charts. Alternative lot sizing techniques that may be used in MRP are then discussed, and the role of safety stock in MRP is analysed. The new roles of the purchasing and inventory control functions in an MRP driven production management environment are next discussed, and different types of change management and time aggregation in MRP systems are described in terms of the differences between regenerative and net change, and time-bucketed and bucketless systems. The chapter concludes with a brief analysis of the typical problems encountered in the implementation of MRP systems.

5.3 THE CONTEXT OF MRP

A master production schedule is basically a statement of what the company intends to produce as output and is expressed in terms of items which are at an appropriate level of the bill of materials as discussed in the previous chapter. The schedule must be translated into some form of detailed action plan to show what needs to happen on the shop floor in order to achieve this output.

A number of different approaches may be taken in developing an action plan depending on the type of company and what particular type of production management philosophy the company is using. Three alternative types of approach exist: the MRP approach, the OPT or synchronous manufacturing approach and the JIT approach. The MRP and the OPT approaches have been applied mainly to batch manufacturing companies and the JIT approach has been used mainly in repetitive manufacturing. However, as we shall see in the next chapter, it can sometimes be possible for batch manufacturers to rationalize and structure their operations in such a way that the use of JIT techniques becomes possible.

All three approaches require that the master production schedule be translated into a detailed operational plan that is achievable within the production resource capacity limitations of the plant. This requires timings and quantities of production orders to be matched against production capacity (i.e. we require a detailed feasible operational schedule for the production of all sub-assemblies, components, etc., that will be required to meet the master production schedule). The form in which this schedule is stated and the mechanics of its production are the factors which constitute the most significant difference between the three approaches mentioned above.

Material requirements planning (MRP), subsequently more commonly known as 'manufacturing resources planning' (and distinguished as an acronym from MRP by being referred to as MRP 2), was developed in the USA in the mid 1960s as an order launching system. The original idea behind MRP was to start from a master production schedule of requirements for finished products, and to compute from this together with bills of materials and inventory status information the detailed requirements for all the individual components and raw materials needed. A schematic diagram of the process is shown in Fig. 5.1. By including in the calculation the inventory status and average lead times for all items and time phasing the requirement dates for all sub-assemblies, components, etc., backwards from the due date of each batch of finished product, the required ordering dates and quantities for all raw materials, components and sub-assemblies to meet the final assembly schedule can be computed, the computation itself being known as the **MRP explosion** process. MRP is essentially a simulation of the detailed effects on individual item requirements of meeting a predetermined finished product assembly schedule extended for several months into the future. Thus in MRP, raw materials are not procured nor components machined simply because they 'may' be required. All stock replenishments, from raw materials onwards, are specifically tied to firm orders or firm demand projections for the finished product. In the 1970s, rising dissatisfaction with the degree of success of MRP in improving productivity led Joe Orlicky and Oliver Wight of IBM

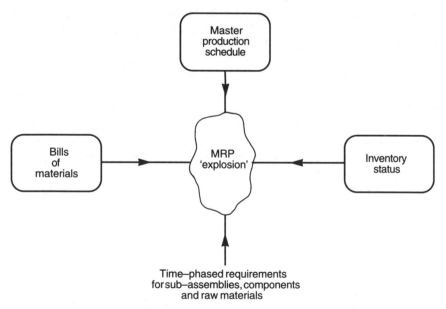

Fig. 5.1 The MRP explosion process.

(the company which produced the first MRP system) to rethink the conceptual foundations of MRP. They came to the conclusion that the reasons for the failure of MRP lay in the fact that an order launching system by itself was not sufficient, and what was required was a system that was more efficient at 'pulling' the urgently needed items through the system. As a result, much more attention was paid from then on to maintaining updated priorities of each order or job, rather than simply using the system to launch orders at the appropriate time and then leaving them to progress at their own rate. This new type of MRP was called **closed loop MRP**, due to the fact that continuing to track orders after they have been launched and 'pulling' through the ones really needed represents a form of closed feedback control loop.

As an increasing number of companies succeeded in implementing closed loop MRP with large gains in productivity, attention was given to integrating the accounting, marketing, engineering and distribution functions into one system. The term given to this approach is **manufacturing resources planning** or **MRP 2**. This chapter will mainly be concerned with the detailed mechanics of closed loop MRP, with brief descriptions where relevant of the interfaces and extensions required for a system to be classed as MRP 2.

5.4 THE COMPONENTS OF MRP

An MRP system is comprised of the following basic components which take the form of computer 'files' containing the data indicated.

- **A master production schedule** which is a statement of what finished products will be manufactured in what quantity and in what time periods over some future planning horizon that may extend from between three months and a year into the future.
- **A bill of materials file** which contains, for each finished product, details of all the individual items (raw materials, sub-assemblies, components, etc.) required before a product can be manufactured, and the lead times needed to procure these items if they are not in stock.
- **A set of valid inventory records** giving the current quantity on hand of each item appearing in the bill of materials file.

For the planning of production capacity requirements in addition to material requirements, two additional files are required:

- **A routeing file** indicating for each item appearing in the bill of materials file the sequence of operations required in its production, and the work centres at which it must be processed. For purchased items, this file could be regarded as containing the name of the supplier, or alternative suppliers.

- **A work centre file** which accumulates against each work centre the actual anticipated production hours in each time period as computed from the time-phased production requirements of each item.

The basic logic of the system is as follows:

1. For each time period over the duration of the planning horizon, the master production schedule for that time period (i.e. the statement of what products will be produced in this time period) is combined with the bill of materials file and the inventory file to give the detailed net requirements and dates for all the individual items needed to satisfy the finished product schedule for that week.
2. Dates at which orders need to be launched to satisfy item net requirements are computed using information on item lead times contained in the bill of materials file.
3. The system refers to the routeing file to ascertain which work centres will be involved in satisfying each net requirement (or production order). The number of actual hours work physically required to produce each order are then accumulated by time period against each work centre in the work centre file.
4. A check is made to establish if the resultant load on any work centre in any time period exceeds its capacity. If so, some rescheduling must be performed.
5. The whole process is repeated for each period of real time. In closed loop MRP the requirement dates for each order are continually updated in the light of changing customer requirements and unforeseen shopfloor contingencies and shortages.

5.5 THE MRP EXPLOSION PROCESS

The 'core' of the MRP process is the combination of the master production schedule with the bill of materials file and the inventory file to produce time-phased net requirements of the individual items needed to assemble finished products as dictated by the master production schedule. This is commonly referred to as the MRP explosion process.

5.5.1 STRUCTURE OF A BILL OF MATERIALS FILE

In order to understand the nature of the explosion process, it is necessary to examine in more detail the structure of the bill of materials file.

Bills of materials for two typical assembled products are shown in Fig. 5.2. Representation of a bill of materials for MRP purposes is in the form of a hierarchical tree structure with various levels. By convention, the finished product is at level 0 (sometimes level 1). The next level down (level 1) shows the items that are directly assembled together to make the

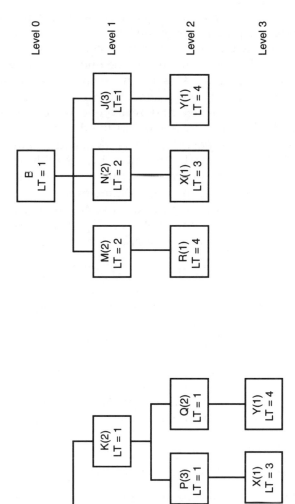

Level 0

Level 1

Level 2

Level 3

B
LT = 1

M(2)
LT = 2

N(2)
LT = 2

J(3)
LT=1

R(1)
LT = 4

X(1)
LT = 3

Y(1)
LT = 4

A
LT = 1

M(3)
LT = 2

L(1)
LT = 1

K(2)
LT = 1

R(1)
LT = 4

R (1)
LT = 4

P(3)
LT = 1

Q(2)
LT = 1

X(1)
LT = 3

Y(1)
LT = 4

Fig. 5.2 Bills of materials for two products A and B.

end product, the number required and the lead time needed to procure each item. Level 2 shows the items quantities and lead times that are required to produce the level 1 items, and so on.

Thus to assemble one unit of finished product A, we require (at level 1 on the bill of materials) three units of M, one unit of L and two units of K. The lead time for product A is given as one week, meaning that provided items M, L and K were available, the required batch of A could on average be assembled and ready one week after receiving the order. Items M, L and K are known as the **daughter** items of item A. Item A is known as the **parent** of items M, L and K. Both M and L are produced (probably by machining) from item R with one unit of R being required in each case. The lead times are two weeks and one week respectively. Thus on average, the elapsed time from when an order for M is launched to when it arrives in stock is two weeks. The corresponding time for L is one week. Item R, at level 2 on the bill of materials, is an externally purchased item with a relatively long lead time of four weeks.

Item K is a sub-assembly comprising three units of item P and two units of item Q, with a lead time of one week to assemble them together, given that they are available. P and Q are produced from purchased items X and Y, a lead time of one week being required for the production in each case. The purchased items X and Y have lead times of three and four weeks, and are at level 3 of the bill of materials.

Finished product B has a slightly simpler structure with no sub-assemblies involved. It does, however, contain some common items also used in product A. Total requirements for these common items will be generated from the master production schedule requirements for both finished products.

5.5.2 COMPUTATION OF GROSS REQUIREMENTS

In order to obtain a simple understanding of the principles of time phasing used in MRP, let us assume initially that production is just starting up, and the only stocks we have are of the purchased items R, X and Y. To see how the requirements and timings of order releases for each item can be computed from a given master production schedule for the finished products A and B, let us assume that a master production schedule for A and B has been prepared for the next 10 weeks and is as follows:

	[Week]									
	[1]	[2]	[3]	[4]	[5]	[6]	[7]	[8]	[9]	[10]
A	0	0	0	0	8	0	0	7	0	0
B	0	0	0	0	0	0	6	0	0	5

The gross requirements for each individual item, on each level of the bill of materials, can now be computed from the bill of materials file. The schedule for finished product A, for example, will generate requirements for M (at level 1) which in turn will generate requirements for R (at level 2) as follows:

	[Week]									
	[1]	[2]	[3]	[4]	[5]	[6]	[7]	[8]	[9]	[10]
A	0	0	0	0	8	0	0	7	0	0
M	0	0	0	24	0	0	21	0	0	0
R	0	24	0	0	21	0	0	0	0	0

Master schedule requirements for 8 and 7 units of A in weeks 5 and 8 will generate requirements at level 1 for 24 units of M in week 4 and 21 units of M in week 7, since 3 units of M are required to produce 1 unit of A. Since the lead time of A is one week, these items must be ready one week before A is due.

The requirement for 24 units of M in week 4 and 21 units of M in week 7 generates in turn, at level 2, a requirement of 24 units of R in week 2 and 21 units in week 7. Only 1 unit of R is required per unit of M, but the lead time for M is two weeks, and so the appropriate number of R must be available two weeks before the batches of M are required, to be ready for the processing of M.

We can now extend the process to compute the gross requirements of each item. If, for simplicity, we separate the requirements generated by product A from the requirements generated by product B, we obtain tables of gross requirements as shown in Fig. 5.3.

Notice that some of the purchased items are required in week 1. If these items are in stock no problem arises. However, if they are not in stock, we can see from the lead times that X, for example, should have been ordered three weeks ago and Y should have been ordered four weeks ago. If we display the bill of materials for each product with lead times on a time axis, as shown in Fig. 5.4, we can see that the maximum time span from ordering the earliest required raw materials (R and Y) to final assembly of the finished product is seven weeks. This is the total 'stacked' lead time of product A. Our master production schedule must therefore extend at least seven weeks into the future so that we can be sure that action can be taken now to order the raw materials required if, for example, an unexpectedly large demand for A is forecast for seven weeks' time.

This concept is similar to the notion of the 'critical path' in PERT and CPM techniques. The difference is that, since in MRP we try to avoid producing an item before it is required by backscheduling from the due date, then if the plan is adhered to, all items on the bill of materials are on the critical path, since a delay in availability of any one of them will delay the finished product.

Requirements generated from product A:

					Week					
	1	2	3	4	5	6	7	8	9	10
A	0	0	0	0	8	0	0	7	0	0
M	0	0	0	24	0	0	21	0	0	0
L	0	0	0	8	0	0	7	0	0	0
R	0	24	8	0	21	7	0	0	0	0
K	0	0	0	16	0	0	14	0	0	0
P	0	48	0	0	42	0	0	0	0	0
Q	0	32	0	0	28	0	0	0	0	0
X	48	0	0	42	0	0	0	0	0	0
Y	32	0	0	28	0	0	0	0	0	0

Requirements generated from product B:

					Week					
	1	2	3	4	5	6	7	8	9	10
B	0	0	0	0	8	0	6	0	0	5
M	0	0	0	0	0	12	0	0	10	0
R	0	0	0	12	0	0	10	0	0	0
N	0	0	0	0	0	12	0	0	10	0
X	0	0	0	12	0	0	10	0	0	0
J	0	0	0	0	0	18	0	0	15	0
Y	0	0	0	0	18	0	0	15	0	0

If we join the two tables together, adding the requirements for the common items, we obtain:

					Week					
	1	2	3	4	5	6	7	8	9	10
M	0	0	0	24	0	12	21	0	10	0
L	0	0	0	8	0	0	7	0	0	0
R	0	24	8	12	21	7	10	0	0	0
K	0	0	0	16	0	0	14	0	0	0
P	0	48	0	0	42	0	0	0	0	0
Q	0	32	0	0	28	0	0	0	0	0
N	0	0	0	0	0	12	0	0	10	0
X	48	0	0	54	0	0	10	0	0	0
J	0	0	0	0	0	18	0	0	15	0
Y	32	0	0	28	18	0	0	15	0	0

Fig. 5.3 Gross requirements for product A and product B items.

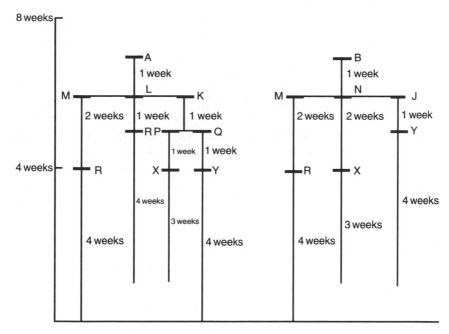

Fig. 5.4 Bills of materials on a time axis.

5.5.3 COMPUTATION OF NET REQUIREMENTS AND PLANNED ORDER RELEASES

In the above example, it was assumed that we had no stock on hand of any items other than raw materials, and so the gross requirements as calculated from the master production schedule and the bill of materials file represented what was actually required to be produced or ordered. If we already have some items in stock, these must be subtracted from the gross requirements before the net requirements can be obtained.

In addition, if we have more stock on hand than is needed for the current requirement, or if items are produced in batches larger than the quantity immediately required so that some stock will be carried into subsequent periods, then the projected net requirements for future periods must be obtained by subtracting the projected gross requirements from the projected inventory balance. Net requirements are computed by setting up a **requirements record** for each item, giving details of projected gross requirements, on-hand balances, net requirements and quantities and timings of expected receipts and orders that need to be launched to satisfy net requirements.

A requirements record is shown on p. 118 for item M assuming that demand for M is generated by the master production schedule for A and

B as indicated previously, and that we currently have a stock on hand of 30 units:

Item: M
Lead time: 2 weeks
Order qty: 45
On hand: 37

Week	[1]	[2]	[3]	[4]	[5]	[6]	[7]	[8]	[9]	[10]
Gross requirements	0	0	0	24	0	12	21	0	10	0
Scheduled receipts	0	0	0	0	0	0	0	0	0	0
On hand	37	37	37	13	13	1	25	25	15	15
Net requirements	0	0	0	0	45	0	20	0	0	0
Planned order receipt	0	0	0	0	0	0	45	0	0	0
Planned order release	0	0	0	0	45	0	0	0	0	0

Gross requirements represent the weekly gross requirements (i.e. the total demand) for item M as generated by the production schedule for the finished products of which item M forms a part (in this case, products A and B). Gross requirements of 24, 12 and 21 units exist for item M in weeks 4, 6 and 7 respectively.

Scheduled receipts give details of quantities that are due to be received as a result of production orders that have already been placed. Such orders are described as **open orders**. There are no receipts scheduled for item M in the 10-week period shown by the record.

On hand gives the projected on-hand inventory balance at the end of each week that will be available to meet requirements in future weeks, after allowing for the arrival of scheduled receipts, planned order receipts and the withdrawal of gross requirements. Item M has a starting balance of 37 units which is reduced to 13 in week 4 by the demand of 24 in that week, and to one in week 6 by the demand of 12. The balance increases to 25 in week 7 due to the arrival of a planned order of 45 and a demand of 21.

Net requirements give the outstanding quantity required each week that cannot be met from the on-hand balance for the end of the previous week and the scheduled receipts due in the current week. A net requirement of 20 for item M arises in week 7 because the on-hand balance at the end of week 6 was insufficient to meet the demand of 21 in week 7.

Planned order receipts represent the quantity that would need to be planned to be received in a particular week to meet the net requirements for that week. The quantity may be a 'standard' order quantity or a multiple thereof, and may therefore be larger than the actual net requirement for that week. A replenishment batch of item M will have to be received in week 7 to satisfy the net requirement in that week. Since the standard replenishment batch size is 45 units, this will be the quantity that must be planned to arrive. After satisfying the net requirement of 21 units, the surplus of 25 units will be carried over to the next week.

Planned order release gives the release dates and quantities of the orders that must be placed such that they arrive as planned receipts in time to satisfy net requirements. In order to receive a batch of 45 units of item M in week 7, the order must be released in week 5 since the lead time is two weeks.

Note that the planned order release will always be for the same quantity as the planned order receipt, and will be timed-phased forward by the lead time of the item (i.e. the order must be released one lead time before it is needed).

Note also that the requirements record is a 'rolling' schedule which is updated each week as we move forward in time. As we move forward in real time by one week, the week 1 entries are deleted, the week 2 entries replace the week 1 entries, the week 3 entries replace the week 2 entries, etc. A new set of week 10 entries must be generated from the master production schedule for finished products in what was last week designated as week 11, but is now week 10. When a 'planned order release' appears in the week 1 column, action must be taken to release the order. The week 1 column is thus the 'action' column. After a planned order release has actually been released, and has disappeared from the week 1 column, the corresponding planned order receipt entry will also be deleted and will appear as a scheduled receipt (i.e. an expected receipt for which the order has already been placed).

The requirements record for item M five weeks later might appear as follows:

Item: M
Lead time: 2 weeks
Order qty: 45
On hand: 13

Week	[1]	[2]	[3]	[4]	[5]	[6]	[7]	[8]	[9]	[10]
Gross requirements	33	0	0	0	0	0	20	0	0	35
Scheduled receipts	0	←45	0	0	0	0	0	0	0	0
On hand	25	25	25	25	25	25	5	5	5	15
Net requirements	0	0	0	0	0	0	0	0	0	30
Planned order receipt	0	0	0	0	0	0	0	0	0	45
Planned order release	0	0	0	0	0	0	0	45	0	0

In this case what were the requirements for week 6 on the original record are now the requirements for week 1 on the updated record. New gross requirements of 20 and 35 have appeared for weeks 7 and 10 (which would have been weeks 12 and 15 at the time the original record was computed). The planned order release in week 5 of an order for 45 units was released last week and the order has been converted to a scheduled receipt due in week 2.

Note that the gross requirement for 21 units in week 7 of the original record should now appear as a requirement for week 2 in the updated record. In fact, the requirement for these items appears in week 1 giving a total requirement of 33 items for that week. This implies that in the intervening five weeks, the requirement date for this quantity of item M has been brought forward by one week, perhaps because the customer who ordered product A or B is asking for early delivery.

Unfortunately, the scheduled receipt of 45 units to satisfy this demand is not due until week 2. The way this problem is solved in MRP is to **expedite** the arrival of the scheduled receipt and arrange for it to be ready in less than the average lead time. This can generally be done because, as discussed in Chapter 3, the lead time as defined for planning purposes is considerably longer than the physical time required to produce the item. The job thus spends a high proportion of its lead time simply waiting in a queue, and the lead time can be shortened simply by arranging for it to jump the queue. As was discussed in section 3.6 in Chapter 3, provided that on average as many jobs can be 'de-expedited' as are expedited, for example through some customers accepting later delivery, the integrity of the overall schedule can be maintained. If, for example, there were no gross requirements for item M until week 4, the scheduled receipt of 45 would not actually be required until week 4, and could be de-expedited. The difference between MRP and more informal systems of expediting is that MRP allows **automatic** expediting of jobs tied to orders required before their original due date, and allows jobs not needed until past their original due date to be automatically de-expedited. All priorities are thus automatically maintained up to date.

5.5.4 LEVEL-BY-LEVEL PROCESSING

The existence of inventory means that a set of gross requirements for level 1 items will not necessarily all be reflected in corresponding requirements for items at a lower level of the bill of materials. Only the net requirement (i.e. the part of the gross requirement that cannot be satisfied from inventory and which is therefore converted into a planned order release) will cause a gross requirement for the parent item to be propagated downwards to cause requirements for daughter items.

We can formalize this statement to say that a planned order release for any item will automatically result in a set of gross requirements for the set of daughter items of which the parent item is composed, in the week that the planned order release for the parent is due for release.

Consider the following requirements records for items M and L as generated by the master production schedule for products A and B considered previously:

Item: M
Lead time: 2 weeks
Order qty: 45
On hand: 37

Week	[1]	[2]	[3]	[4]	[5]	[6]	[7]	[8]	[9]	[10]
Gross requirements	0	0	0	24	0	12	21	0	10	0
Scheduled receipts	0	0	0	0	0	0	0	0	0	0
On hand	37	37	37	13	13	1	25	25	15	15
Net requirements	0	0	0	0	0	0	20	0	0	0
Planned order receipt	0	0	0	0	0	0	45	0	0	0
Planned order release	0	0	0	0	45	0	0	0	0	0

Item: L
Lead time: 1 week
Order qty: 15
On hand: 5

Week	[1]	[2]	[3]	[4]	[5]	[6]	[7]	[8]	[9]	[10]
Gross requirements	0	0	0	8	0	0	7	0	0	0
Scheduled receipts	0	0	0	0	0	0	0	0	0	0
On hand	5	5	5	12	12	12	5	5	5	5
Net requirements	0	0	0	3	0	0	0	0	0	0
Planned order receipt	0	0	0	15	0	0	0	0	0	0
Planned order release	0	0	15	0	0	0	0	0	0	0

Item: R
Lead time: 4 weeks
Order qty: 30
On hand: 5

Week	[1]	[2]	[3]	[4]	[5]	[6]	[7]	[8]	[9]	[10]
Gross requirements	0	0	15	0	45	0	0	0	10	0
Scheduled receipts	0	0	0	←30	0	0	0	0	0	0
On hand	5	5	20	20	5	5	5	5	5	5

Week	[1]	[2]	[3]	[4]	[5]	[6]	[7]	[8]	[9]	[10]
Net requirements	0	0	0	0	25	0	0	0	0	0
Planned order receipt	0	0	0	0	30	0	0	0	0	0
Planned order release	30	0	0	0	0	0	0	0	0	0

Item A is required to produce both items M and L (one unit of item R per unit of item L or M). The planned order releases for 15 units of L in week 3 and 45 units of M in week 5 thus generate gross requirements for the corresponding quantities of item R in the corresponding weeks. Although the batches of items L and M will probably not be produced until towards the end of their lead times, sufficient of item R (which is the raw material) must be actually available at the time the orders for L and M are released in case it is necessary to produce the batch slightly earlier for capacity scheduling reasons. For example, the plant might be overloaded in week 4 but spare capacity may be available in week 3, indicating it may be more convenient to produce the batch of 45 units of item M in week 3 rather than in week 4.

The requirements record for item R shows a net requirement of 25 appearing in week 5 which means an order must be released in week 1. Note that the scheduled receipt of 30 units in week 4 has been expedited to week 3 to meet what would otherwise appear as a net requirement. Since item R is a purchased item, it is assumed that the supplier was persuaded to deliver one week earlier than the normal lead time.

Note also that it is only the planned order release row of a parent item that generates gross requirements for the daughter items. If a scheduled receipt of, say, 30 units of item M was due to arrive in week 3, this would not have generated any requirement for item R since it is assumed that the requisite amount of item R would have been available and subtracted from the 'on hand' of the item R requirements record at the time the order for item M was released (and hence converted to a scheduled receipt).

If we refer back to the original gross requirements table on page 114 which was developed on the assumption that there was no current stock of any item, we can see that the gross requirements for item R are quite different from those we have generated from the situation where items M and L had current on-hand balances. This is because meeting part of the gross requirement for items M and L from stock reduced the requirement for item R since it was already present (in its converted form) in the stocks of L and M.

In order to ensure that the correct quantities of all items at each level are worked out in a consistent and efficient manner, MRP uses the concept of **level-by-level processing**. This means that the net requirements and planned order releases over the full time horizon of all items on one level must be computed before moving to the next level. If we consider again the bills of materials for products A and B shown in Fig. 5.2, it should be apparent that a policy of 'depth first' processing as opposed to 'level-by-level' processing would involve processing the requirements records of each item in product A down to the lowest level before looking at product B. In the case of item R, for example, this would involve recomputing the requirements record from scratch each time it appeared since each additional gross requirement for item R may involve changing or adding to the planned order releases already computed. The same of course would be true for items M, L, X and Y. With level-by-level processing, all the gross requirements for an item are computed by processing all the items on the level above before the requirements record for the lower level is processed, thereby ensuring that processing need only be performed once.

A slight complication occurs in the level-by-level processing approach when an item appears on more than one level. This is true of items X and Y in Fig. 5.2, which both appear on level 3 for product A and level 2 for product B. This is usually handled by noting the lowest level in any bill of materials at which the item occurs, and by storing this information together with the order quantity, lead time, etc., at the head of the requirements record for that item. Although gross requirements for this item (generated by its different level parents) will be accumulated in the gross requirements row of the record in the usual way, the requirements record itself (giving computed on-hand balances, net requirements and planned order releases) will only be processed when the lowest level at which the item occurs has been reached. This ensures that all the gross requirements on that item will have been generated before the item itself is processed.

5.5.5 INDEPENDENT DEMAND ITEMS

It is possible to have a demand (i.e. a gross requirement) for component items at a low level of the bill of materials that are not generated by the parent item. This happens most frequently where the item concerned is sold direct to the customer in the form of spare parts. In this case the item is termed to have an **independent demand** on it (i.e. independent of the demand for any higher level items). This independent demand must be estimated for each week of the planning period, and must be added to the gross requirements generated by the parent items in the normal way.

5.6 CAPACITY REQUIREMENTS PLANNING

5.6.1 BASICS OF CRP

We have seen in section 5.4 of this chapter how MRP combines the planned production schedule (MPS) for each item with routeing information that indicates which work centres are involved in the production of that item. The expected number of hours' work involved for each production order can then be accumulated against the appropriate work centre. For capacity planning purposes, the number of hours' work involved in each order will be assigned to the week immediately prior to that in which the order is due, even though the actual physical production may actually take place at any time between the week that the order is released and the week it is due.

The result of this process will be a planned **work centre load profile** for each work centre over as many weeks as the MRP planning horizon extends. A check can be performed to ascertain whether any work centre is overloaded in any particular week, and appropriate action can be taken.

An example of a work centre load profile is shown in Fig. 5.5. The weekly capacity of the work centre is shown by the dotted line. It will be seen that the current MPS results in work centre WC.3 being overloaded in weeks 1 and 4. Note how the MRP process allows us to predict overload problems well in advance and plan accordingly.

If a work centre is overloaded in any particular week, three possible courses of action present themselves:

1. Establish if the load can be levelled by shifting some work from the overloaded periods to periods with spare capacity within the 'slack' allowed by the lead time of the item concerned (i.e. without having to change the MPS).
2. If this fails, use a set of priority rules to level the load by scheduling lower priority work to the first period with spare capacity, and change the master production schedule accordingly.
3. If the change to the master production schedule is unacceptable in terms of the resulting delays in satisfying customer demand, then

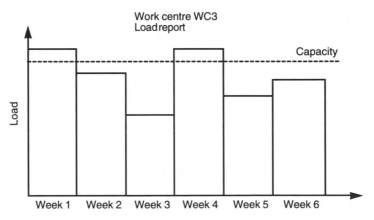

Fig. 5.5 Work centre load profile.

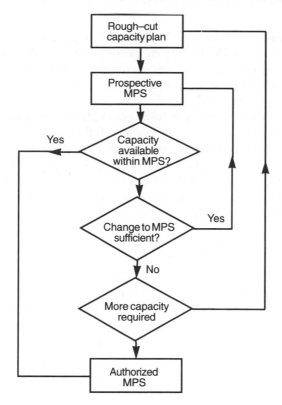

Fig. 5.6 Capacity requirements planning – interaction with MPS.

plan to increase capacity by overtime work, hiring extra labour, subcontracting etc.

This process is shown schematically in Fig. 5.6. If option 3 has to be exercised, MRP allows the possibility of the capacity problem to be predicted well in advance, so that action to increase capacity can be taken in good time.

5.6.2 FINITE AND INFINITE LOADING

In the approach outlined above, a so-called **infinite loading approach** has been taken. Infinite loading simply allows the computer system to load each work centre with the jobs generated by the current MPS without any regard for the capacity of the work centre. The feasibility of the load schedule is then assessed by the shop foreman who checks whether the load can be levelled by transferring work from overloaded to underloaded periods. Jobs are then scheduled in order of priority.

Most CRP systems also have an option for **finite loading**. Finite loading allows the computer system to level the loading between periods automatically by rescheduling jobs from overloaded periods to underloaded periods in some mathematically optimum way, and automatically changing the MPS where necessary. The precise order in which jobs will be processed is thus computed.

Experienced MRP users generally advocate the infinite loading approach, since this allows more flexibility and direct control over shopfloor operations by the foreman and the production controller. However, to understand the principles of work centre load levelling within an existing MPS, it is important to understand the role of the lead time in MRP and how it is employed to generate **slack** within which flexibility to change loadings can be maintained.

5.6.3 LEAD TIMES IN MRP

Up to now, we have used the notion of lead time in MRP to back-schedule order releases for items based on requirement dates for their parents, without saying much about how lead times are actually determined. In reality, the lead time of an item is made up of a number of components as shown in Fig. 5.7.

The lead time is thus composed of:

1. 'wait' time in a queue of orders waiting to be processed;
2. 'move' time in which the required materials are moved from stores to the processing work centre;
3. set-up time in which the work centre is set up for the job;
4. processing time on the work centre;
5. 'move' time of the finished item from the work centre back to stores.

Components 2 to 5 represent the 'physical' part of the lead time. For the remainder of the time, the order exists only as a piece of paper waiting in a queue of similar orders. Typically, this 'wait' time can represent up to 90% of the total lead time.

When in MRP we specify the lead time of an item as, say, three weeks, we are implying that although the physical production time of the order may be only a matter of hours, all the lower level 'daughter' items are

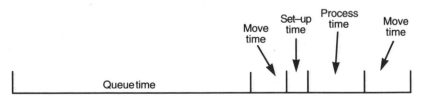

Fig. 5.7 Lead time composition.

required to be ready three weeks before the parent item is actually re-quired to be ready.

What is the purpose of extending our planning lead times to be so much longer than the physical production time of the item, and allowing its components to wait so long in a 'queue'?

The reason is to retain more flexibility in the loading of work centres, so that actual production of orders can be effected before the week in which they were initially loaded in order to help level the load from week to week. By having all items needed for the production job available three weeks in advance, although the order will initially be loaded in the week immediately before it is due, we are effectively allowing flexibility to transfer actual production of the order, for load levelling purposes, to either of the two weeks before the week in which it was initially loaded, depending on the work centre loading over that period and the urgency of the job. Thus provided an order can be reallocated from an overloaded period to an earlier underloaded period within the bounds of the lead time of the order, then we know that the load can be accommodated within existing capacity without changing the MPS. This is shown schematically in Fig. 5.8.

This point is best illustrated in more detail with the simple example shown in Fig. 5.9. Consider two products A and B with the structures shown, both containing a common component D. Assume further that the lead time for assembly of both A and B from their component items is relatively short (a matter of hours).

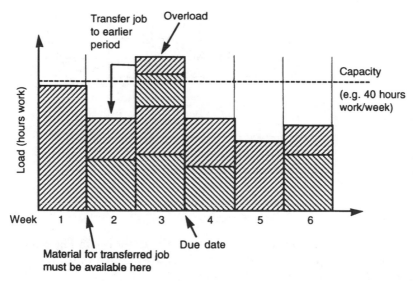

Fig. 5.8 Transferring loads between time periods.

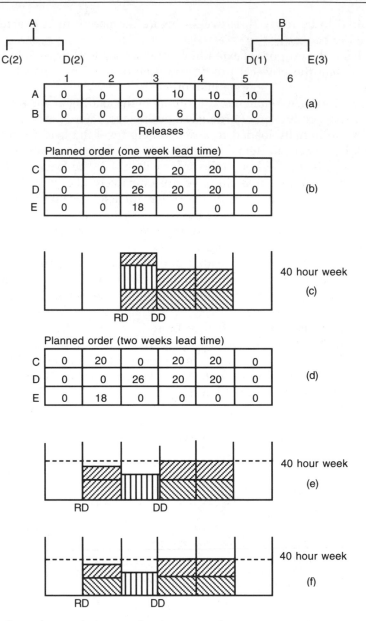

Fig. 5.9 Capacity requirements planning example.

A master production schedule for A and B as shown in Fig. 5.9(a) will then generate requirements for the appropriate number of components to be available for assembly in the same week.

If we assume the lead time of all components is short, say one week, orders for production of components to satisfy the MPS for A and B must be launched a week earlier than the finished product requirements as shown in Fig. 5.9(b). If we further assume that one unit of each component of any type needs one hour of processing on work centre WC1, the load profile for work centre WC1 is as shown in Fig. 5.9(c).

Consider the orders due in week 4. Since materials for the production of components C, D and E will not be scheduled to be available until the start of week 3, and we assume the machined components must be ready for assembly at the start of week 4, the machining of these components can take place only in week 3 giving us a load of 64 hours of work in that week. If the load capacity of WC1 is only 40 hours per week, we should be unable to meet the schedule. With the current lead time of one week, we only have a very small time window of one week between the release date and the due date (RD and DD in Fig. 5.9), and this gives us no flexibility for moving some of the load to an earlier period. We could of course ask for the materials needed for these components to be available at the start of week 2 so that some of the overload could be transferred to week 2. But what we are doing here is effectively increasing the lead time of our components after discovering that capacity in a particular week was insufficient. This would not matter once in a while. But if we found that we were continually having to plan for an earlier than usual arrival of raw materials, it would be an indication that a lead time of one week for our components was too short. This would normally be due to irregular loading of production orders on WC1 (e.g. clusters of orders all required in the same week, interspersed with periods during which no orders are due). To cope with this problem, the lead time must be extended so that orders can be rescheduled to earlier underloaded periods and that materials will still be available for work to start. Put in another way, it means that the 'queue' of jobs waiting to be processed on WC1 can frequently represent more than a week's work, meaning that the average actual lead time is more than a week.

To take a 'queuing' perspective on work centre loading can in fact be quite instructive. In any system in which arriving entities are processed in some way before leaving the system and in which the potential processing rate is greater than the arrival rate (i.e. the system has sufficient capacity to cope with the arrivals) a queue tends to build up only if the arrivals are irregular in their timing. If arrivals are perfectly regular, there is no queue. There is also no queue (or a very low probability of a queue) if the potential processing rate is much greater than the arrival rate (i.e. we have excess capacity). Similarly, if jobs arrive at or are loaded on to a work centre at precisely regular intervals, and the capacity is sufficient, no queue of work will build up because there will never be any time period in which the load on the work centre is greater than its capacity. This is shown in Fig. 5.10.

The length of the queue of jobs waiting to be processed (or the 'backlog') is thus a measure of the irregularity of arrivals of individual jobs. This is

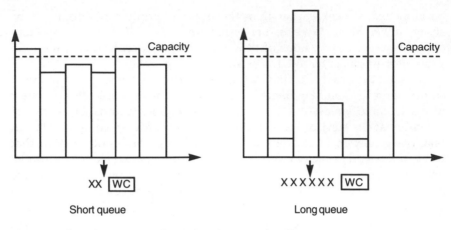

Fig. 5.10 Queuing perspective on work centre loading.

of course indicated by the magnitude of the load fluctuation from week to week as displayed on a load profile report such as that shown in Fig. 5.5. For widely fluctuating weekly loads, we will have a significant amount of shifting of jobs between periods to level the load, and we shall thus need to increase lead times. From the queuing perspective, the time spent in the queue is longer. If we assign planning lead times correctly based on the degree of weekly variability of work centre load, then we should be able to schedule jobs into existing capacity within the times allowed by their lead time without needing to change the MPS.

If we now refer back to Fig. 5.9, we can see what happens if we increase the lead time of all components to two weeks. Planned orders for components are now launched a week earlier as shown in Fig. 5.9(d). We can now transfer two of the orders from the overloaded week 3 to underloaded week 2 as shown in Fig. 5.9(e) (the materials will now be available at the start of week 2 due to the increase in lead time) resulting in the load profile shown in Fig. 5.9(f) which is within capacity.

Alternatively, if the capacity limit of 45 hours'work had represented the capacity of WC1 on normal shift working, it may have been possible to meet the overload by working overtime. The advantage of the MRP capacity planning process is that it allows these decisions to be made well in advance.

5.6.4 PRIORITY PLANNING

Having developed a capacity plan and established with the aid of the work centre load reports whether existing jobs can be fitted into the planned capacity, it is necessary to actually execute the plan.

As we move forward in time, and each future week of our MRP requirements plan (represented by the individual requirements records for each item) becomes in turn the current week, the planned orders for the current week are released. The current week becomes what is called the **action bucket**. Actions can be the release of either purchase or production orders appearing in the planned order release row for week 1 of each requirement record.

The release of a production order means that it will simply join the 'queue' of work waiting to be processed at the appropriate work centre. If our planning lead times have been set to give a good reflection of the average length of this queue, then on average the order should reach the head of the queue to be processed just before it is required. Provided there is always a backlog of work in front of the work centre, and we always keep the work centre running, the periods which according to our infinite loading work centre load profile were underloaded will be automatically loaded to capacity because the work centre will always be working off the backlog. When it has finished the orders that the infinite capacity plan had loaded for the current period, it will start on the orders for the next period provided the required materials for these orders are ready (i.e. we are 'within' the planned lead time period for those orders). We must simply make sure that the orders we work on in that period are the ones that are really needed to ensure the MPS is adhered to. It should thus be apparent that the problem of executing the detailed loading of orders is reduced to the problem of selecting the highest priority order from the queue of orders waiting (i.e. we have a problem of priority control).

A number of **priority rules** have been suggested to give the sequence in which a queue of orders should be loaded on to a particular work centre. There is no universal agreement about the precise nature of the priority rules that should be applied, other thàn that the rule should rank the orders according to the urgency within with which they are required to meet the original MPS, and that priorities should be kept current. It is generally recommended that priorities should be updated on a daily basis to reflect changing demand dates and conditions on the shop floor.

The need dates of individual orders are generally tied to the need dates of the parent items. A change in the requirement date of the end product will thus result in a change in the need dates of all the lower level items.

A further type of event that can change the need date of an item is the situation where a particular component is unavailable at its required time due to an unavoidable delivery delay or a machine breakdown. This may have an effect on the timing at which an end item can be produced. A delay in a component may cause an unavoidable delay in an end item which in turn can affect the need dates of all other lower level items needed in this particular product. Their priorities will be reduced because they will not actually be required until the delayed item is ready. This

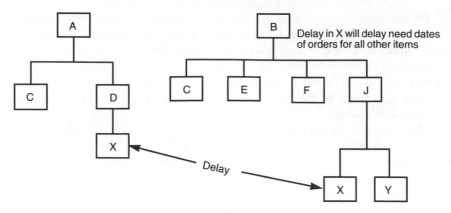

Fig. 5.11 Pegging.

type of priority update is also performed automatically in MRP by a process known as **'pegging'**. The requirements record of each lower level item has access to 'pointers' to all the higher level items in which it is used. If a particular item is delayed, the higher level item that might be affected by this delay can be tracked, current orders for these items can be located, and the need dates of these orders and all the other associated lower level orders that will be affected via the common parent can be updated. This process is shown schematically in Fig. 5.11.

5.6.5 SHOPFLOOR CONTROL

The flow of work through a work centre is monitored by a process known as **input/output control**. This is a procedure whereby a running record is kept of the weekly planned and actual input to the work centre, the weekly planned and actual output from the work centre, and the current backlog. A specimen input/output report is shown in Fig. 5.12.

The planned output will usually be constant (apart from periods of maintenance etc.) and will be the planned capacity of the work centre. The planned input will be generated from the work centre loading report and will reflect the planned future job arrivals as deduced, for example, from Fig. 5.5. The actual job arrivals (in terms of hours' work), and the amount of work processed, will be recorded as the plan is executed. By this means, we can monitor the length of the backlog or 'queue' at a work centre to establish if lead times are starting to get out of control. We can specify control limits for the backlog which, if exceeded, will trigger some form of corrective action. An excessive and increasing backlog may be due to an increase in actual compared to planned input (too much work coming in) or a decrease of actual compared to planned input (work centre running below capacity). Lead times may have to be increased if

Work centre WC1

	Wk 1	Wk 2	Wk 3	Wk 4	Wk 5
Planned input	30	40	35	20	40
Actual input	40	60			
Deviation	+10	+20			
Planned output	40	40	30	40	40
Actual output	40	40			
Deviation	0	0			
Planned backlog	90	90	95	75	75
Actual backlog	100	120			

Fig. 5.12 Input/output report.

too much work is coming in, or if the work centre output cannot be restored to its planned level.

A decreasing backlog means the work centre may be in danger of running out of work due to too little input. Again some form of corrective action would need to be taken to keep the machine running. On the other hand if the long term input is actually lower than capacity, lead times could be reduced.

5.7 LOT SIZING IN MRP

5.7.1 LOT SIZING CONSIDERATIONS

Whereas the estimation of the economic size of a production or purchase order may be one of the dominant concerns of more traditional approaches to production planning, much less attention is paid to this particular problem in MRP. The three main reasons for this are:

- a recognition that the timing of an order is much more important than its quantity;
- a recognition that the difficulty of objective cost measurement makes accurate determination of the economic batch size impossible;
- the increasing use of set-up engineering techniques to greatly reduce set-up times and thus make smaller batches economic.

Although emphasis on economic batch quantity (EBQ) determination in MRP is reduced, it is nevertheless essential to have some ordering policy associated with each item that is purchased or produced. Each requirements record used as an example in the previous section had an order quantity as one of the characteristics of that particular item. The purpose of this section is to explain the different criteria and methods that may be used to set the order quantity.

Ways of estimating batch sizes may be divided into **static** and **dynamic batch sizing policies**. Static policies rely on the determination of a fixed

(a) Classical EBQ

Week	1	2	3	4	5	6	7
Demand	50	5	0	65	10	55	50
EOQ (117)	117			117			117
Onhand	67	62	62	114	104	49	116

Mean inventory = 82 (£41)
        Set–ups = 3 (£42.9)

(b) Lot for lot

Week	1	2	3	4	5	6	7
Demand	50	5	0	65	10	55	50
Lot for lot	50	5	0	65	10	55	50
Onhand	0	0	0	0	0	0	0

Mean inventory = 0 (£ 0)
        Set–ups = 6 (£85.7)

(c) Period order quantity

Week	1	2	3	4	5	6	7
Demand	50	5	0	65	10	55	50
POQ (4 wks)	120				115		
Onhand	70	65	65	0	105	50	0

Mean inventory = 51 (£25.5)
        Set–ups = 2 (£28.6)

(d) Part period balancing

Week	1	2	3	4	5	6	7
Demand	50	5	0	65	10	55	50
PPB	130				105		
Onhand	80	75	75	10	0	50	0

Mean inventory = 41 (£20.5)
        Set–ups = 2 (£28.6)

Fig. 5.13 Lot sizing in MRP.

batch size which is always adhered to regardless of any unevenness in the demand. The simple economic batch size technique is the best example of this approach. Dynamic batch sizing techniques use knowledge of probable forward demand variability to estimate batch sizes that will minimize set-ups and at the same time avoid carrying 'remnants' (excess inventory carried for several periods without being sufficient to cover a future period's requirements in full).

5.7.2 COMPARISON OF POLICIES

(a) Economic batch quantity

We have observed in Chapter 3 that the EBQ approach can perform poorly in situations where the demand is highly irregular. Use of the classical EBQ approach is nevertheless possible in MRP for items whose demands are fairly regular, provided of course it is felt that the relevant cost parameters can be reasonably estimated. Figure 5.13(a) shows the performance of an EBQ policy for a typical demand pattern in a situation in which the set-up cost for the item is £100 and the inventory carrying cost is £0.5 per unit per week. We assume that there is zero stock in week 0 and no safety stock is carried. It can be seen that the mean inventory carried with this policy is 82 units (cost per week £41) and that three set-ups are required giving an average weekly set-up cost of £43.

(b) Lot for lot

A 'lot-for-lot' batch sizing policy is a policy that produces items as required without carrying any excess stock from one week to the next. Lot-for-lot policies generally require that set-up costs and times be fairly low or they can be expensive. A lot-for-lot policy on the same demand pattern is shown in Fig. 5.13(b). The mean inventory cost is zero, but six rather than three set-ups are required, giving an average weekly set-up cost of £85.7. This makes the total weekly cost of the lot-for-lot policy slightly more than the EBQ policy.

(c) Period order quantity

This approach involves first determining the EBQ based on the average demand pattern (as in the first example) but then translating this into the number of weeks' demand that this represents. When an order is placed, it is placed for this number of weeks' demand. Assuming that there is some variability in the demand, and that this is at least partially predictable, the quantity represented by a fixed number of weeks' demand will itself be variable. Thus to cover a three-week period over which the demand is known will be low, a smaller batch is ordered. This approach avoids carrying unneeded inventory for long periods of time as can happen if the fixed EBQ is ordered in a situation where the demand is 'lumpy'. At the same time, we are not increasing the number of set-ups per year. Inventory is reduced by explicitly recognizing that demand variability exists. The effect of a period order quantity policy is shown in Fig. 5.13(c). The EBQ of 82 calculated from the average demand rate represents (to the nearest week) four weeks' demand. Hence four weeks' actual (assumed known) demand is ordered at four-weekly intervals to cover the following four weeks. As can be seen, both set-up cost and inventory cost are considerably lower than in the EBQ case.

(d) Part period balancing

This approach attempts some crude form of optimization on a dynamic or 'rolling schedule' basis. The idea behind the approach is that if requirements can be predicted in advance, then whenever the projected 'on-hand' situation indicates an order will need to be received, a trial and error calculation can be made of the maximum number of weeks' supply that can be ordered before the average inventory cost associated with the excess inventory exceeds the additional set-up cost that would be incurred if an additional batch had been made.

This can best be illustrated by reference to the example in Fig. 5.13(d). We clearly need to place an order in week 1. For how many weeks' supply should this be? If we order one week's supply, we carry no excess inventory, but the set-up cost of £100 must be repeated in week 2 to meet the week 2 requirement.

If we order two weeks' supply, then we are carrying five excess units from week 1 to week 2. The cost of doing this is $5 \times 0.5 \times 1 = £2.5$ for the week. We are substituting this small carrying cost for the additional cost of £100 had we decided to make a separate batch in week 2. It is therefore certainly cheaper to make at least two weeks' supply.

If we order three weeks' supply, we are in fact ordering the same quantity as for two weeks, since the demand in week 3 is zero. The next policy to consider therefore is to order four weeks' supply to see whether this is cheaper than ordering two weeks' supply. If we order four weeks' supply, we incur a carrying charge of £2.5 on our initial five units carried from week 1 to week 2 and a further charge of $65 \times 0.5 \times 3$ on the 45 units we shall be carrying from week 1 to week 4. This gives us a carrying cost of £97.5 on the additional 45 units made with the first batch which is still cheaper than the cost of £100 on the additional set-up that would have been required if we had decided to produce the 45 units as an extra batch.

If we now consider ordering five weeks' supply, we will require to make an additional 10 units to hold until week 5. The cost of doing this is $10 \times 0.5 \times 4 = £20$ which is again cheaper than the cost of an extra set-up.

If, however, we order six weeks' supply, we must carry an additional 55 units from week 1 to week 6 at a cost of $55 \times 0.5 \times 5 = £137.5$. This is more expensive than the cost of an extra set-up for the 55 units and so we order only five weeks' supply. At the start of week 6, we repeat the calculation on the demand from week 6 onwards.

The weekly inventory cost of this policy is £20.5 and the set-up cost averaged over the seven weeks is £28.6. This is the cheapest of all the policies.

It should be stressed that part period balancing does not give a true optimal solution, since it only looks at the demand from one order to the next, and does not evaluate all the possible sets of different timings and quantities of batches that would meet the demand over the total planning horizon. An algorithm called the **Wagner-Whitin algorithm** does perform an efficient search of all possibilities, and is guaranteed to arrive at the optimal solution in terms of minimizing the sum of inventory and set-up costs. Comparative tests have shown that, on average, policies using the Wagner-Whitin algorithm show an 8% cost reduction over policies using the part period balancing approach. Bearing in mind the extra computational complexity of the Wagner-Whitin algorithm and uncertainty in the values of the cost parameters, it is not surprising that part period balancing and period order quantity techniques are much more common.

In summary, it can be stated that the best batch size to order or produce in an environment in which MRP is employed is a quantity that will require some degree of judgement in its determination. A variety of conflicting considerations will influence the quantity chosen, the familiar tradeoff between inventory and set-up cost being only one example. In general MRP emphasizes the timing rather than the quantity of an order, and stresses flexibility rather than rigid attempts to achieve 'optimality' in an environment that in practice is so rapidly changing as to make such attempts redundant.

5.8 MRP AND SAFETY STOCK

One of the aims of MRP is to eliminate the need for safety stock that arises from the assumption that demand on all items is an independent random variable. By making the variability of the demand on dependent items predictable from the end item master production schedule, we are removing most of the uncertainty on demand that in a simple reorder point system would have called for high safety stocks.

We cannot of course eliminate uncertainty entirely. There will still be some uncertainty as to whether the master production schedule is adequate to meet the end item demand, and as a hedge against this type of uncertainty it is customary to 'overplan' at the MPS level (effectively this means developing a schedule to produce, say, 10% more of an end item than the expected requirement). When such a schedule is 'exploded' down to individual requirements for lower level items, this 10% safety factor will be reflected all the way down. We are effectively planning to have sufficient extra materials available to be able to build 10% more end items than our forecast in case the need arises. If the lead time for final assembly is short, there is of course no need to actually build the extra 10% if the extra demand does not materialize. We will, however, be in a position to build it if necessary. This can be a great advantage if long lead times exist on purchased items for example. By planning safety stock at the MPS level and transmitting the extra requirements downwards via the bill of materials, we are ensuring that resulting safety stocks of lower level items are carried in **matched sets**, i.e. for every additional unit planned at the MPS level, a matched set of lower level components required to build that item will be scheduled by the MRP explosion process. Under simple statistical reorder point systems the assumption of independence of demand of lower level items would cause the resulting levels of planned safety stock to be random. This would not reflect the way in which components were actually put together to make end items and would lead to carrying needlessly large quantities of some items and too few of other items.

Overplanning at the MPS level gives us a hedge against uncertainty in the quantity of the requirements of a particular item. The other type of uncertainty that can exist is in the timing at which individual quantities are required. The requirement date for a particular end item may be put forward or back, and a machine breakdown may delay the requirement date for all related items that are assembled with items produced on the broken machine. Uncertainty in requirement dates are handled through the safety factor implied by the planning lead time which, as we have seen, is considerably longer than the physical lead time. The setting of planning lead times to be longer than the physical lead time actually required to produce the item means of course that the lower level items required for a given production order will be available some time before they will actually be needed. This allows lead times to be 'collapsed' internally if necessary, with the order being rushed through the shop in the quickest possible time rather than in the 'average' time. Unexpected demand peaks can actually be met by bringing forward the timing of a requirement (expediting) rather than by increasing the quantity and it is the concept of the 'planning' lead time that allows this to be done.

The planning lead time means we are again carrying more stock than we strictly need. Having items ready earlier than required represents effectively a form of safety stock. Safety stocks are 'hidden' in the lead times of the items. We are carrying safety stock of an item not in the form of that item itself, but in the form of the daughter items required to produce it. This is of course not explicitly recognized in simple reorder point systems where safety stocks based on the demand variability over the lead time are carried in addition to the safety stock inherent in the lead time itself.

Is there any role at all in MRP for safety stocks computed according to the techniques described in Chapter 3? In fact we do have a section of the lead time that is irreducible which corresponds to the physical production time of the item. Any safety stock carried in the conventional sense should be based on the demand variability over the physical lead time over which no further 'collapse' is possible. Small safety stocks based on physical lead times are normally associated with the requirements records of individual items. Planned order releases are generated when the 'on hand' is reduced to below this safety stock level.

The concepts described in this section may be illustrated with reference to Fig. 5.14 which shows requirements generated by product A on a time axis. It will be seen, for example, that since the lead time for C is four weeks, 900 units of G must be ready four weeks before the 300 units of C are required. These 900 units are actually carried in stock over most of that period in an 'allocated' status (not appearing as an 'on-hand' balance). These 900 units of G represent the 'hidden' safety stock of item C. If C is required two weeks earlier than expected, the requisite amount can be produced because sufficient G is already available. Similarly, the 300 units of C and the 200 units of B represent 'hidden' safety stock of item A. If, as we move forward in time, demand on A is greater than expected and it appears that a stockout will occur, we can convert our 'hidden' safety stocks of B and C into A provided that we are inside the planning lead time of A. Stockouts can be avoided if we have knowledge of the imminent shortage at least one physical lead time before it is likely to occur, giving us a chance to convert our 'hidden safety stocks' of B and C into A. This justifies the carrying of small conventional safety stock as an extra

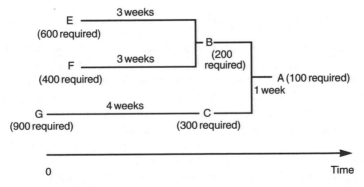

Fig. 5.14 MRP and safety stock.

hedge against additional extra demand over the physical lead time. An unexpected extra demand required at a time from now within the physical lead time of the final assembly would not give us time to convert stocks of B and C into A, even if they were available.

Overplanning at the MPS level would be based on the expected demand variability over the total stacked lead time of the product, since this gives us a safety margin in terms of purchasing slightly more raw materials than required. Purchasing is an action that must be taken when we still have a complete stacked lead time's worth of uncertainty present in our demand estimates for the end item. Overplanning of 10 units of item A would mean purchasing an extra 90 units of G, 60 units of E and 40 units of F. Whether we actually assemble the full extra 20 units of B, 30 units of C, and 10 units of A depends on our current estimate of the uncertainty in the end item demand when the time comes to physically assemble the daughter items into the parent. By the time we are ready to assemble the extra 10 units of A, we may have established that they will definitely not be needed, and we can therefore leave the additional stock in the form of E and C. Similarly it may not be necessary to assemble the full overplanned amount of E and F into G, since by the time we are ready to perform this assembly we only need to hedge against demand uncertainty on A over the remaining cumulative lead time, and this is less than the total stacked lead time on which the overplanning for raw materials purchase was based. Overplanned amounts that are not used simply become part of the projected 'on-hand' balance for future periods.

For the case of purchased items, we must not only have a hedge against demand uncertainty on the end item, but also against uncertainty in the delivery capability of the supplier. Supplier lead times are not as controllable as internal lead times and some degree of additional safety stock is advisable to cover this. Likewise allowances for rejects and scrap must be built in by automatically overplanning by a fixed amount based on elementary statistical analysis of past performance.

5.9 MRP AND PURCHASING

Use of MRP for forward planning of requirements has considerably changed the conception of the purchasing function in an organization. By performing 'rough-cut' planning, it is possible to estimate the approximate quantities of all purchased items that will be required over a planning horizon of up to one year ahead. This information can be used as the basis of **blanket ordering** from an individual supplier.

Blanket ordering is effectively a means of giving a supplier planning information about one's approximate future requirements to assist him in his own planning. The idea here is that if one places a blanket order for a year's supply, it is generally possible to negotiate an agreement whereby one does not take delivery of a year's supply in one batch; one simply orders individual deliveries to be made at very short notice, once the precise quantities and requirement dates have been fixed. The extra long-term planning information and the commitment given to the supplier enables him to firm up his own demand forecasts and cut his lead times drastically for individual deliveries, particularly if he is operating his own MRP system. There can be considerable advantages to both parties by exchanging the information and giving the commitment required to operate in this manner that many people feel outweighs the disadvantage of tying oneself to a single supplier for a particular item. It does, however, require the identification and cultivation of individual suppliers whose prices and standards of reliability and quality assurance are acceptable.

MRP used in conjunction with blanket ordering has been termed **scheduling the outside factory** since it almost regards the supplier as being subject to an extension of one's own planning and control system.

5.10 MRP AND INVENTORY CONTROL

In order to operate MRP successfully, it is essential that inventory records should be accurate, and that the 'on-hand' balance in the computer system for each item corresponds to the actual quantity of the item physically in stock. Any lack of correspondence will quickly destroy the integrity of the system and will lead to the re-emergence of 'informal' methods of planning and control. It is generally recommended that stock records for MRP purposes should be accurate to a level of 99%. It is not uncommon, however, to find manufacturing companies using informal systems whose stock records show discrepancies of 30% or more from what is physically held.

In order to achieve the desired degree of accuracy a method of stock control called **cycle counting** has been proposed for use with MRP. Rather than rely on an annual stock count taking perhaps several days for the reconciliation of actual and recorded stock, cycle counting involves selected personnel on a rotating basis spending the first half hour or so every day physically counting selected items. The counting schedule is arranged in such a way that each item is counted at least once a year. This effectively spreads out the annual stocktake over the complete year rather than concentrating it in a few days.

Items can be classified as 'high' usage (A items), 'medium' usage (B items) and 'low' usage (C items) and it can be arranged for the A items to be counted, say, three times per year, the B items twice per year and the C items once per year. Furthermore the computer can be used to indicate which items should be counted on a particular day. Since time can be saved by counting items whose current stock levels are low, the computer can search for items with the lowest stock levels and indicate that these items should be counted, consistent with the constraint on the number of times per year that a count on each item should take place.

Cycle counting is as much a quality assurance technique for checking the accuracy of inventory records as it is a physical reconciliation. Discrepancies can be closely monitored and if they become more than a certain magnitude (which can be different for A, B and C items), action can be taken to investigate the causes rather than waiting for the end of the year to discover the discrepancy. Continuous counting is thought to raise the general level of awareness in the organization of the importance of accurate inventory records.

One of the difficulties of stocktaking in informal systems is caused by staging the physical withdrawal of items from stock as soon as an order is received, regardless of whether they are ready to be processed. In MRP, release of a planned order automatically causes the corresponding gross requirements of lower level items to be subtracted from the 'on-hand' balances at the time the order is released, even though these items will not necessarily be required at once, since the order might not be due as a scheduled receipt until several weeks later. The stock effectively 'disappears' from the record since it is not 'available' for other orders. In fact a record of this stock is kept in a special 'allocated' field which for simplicity has been omitted from the examples of requirements records given earlier in this chapter. The stock should remain on the shelf until it is physically required, but it will not appear as part of the available 'on-hand' balance. Thus when physical inventory is checked against the records, the total of the 'on-hand' and the 'allocated' fields must be compared with the physical inventory. When stock is physically released from the store just before processing, the corresponding quantity will be removed from the 'allocated' field. This system allows more flexibility in the reallocation to other priority jobs of, for example, parts that cannot be assembled on schedule in their original job because of an essential missing component. At the same time, strict controls must be maintained in the storeroom to ensure that allocated stock is not withdrawn and used for other purposes without the MRP system being informed.

5.11 REGENERATIVE AND NET CHANGE SYSTEMS

In terms of the way that MRP systems implement the effect on lower level requirements of changes made in the master production schedule, we can identify two different methods. These are the **regenerative method** and the **net change method**.

The characteristics of regenerative MRP systems are that a complete MRP explosion process generating all lower level item requirements is performed only once in each time period (normally weekly). The entire process is carried out on a level-by-level basis, and each time period the explosion is performed from scratch. Each explosion represents a replanning from scratch of all net requirements, planned order releases, etc., and a fresh projection of on-hand balances is made. Such MRP systems rely on a batch processing approach (in the computer sense) and are often associated with voluminous printed output (although in modern regenerative systems, the status of requirements records can be accessed on screen from remote terminals). It should also be noted that inventory files in a regenerative system are normally updated on a transaction-by-transaction basis as would occur in any conventional stock control system. It is the requirements that are replanned only on a periodic basis. The important fact about a regenerative system is that changes in the MPS etc. that occur in between regenerations of requirements must be accumulated until the next regeneration takes place before their effects on lower level requirements can be implemented. Thus the picture of lower level requirements obtained by interrogating the system (either by remote terminal or by inspecting batch printed output) is liable to be out of date by a length of time up to the regeneration period. Such systems are sluggish in response and are difficult to operate in an environment characterized by rapid change. Most of the earlier MRP systems were of the regenerative variety since the programming task is considerably easier. In companies with a large number of products of high complexity, it would be normal to let a regenerative system run over the weekend, since a large number of hours of computer time might be required to perform the complete explosion. There has been a tendency for more recent systems to be of the net change type for faster response to increasingly rapidly changing manufacturing environments.

Net change systems, as the name implies, rely on the implementation of individual updates as they occur, on a real-time basis. Thus changes to the MPS, for example, are implemented as soon as they occur by performing the partial explosion required to carry the effects of the change through to the lower level items. The MPS can thus be viewed as one plan in continuous existence, rather than as successive versions of the same plan. The weekly 'regeneration' of requirements from scratch is avoided because all requirements are being continuously updated. One of the main problems with net change MRP systems is system 'nervousness'. Continual changes to the MPS, combined with events occurring on the shop floor which do not correspond precisely with the plan, mean that detailed shopfloor schedules will be in a continuous state of flux. A dozen or more changes involving current actions may occur in the space of half an hour. If every single change is acted upon, it may be found that many changes turn out to be self-cancelling. A job may be rescheduled, only to find that an hour later it is scheduled back to its original time. In many cases, much of the rescheduling would have been unnecessary, and could have been accommodated within system 'slack'. Some form of 'damping' of action notices generated by a net change system is therefore usually required. The most common form this takes is in the use of **action cycles** on the shop floor. Although any information that may affect the material requirements plan can be input to the system as soon as it is known, and individual requirements are updated accordingly by a partial explosion, the required actions implied by the changes are accumulated by the system and generated to the shop floor on a periodic basis (for example six hourly) thus allowing some of the mutually self-cancelling actions to be resolved within the system before the shop floor is informed.

In a similar way, planning changes need not be executed immediately, but can be accumulated until a sufficiently large number exist before a partial explosion takes place. Partial explosions can also be arranged to occur at fixed time intervals (for example daily) in which all changes during the time interval are accumulated and then executed together. The fixed time interval would represent the 'planning cycle'.

Planning and action cycles (which do not have to be of the same length) can vary and are established on a more or less arbitrary basis depending on the degree of 'volatility' of the company's operations.

5.12 TIME-BUCKETED AND BUCKETLESS SYSTEMS

The concept of the 'action cycle' introduced in the previous section leads us to make a further distinction between **time-bucketed** and **bucketless** systems. In a time-bucketed system, all planned transactions are accumulated by 'time bucket' which is usually a period of one week. Thus the time at which an individual transaction is due to take place, whether it be a stock replenishment or a planned order release, can only be specified in terms of the week number (assuming the 'bucket' is one week). No further resolution takes place into the specific day the order is due to be released or the stock to be replenished. At the start of the current week, a list of all the actions for that week is generated without any specification as to when during the week they should be performed.

In a 'bucketless' system, on the other hand, each individual planned transaction is tracked by its date (in some more advanced systems, even by the hour). Lead times can be specified in days rather than weeks. The idea of the requirements record being time-phased on a weekly basis becomes redundant since all transactions are specified by individual date rather than week. Weekly transaction summaries can of course be produced in which the effect of individual planned actions are aggregated. In this way, weekly summary planning reports similar to those produced in the time-bucketed system can be obtained, but the underlying degree of detail represented is of course much greater.

Use of the 'bucketless' approach eliminates some of the problems of time resolution associated with the time-bucketed system. For example, a gross requirement for the first day of a week and a scheduled receipt due on the last day of the week would not appear as an expediting problem in a time-bucketed system, since as far as the system was concerned both events would happen at the same time. In the 'bucketless' system, the problem would be recognized and an action notice raised. An important beneficial effect of the 'bucketless' approach is that it does not freeze the planning horizon to a fixed number of buckets as must happen in the time-bucketed system. In the latter approach, if the planning horizon extends over, say, 12 weeks then each requirements record will normally extend out over only 12 weeks, and a gross requirement for, say, week 15 will have no way of being entered into the record. In a bucketless system, however, we are not tied down to a fixed format, finite length planning horizon, and such a requirement could simply be entered as a requirement for week 15.

Regardless of whether a 'time-bucketed' or a 'bucketless' system is used in MRP, if we wish to operate a true 'closed loop' system, for the purposes of shopfloor control, it is essential to maintain individual job priorities on a daily basis so that the correct jobs can be loaded on each machine. As a result, more modern time-bucketed systems normally have a **daily dispatch list** in which the current due dates of each job waiting to be processed are updated. In a system which is otherwise time-bucketed, the due dates (as opposed to due weeks) of each scheduled receipt are the only items of information that are not aggregated by week. In both bucketed and bucketless systems, the daily dispatch list is a list produced daily by the system and transmitted to each work centre giving the current priority ordering of each job queuing to be processed at that work centre.

5.13 MRP IN PRACTICE

MRP (Material Requirements Planning) was subsequently expanded from material and capacity requirements planning to include computerization of all the planning activities of a manufacturing organization. These included demand forecasting, aggregate production planning and the development of the master production schedule itself (all of which we examined earlier in this chapter) and principles similar to the MRP explosion and CRP procedures are used to compute the implications of a given aggregate production plan and/or master production schedule on human resources, financial resources, purchasing and distribution requirements. The system in its extended form was termed Manufacturing Resources Planning, or MRP 2. The schematic structure of a typical MRP 2 system is shown in Fig. 5.15.

When MRP 2 became commercially available it was seen as a break-

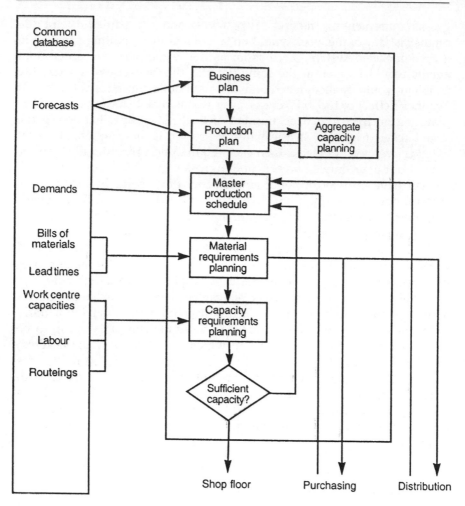

Fig. 5.15 MRP 2 schema.

through for the effective management of manufacturing. However, over time various surveys began to show several problems with MRP 2 system implementations. The results of such surveys were conventionally expressed in terms of the proportion of users falling in four distinct classes, from class A which represents excellence to class D in which the only people who use the system are those in the MIS (management information systems) department.

The surveys showed typically the following results.

- Many users did not consider themselves to be successfully operating the system. In other words, the system was installed but not necessarily being used. Less than 10% of users surveyed considered themselves class A users while over 60% considered themselves class C and class D users and to be deriving little benefit from the system.

- A large proportion (nearly 40% in a 1991 survey) had not computerized master production scheduling.
- Capacity requirements planning has a relatively low utilization with less than half those surveyed having computerized systems that function.
- Approximately half those surveyed had not computerized the shopfloor control function.

Despite these findings the same MRP 2 users reported significant improvements resulting from the use of the system including:

- average inventory turns improved from 3.2 to 4.3;
- average delivery lead times fell from 71.4 days to 58.9 days;
- average delivery performance rose from 61.4% to 76.6%;
- the average number of expediters fell from 10.1 to 6.5;

From the above it would appear that MRP has brought benefits to users and this would explain why even C and D class users would prefer to have the system than not have it. Having said this, however, it is also clear that there are many poorly implemented MRP systems. It is now generally agreed that the failure of MRP implementations may be traced to a number of basic issues, the most common being:

- lack of top management commitment;
- lack of MRP education for the users of the system;
- inaccurate data, particularly bill of materials and inventory data.

In practical terms there are a number of important additional related problems in the structure and logic of MRP 2. These include the following.

- There are few guidelines as to how long lead times need to be in order to 'level' the uneven loading of resources within the slack provided by the queue of orders waiting to be processed. In these circumstances people tend to err on the safe side leading to long lead times and high stock levels.
- In the same way that lead times are assumed to be a fixed input to MRP both batch sizes and routeings are also assumed to be fixed when in fact they are variable, and can be changed to overcome local production overload problems.
- The CRP module of MRP 2 tends to rely on solving local overload problems identified during the capacity requirements planning phase by the use of overtime or by making adjustments to the MPS. In reality, flexible lead times, flexible batch size policies and flexible routeings can be used to solve these problems without either using overtime or

changing the master production schedule. However, CRP itself gives little guidance as to how this can be done.

5.14 CONCLUSION

We have looked at one approach (MRP 2) to translating a master production schedule into a detailed action plan for what needs to happen on the shop floor, and how these actions can be monitored and controlled. We have also looked at some of the problems associated with this approach, particularly in the context of shopfloor implementation. In the next chapter, we shall move on to examine other approaches to implementing a master production schedule that do not suffer so much from these limitations, and in what types of company these approaches are most applicable.

FURTHER READING

Berry, W. (1972) Lot sizing techniques for requirements planning systems. *Production and Inventory Management*, Vol. 13, No. 2.

Browne, J., Harhen, J. and Shivnan, J. (1988) *Production Management Systems – A CIM Perspective*. Addison-Wesley, Workingham.

Latham, D. (1981) Are your among MRP's walking wounded? *Production and Inventory Management*. Vol. 22, No. 3. pp. 33–41.

Melnyk, S.A., Carter, P.L., Dilts, D.M. and Lyth, D.M. (1985) *Shop Floor Control*. Dow Jones-Irwin, Homewood, Illinois.

Orlicky, J. (1974) *Material Requirements Planning*. McGraw-Hill, New York.

Sartori, L.G. (1988) *Manufacturing Information Systems*. Addison-Wesley, Wokingham.

Wight, O. (1984) *Manufacturing Resource Planning MRP 2*. O. Wight Publications, Williston VT.

OPT and synchronous manufacturing

6

6.1 OVERVIEW

In this chapter, we continue our examination of the methods available for planning and controlling production that we started in Chapter 4 with an examination of a system for production management which in some respects can be regarded as an alternative to the MRP system, and which addresses itself to attempting to overcome some of the limitations of MRP, particularly in relation to the assumption of fixed lead times and effectively infinite production capacity. This approach is grounded in a proprietary technology developed by an Israeli physicist Eli Goldratt, originally termed **O**ptimized **P**roduction **T**echnology or OPT. Although the core of OPT is a secret computer algorithm used for finite scheduling of the bottleneck resource, the underlying principles and assumptions on which the algorithm is based are universally valid and can be beneficially applied in most manufacturing environments without the necessity of implementing the algorithm itself. The philosophy of OPT has been developed into a more general system of manufacturing management that has been variously termed the **theory of constraints** or **synchronous manufacturing**, and which does not rely on the proprietary OPT scheduling algorithm for its implementation.

The original OPT philosophy consisted of nine basic principles centred around the general implications for production management and production scheduling of the existence of a clearly defined bottleneck resource.

The principles and their consequent system of manufacturing mainly serve to emphasize the fact that priority should be given to planning and scheduling the flow of work through the bottleneck resources (which will act as the major constraints on what is achievable by the factory as a whole) and that these should therefore be managed much more carefully than non-bottlenecks. The detail of how this is actually achieved can vary from situation to situation, and the operationalization of the nine principles designed by Goldratt in the form of his proprietary OPT system is only one way in which this can be achieved. This chapter therefore concentrates on an elaboration of the nine principles and their implications, with an example of a simplified sytem of scheduling closely following the OPT system. This is followed by a brief description of the more general management approach termed synchronous manufacturing which uses a concept called the **drum–buffer–rope** analogy to identify and manage the critical constraining resources in a plant in such a way as to have the maximum impact on profitability.

6.2 CHAPTER STRUCTURE

This chapter is divided into the following sections:

- the objectives of OPT – maximizing global manufacturing performance;
- bottlenecks, non-bottlenecks and capacity constraint resources;
- the nine OPT principles;
- development of a typical OPT schedule;
- the drum–buffer–rope analogy.

The chapter commences with an overview of the objectives driving the formulation of the nine OPT principles, through an introduction to the global manufacturing performance measures that should be optimized by any manufacturing company in order to maximize 'bottom-line' business performance, and the implications these measures have on how this function should be managed. This is followed by a brief description of the distinction the philosophy makes between bottleneck, non-bottleneck and capacity-constraining resources and their significance. The nine basic OPT principles are then introduced, with each principle being elaborated in terms of its specific implications for production management and what should happen on the shop floor in order to result in optimized behaviour of the global manufacturing performance measures. A typical plant schedule that might be developed according to the principles used by the original OPT production management software is then presented. Finally, the more general approach of 'synchronous manufacturing' using the 'drum–buffer–rope' analogy is described, and an overall assessment of the approach is made in terms of its relationship with MRP.

6.3 THE OBJECTIVES OF OPT – MAXIMIZING GLOBAL MANUFACTURING PERFORMANCE

The OPT philosophy was derived from a view of the manufacturing function and the measures characterizing its performance which were enunciated by Goldratt in order to try and direct attention away from the more traditional accounting-based view of the company's activities. These, Goldratt claimed, were inhibiting the competitiveness of Western manufacturing industry.

The overall objective of a manufacturing company is to make money, both in the present and in the future. According to the terminology developed by Goldratt (which uses familiar terms but in a very specific way), this occurs by the investment of money in **inventory** (raw materials), which are then converted into **throughput** (income from sold products) by incurring various **operating expenses** which add value to the raw materials. It should be noted here that the definition of 'inventory' deliberately excludes any component of added value that may be associated with materials that have been processed, and that throughput is associated only with goods actually sold, not goods produced. Maximization of the 'bottom-line' business performance measures of net profit, return on investment and cash flow can be achieved by maximizing throughput (goods sold) at the same time as simultaneously minimizing inventory and operating expenses. Thus all manufacturing activities should be directed towards these latter objectives. Any activity that has a deleterious effect on any of these performance measures should be re-evaluated.

Although this may seem to be intuitively rather obvious, Goldratt pointed out that many traditional manufacturing objectives, particularly those related to local minimization of the costs of running individual work centres by keeping them operating (i.e. maximizing utilization) were in fact not contributing to maximizing throughput but were only increasing inventory if the goods produced could not be sold. Thus the sum of a series of decisions optimal at the local level (e.g. individual machine schedules developed in order to maximize their utilization) does not necessarily lead to a global optimum for the entire plant. This applies particularly to plants whose total output is limited by a bottleneck resource. In this situation, to attempt to fully utilize the non-bottleneck resources without coordinating them with the rate of production of the bottleneck will merely result in a surplus of items accumulating in front of the bottleneck with an increase in inventory but no increase in throughput. The latter is determined by the rate of production of the bottleneck resource.

The objectives of manufacturing should therefore be:

- to maximize throughput by scheduling the bottleneck resource in such a way as to maximize its utilization;
- to reduce inventory by synchronizing production at the non-bottleneck resources to support production at the bottleneck;
- to reduce operating expenses by utilizing idle time at non-bottleneck resources for such things as preventative maintenance and other improvement programmes, or by reducing non-bottleneck capacity.

In general a tradeoff exists between inventory and operating expenses for any given throughput. Thus it is always possible to decrease inventory by increasing operating expenses, and conversely, operating expenses can generally be decreased by increasing inventory. The task of a manufacturing company is to try and find an operating mode which gives the best possible tradeoff.

6.4 BOTTLENECKS, NON-BOTTLENECKS AND CAPACITY CONSTRAINT RESOURCES

In the original OPT formulation, bottleneck and non-bottleneck resources are defined as follows:

- **Bottleneck resource**: any resource whose capacity is equal to or less than the demand placed upon it.
- **Non-bottleneck resource**: any resource whose capacity is greater than the demand placed on it.

As seen from the brief analysis of the properties of bottlenecks given in Chapter 3, any idle or wasted time at the bottleneck will lead to unavoidable loss of throughput. Furthermore, any action resulting in additional productive time on a bottleneck will allow the plant to process additional throughput. On the other hand, non-bottleneck resources will always have excess capacity. This idle time can, however, be used in a productive way which represents an important key to the overall OPT approach. By tolerating more set-ups (which can usually be accommodated within the idle time) smaller batch sizes can be tolerated at non-bottleneck resources which can provide greater flexibility for coordinating these resources with the activities of the bottleneck, thus leading to inventory reductions. The mechanics of how this can occur will be seen in section 6.6 in which a typical OPT schedule is developed.

Bottlenecks act as potential **constraints** on the performance of the system, and need not necessarily be production machines. They might also take the form of labour, material availability, materials handling systems, information processing or even management policies. The objective of the OPT approach is to focus on the constraining resources and effectively manage both them and the interactions they have with non-constraining resources.

The definition of a bottleneck as given above does not necessarily imply that all bottleneck resources will at all times be equally important in controlling throughput. Consider the following example in which products must be processed sequentially through four work centres having the processing capacities shown in Fig. 6.1.

If the market demand is for 60 units per hour, in this case work centres B and D would both be defined as bottlenecks as their capacity is less than

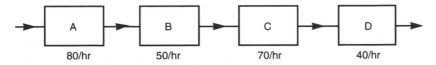

Fig. 6.1 Work centre processing capacities.

the demand. However, in the situation in which this production line is run, i.e. to service that proportion of the demand of which it is capable, the actual product flow is controlled by the most severe bottleneck, which in this case is work centre D. Although work centre B is technically speaking a bottleneck, it is not an active constraint on the process since with the major bottleneck, work centre D, operating at full capacity, work centre B (which can only work at the bottleneck rate of 40 per hour) is only operating at four-fifths capacity, and hence minor disruptions occurring at this work centre will not affect the throughput. Hence although work centre B is a 'bottleneck' according to our original definition, it does not represent a capacity constraint in the above situation. This leads to the notion of a 'capacity constraint resource' which in OPT has the following definition.

- **Capacity constraint resource**: any resource which, if not properly scheduled and managed, is likely to cause the actual flow of product through the plant to deviate from the planned flow.

Thus in situations where the production capacity of the plant is well below market demand, it is possible to have bottlenecks which are not in fact capacity constraint resources. Conversely it is also possible to have non-bottlenecks whose capacity is less (but not much less) than market demand, but which because of possible variations in product mix, could disrupt product flow if not scheduled carefully. It is in fact the capacity constraint resources rather than the bottlenecks which are the key resources to plan and schedule very carefully, and these are sometimes rather difficult to determine since the relationship between the two is dependent on product volumes and mixes and the dynamics of the interaction between resources and cannot necessarily be determined from a static loading analysis. This has given rise to a phenomenon known as the **wandering bottleneck**. Experiences in implementing OPT have shown that it is easier to detect capacity constraint resources by looking for certain well defined 'symptoms' in the behaviour of the actual plant. These 'symptoms' for the case of V, A and T plants were briefly described in section 3.10 of Chapter 3.

From here on, the term 'bottleneck' will be retained for brevity, but it will be used to denote the capacity constraint resource(s) of a plant rather than a bottleneck as in the original definition.

The underlying philosophy has become embodied in the so called **nine principles of OPT** which have subsequently given rise to the term 'synchronous manufacturing' to describe their application (although for brevity we shall continue to use the term OPT rather than synchronous manufacturing in this chapter).

The OPT Scheduling System is a proprietary computer scheduling algorithm also developed by Eli Goldratt. Although the algorithm is supposedly secret and owned by Creative Output Inc., the importance of OPT is generally associated with the nine principles and their significance, and the general OPT framework within which planning and scheduling takes place, rather than with the algorithm itself. Over 100 major companies worldwide have installed OPT, including Kodak, ITT, General Electric, Ford and General Motors, and this has resulted in it becoming a widely discussed approach which is now being considered as being of equal significance to manufacturing management as MRP or JIT.

6.5 THE NINE OPT PRINCIPLES

The nine principles embodying the OPT philosophy are as follows.

1. Balance flow not capacity.
2. An hour lost at a bottleneck resource is an hour lost for the entire system.
3. Time saved at a non-bottleneck resource does nothing for the total system.
4. Bottlenecks determine both total system throughput and inventory.
5. Schedules should be determined after examining all constraints/ factors simultaneously.
6. Resource utilization and resource activation are not synonymous.
7. The level of utilization of a non-bottleneck is not determined by its own potential but by some other constraint in the system.
8. The process batch should be variable not fixed.
9. The transfer batch should not necessarily be equal to the process batch.

These principles will now be examined individually in somewhat more detail.

PRINCIPLE 1: BALANCE FLOW NOT CAPACITY

In Chapter 3, section 3.11 on the effect of process variability on materials flow, it was shown that, although several different work centres which process parts in sequence may have equal capacity, the effect of process variability means that production time is lost due to irregular arrivals at work centres causing possible work starvation. This implies in turn that the maximum flow achievable through the system will be less than the theoretical capacity of the system in the presence of uniform (i.e. non-variable) flow. The average flow through each work centre will actually be determined by the combined variability of its processing time and its input. Because of this, balanced flow will generally require different capacities at different work centres depending on their positioning in the process.

This tends to run counter to the traditional approach of attempting to balance the capacity of the different work centres on a production line. As can be seen from the arguments above, balancing capacity in a static sense in the presence of process variability will not lead to synchronized flow. To do the latter, it is necessary to take a dynamic view.

PRINCIPLE 2: AN HOUR LOST AT A BOTTLENECK IS AN HOUR LOST FOR THE ENTIRE SYSTEM

This should be self-evident from the discussion on bottlenecks. Since the bottleneck determines the total flow, any downtime on the bottleneck will result in loss of total system output. This in turn implies that every effort should be made to keep the bottleneck resource running, and to avoid disruptions such as breakdowns or work starvation. Also, the minimization of set-ups on a bottleneck will increase throughput.

PRINCIPLE 3: TIME SAVED AT A NON-BOTTLENECK RESOURCE DOES NOTHING FOR THE TOTAL SYSTEM

This is the corollary of principle 2. Provided the downtime of the non-bottleneck is not sufficiently long that it becomes the bottleneck itself, the non-bottleneck must by definition spend a proportion of its time idle, hence there is little point in trying to save time on a non-bottleneck. This also means that non-bottlenecks can be set up more frequently than bottle-necks leading to more flexibility in batch sizing and scheduling policies.

PRINCIPLE 4: BOTTLENECKS DETERMINE BOTH TOTAL SYSTEM OUTPUT AND INVENTORY

Bottlenecks quite clearly determine total system output. However, they also determine inventory. Firstly, bottlenecks will often be scheduled with larger batch sizes than other resources to maximize their utilization. This will have an influence on inventory levels carried. Secondly, some safety stock may often be inserted in front of the bottleneck to keep it from being starved of work – this again will influence overall inventory levels.

PRINCIPLE 5: SCHEDULES SHOULD BE DETERMINED AFTER
EXAMINING ALL CONSTRAINTS/FACTORS SIMULTANEOUSLY

In the MRP approach, planning lead times and batch sizes are fixed, and
then a capacity requirements plan is computed and tested for feasibility. If
the plan is not feasible, the master production schedule must be changed
or the process must be repeated for different lead times and/or batch
sizes, i.e. the planning process is sequential. A better way, on the other
hand, would be to regard lead times and batch sizes as variable rather
than fixed, and by considering all constraints simultaneously, compute
lead times and batch sizes that give a feasible plan first time round.

PRINCIPLE 6: RESOURCE UTILIZATION AND RESOURCE ACTIVATION
ARE NOT SYNONYMOUS

A non-bottleneck might be regarded as 'activated' when its output is
actually required by a downstream resource (e.g. a bottleneck). There is a
distinction here between 'activation' (producing work actually needed)
and 'utilization' in which the resource is merely producing output
whether it is actually required or not. In traditional manufacturing, there
is a tendency to try and maximize utilization of all resources as this
minimizes the unit cost of what is produced. However, if the resource
has not been activated by a specific downstream requirement, surplus
inventory will result.

PRINCIPLE 7: THE LEVEL OF UTILIZATION OF A NON-BOTTLENECK
IS NOT DETERMINED BY ITS OWN POTENTIAL BUT BY SOME OTHER
CONSTRAINT IN THE SYSTEM

Clearly the non-bottleneck resources should only be utilized to the extent
required to keep the bottleneck busy; the capacity of the bottleneck is thus
the constraint that should determine the level of utilization of the
non-bottleneck.

PRINCIPLE 8: THE PROCESS BATCH SHOULD BE VARIABLE
NOT FIXED

In MRP the batch size of a particular order is assumed to stay fixed as it
travels through different processes. However, in reality, if some of these
processes are performed on the bottleneck machine and others on non-
bottlenecks, it might be important to produce in larger batches on the
bottleneck to make maximum use of its productive capacity. Non-bottleneck resources can, however, tolerate smaller batch sizes since lost productive time due to set-ups will not be so important. The batch size should

thus depend on the processing resource. Larger batch sizes can be used on the bottlenecks, and these are split into smaller batches on non-bottlenecks for greater scheduling flexibility.

PRINCIPLE 9: THE TRANSFER BATCH SHOULD NOT NECESSARILY BE EQUAL TO THE PROCESS BATCH

Waiting for a complete process batch to be finished before transferring any units to the next work centre can result in unnecessarily long lead times, particularly if the batch is large. Lead times could be shortened by transferring units from one process to the next as they are produced. The 'transfer batch' is then the number of units that are transferred at a time.

6.6 DEVELOPMENT OF A TYPICAL OPT SCHEDULE

The basic data required to run the OPT system is similar to that of the MRP 2. For example OPT uses a **product network** which is similar to a combination of the bill of materials (BOM) and routeing files in MRP 2. OPT also requires very detailed descriptions of each production resource (machine, worker or both combined) and allows a large number of variables to be specified including desired stock levels, minimum batch quantities, alternate routeings, due dates and so on.

As with MRP, the OPT approach starts from a master production schedule of end items. However, in contrast to MRP, no assumptions are made about production lead times in order to set up a time-phased set of material requirements and planned production orders prior to checking these against production capacity. In the OPT approach, the establishment of lead times and the planning of the timings of production orders are considered simultaneously rather than sequentially. This is done by using the proprietary OPT scheduling system to develop a very tight feasible schedule for the bottleneck resource, and using the time that a particular order can be scheduled on the bottleneck to determine the time windows within which it should be processed on the resources upstream and downstream of the bottleneck. Thus lead times are outputs from the planning process rather than being inputs to it.

In a highly simplified version, the OPT approach consists of the following steps. Steps 3 and 4 may be studied in relation to Fig. 6.2 which shows a typical OPT schedule for a series of orders requiring sequential processing on three work centres, the middle one of which is the bottleneck. The schedule is developed in the form of a simple Gantt chart.

1. Using the OPT product network (equivalent to a combination of the bill of materials and routeing files in MRP), perform a requirements explosion and resource loading in a similar way to MRP 2 but without

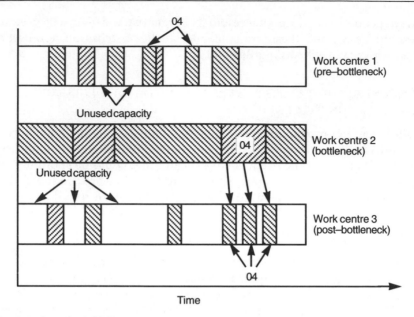

Fig. 6.2 A typical OPT schedule.

any time phasing of requirements, in order to determine the bottleneck (most heavily loaded) resource.

2. Develop a detailed finite (i.e. feasible) schedule for the bottleneck resource in which all orders processed on that resource are scheduled at precise times (which are expected to be adhered to). Large batch sizes and combination of batches with similar set-ups are used in order to minimize the downtime of the bottleneck resource (an hour lost on the bottleneck is an hour lost for the entire system!). The diagram shows a bar chart of the schedule, showing the middle operation as the bottleneck. Orders are scheduled on the bottleneck in priority sequence, and the scheduled start time of an order on the bottleneck acts as an anchor point for when it should be processed on the other work centres.

3. Orders are back-scheduled on pre-bottleneck resources from the expected time that they will be processed on the bottleneck resource (i.e. as late as possible consistent with their scheduled processing time on the bottleneck so as to minimize the time the order will spend as work in progress between the pre-bottleneck and the bottleneck). This back-scheduling is rather similar to MRP with a lead time being allowed to determine when raw materials should be available, although this lead time is considerably shorter than the lead times common in MRP. Since pre-bottleneck resources are, by definition, not utilized to full capacity, batches can be split for greater flexibility of

scheduling. Thus in Fig. 6.2 order 04 is processed in one batch on the bottleneck so as not to lose valuable bottleneck production capacity in extra set-ups, but has been split into two batches on the pre-bottleneck resource for greater scheduling flexibility and to take advantage of gaps in the existing schedule on the pre-bottleneck resource. The additional set-ups on the pre-bottleneck resource can be accommodated (an hour gained on a non-bottleneck resource is a mirage). In order to ensure that the bottleneck resource is never starved of work (due, for example, to a breakdown of a pre-bottleneck resource that feeds it) orders are scheduled to be ready for processing on the bottleneck slightly before their scheduled time (i.e. a **safety time** is left resulting in the accumulation of a small buffer in front of the bottleneck resource).

4. Orders are scheduled on post-bottleneck resources as early as possible after having been processed on the bottleneck. Since the bottleneck operation (which constrains the earliest time at which the order as a whole can be shipped) has already been performed, the order should obviously pass through the post-bottleneck resources as soon as possible as any further queuing time from here on will unnecessarily delay shipment. In Fig. 6.2, order 04 starts processing on the post-bottleneck resource before it has finished on the pre-bottleneck resource, by using transfer batches to move completed units to the post-bottleneck resource as soon as a sufficient quantity has accumulated. Since the processing time on the post-bottleneck resource is shorter than that on the bottleneck, the order will again be processed as a split batch on the post-bottleneck, with time gaps between the individual transfer batches.

The basis of the above philosophy is that all non-bottleneck resources will by definition have excess capacity, and so there will be plenty of slack time available for them to be scheduled without difficulty. The critical resource as far as scheduling is concerned is the bottleneck.

Note that the total lead time of an order (the difference between the scheduled start time of the first pre-bottleneck operation and the finish time of the last post-bottleneck operation) and the lead times of each individual operation are determined by the planning process, whereas in MRP these times are inputs to the planning process. Lead times in OPT can thus vary according to plant loading, and can thus be considerably shorter than in MRP.

This schedule will differ from an MRP schedule in the following ways:

1. In the MRP approach orders will be back-scheduled sequentially on each resource starting from the final operation which is timed to correspond with the date the order is due to be delivered, rather than around the expected processing time on the bottleneck.

2. In MRP, a queue time is allowed between each work centre which is usually several times the physical processing time.
3. In MRP, the whole batch is assumed to be transferred at one time from one work centre to the next, rather than using transfer batches.

The above will result in the MRP schedule being much more extended than the OPT schedule.

6.7 THE DRUM–BUFFER–ROPE STRATEGY

The OPT philosophy has since been generalized into a structured approach to manufacturing management by which most of the benefits of OPT can be achieved without the necessity of using the proprietary scheduling software. This approach uses what has been termed the **drum–buffer–rope strategy**.

The objective of the drum–buffer–rope (DBR) strategy is to achieve two things:

1. to enable the plant to execute a planned product flow over a given period of time;
2. to handle deviations from the planned product flow.

The DBR strategy commences with the development of a feasible master production schedule that does not overload the resource processing capabilities of the plant. This MPS is termed the **drum** and it contains detailed schedules for the bottleneck resources since these will determine the throughput achievable.

In order to hedge against disruptions in the flow of products, time **buffers** are used to schedule the arrival of materials at critical points in the flow slightly earlier than that required by the schedule.

To ensure the required synchronization of production at non-bottlenecks, a concept referred to as the **rope** is used to 'tie' production at these resources to production at the bottleneck by generating the release of just the right materials at the right time.

The DBR strategy is thus as follows:

1. **Drum**. Develop the MPS so it is consistent with the constraints of the system.
2. **Buffer**. Protect the throughput of the system from fluctuations by means of time buffers at a relatively few critical points in the system.
3. **Rope**. Tie the production at each resource to the drum beat.

6.7.1 THE DRUM BEAT

The master production schedule represents the 'drum beat' for the plant. After determining an aggregate level of production that is consistent with market demand and is within the capacity of the plant (or the bottleneck(s)) of the plant, the critical activities in setting the drum beat are the determination of the following parameters for the bottleneck resources:

• the process sequence;
• the process batch size;
• the transfer batch size.

Decisions on these planning parameters are interrelated, particularly those on process sequence and process batch size, since an increase in the latter will involve combining current with future orders for a given product, thus having an influence on process sequence.

The approach recommended by the DBR strategy for determination of good general policies concerning these parameters is by the diagnosis of existing policies by means of so-called **schedule performance curves**, with subsequent policy adjustment in line with the information obtained from an analysis of these curves. A schedule performance curve is a plot over time of the scheduled completion date of orders against their due date. In a perfectly synchronized plant, this plot would be a straight line with a gradient equal to 1 as shown in Fig. 6.3(a). However, because of the application of batch sizing policies which combine different orders with the same or similar set-ups, the plot will actually differ from the ideal case shown. Deviations which appear to be random in nature tend to indicate a lack of any coherent policy in relation to the above planning parameters. However, in plants which do have policies of combining orders with common set-ups, such curves tend to show fluctuations as shown in Fig. 6.3(b), in which the necessity of processing orders out of due date sequence to take advantage of set-up characteristics will result in some orders being early and some being late. In cases where such regular patterns exists, some basic inferences about current policies can be made from the nature of these patterns. The patterns are characterized by:

• the location of the curve;
• the oscillations of the curve;
• the overall slope of the curve.

The location of the curve (in terms of its intercept on the y-axis) is influenced by the size of product transfer batches. Reduction of transfer batch size will result in earlier completion of orders which will tend to move the schedule performance curve down and to the right. Conversely, larger transfer batch sizes will result in later completion of orders which will move the curve up and to the left. Thus for the situation shown in Fig. 6.3(c) performance could be improved by reducing the transfer batch size thus moving the curve more in the direction of the ideal situation.

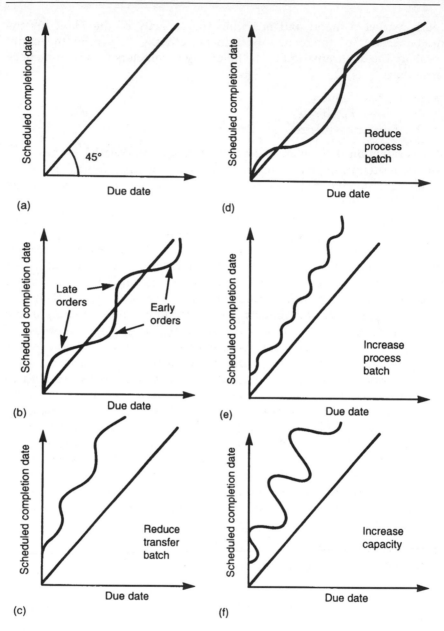

Fig. 6.3 Schedule performance curves.

Both the period of oscillation of the curve and its gradient are influenced by the process batch size. Small process batches will result in increased set-ups and will allow orders to be processed more in line with due dates. This reduces the tendency for some orders to be early at the expense of others being late, and hence reduces the period and amplitude of oscillation of the curve. At the same time, the increased set-ups will result in progressive loss of throughput, resulting in a progressive deterioration of performance with time as orders become progressively later, resulting in a curve which is steeper than the ideal curve. Conversely, large process batches will result in improved throughput shown by a curve of gradient less than 1, but at the expense of bigger deviations from the due dates as a result of the larger number of orders that must be processed out of due date sequence, resulting in larger oscillations of the curve. Thus Fig. 6.3(d) shows a situation in which the process batch is too large. Most orders here are being completed early, and only a few are late, with large oscillations in the curve. This tendency is also increasing with time indicating that the large batch sizes are resulting in excess capacity at the resource. The recommendation in this case would be to reduce the process batch size. On the other hand in Fig. 6.3(e) small batch sizes are causing small but frequent oscillations with scheduled completion of orders consistently lagging behind due dates, and with the situation tending to become worse with time due to the reduction in capacity caused by the many set-ups. The recommendation in this case would be to increase the process batch size which will bring the curve more in line with the ideal curve but will increase the size of the oscillations. The final example, shown in Fig. 6.3(f), shows a situation where the curve lies above and to the left of the ideal curve, with large oscillations and progressive worsening of delivery performance. In this case, large process batches are already being used as indicated by the large oscillations. This indicates that the scheduled throughput of the plant is insufficient to meet the demand and must either be reduced or the capacity of the bottleneck increased.

These schedule performance curves are only intended to give a fairly rough-cut and general indication of the direction in which to adjust policy parameters to achieve throughput and inventory improvements, and rely on close monitoring of performance using the existing policies, with a series of ongoing iterative adjustments to the latter. They essentially provide a substitute method for the computer-generated OPT bottleneck schedule described in the previous section, and if intelligently used allow many of the benefits of the former to be achieved in a cruder but potentially very effective manner.

6.7.2 PLACEMENT OF TIME BUFFERS

The technique for the placement of time buffers in the DBR strategy utilizes the fact that, although time buffers placed equally in front of each resource in a sequential process will protect the overall system to some extent against individual disruptions, a greater degree of protection can be obtained by replacing the individual buffers with one large buffer positioned after the final process, and of size equal to the sum of the individual buffers. This can be seen by considering the flow of a product through four sequential processes as shown in Fig. 6.4.

In Fig. 6.4(a) a single time buffer of six hours has been placed in front of each of the four resources A, B, C and D. If each individual process takes 10 hours, the total lead time for the product will be 64 hours (process time plus time buffer). Some protection is provided for each process, so that, for example, if the process on work centre A is 6 hours late, work centre B is not affected. Furthermore, if there is an 18-hour delay in processing an order on work centre A, final shipment of the order will not necessarily be late since this time can be made up in the subsequent buffers. Thus the protection provided to the overall system is greater than that provided to any individual work centre. However, with the buffers arranged as they are, the later in the processing sequence the disruption occurs the less the degree of protection. If a disruption of 18 hours occurs at work centre C, the order will be 6 hours late, since only 12 hours worth of buffer remain before shipment.

The degree of protection can be increased by changing the buffering to the situation shown in Fig. 6.4(b) in which the individual 6-hour buffers are replaced by a 24-hour buffer positioned just before shipment. An 18-hour disruption can now occur at any stage of the process prior to shipment without causing the order to be late. In this particular case, however, there is no protection to any of the individual work centres.

If, however, one of the four work centres (say C) is a clearly defined bottleneck, then it becomes of the utmost importance to protect the bottle-

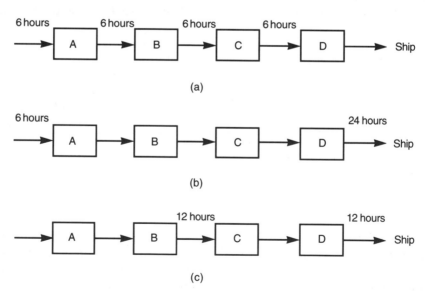

Fig. 6.4 Locating time buffers.

neck from disruption, since this will result in reduced throughput. Thus in this case, we might split the 24-hour buffer into two 12-hour buffers, one before work centre C and one before shipping, as shown in Fig. 6.4(c).

The synchronous manufacturing philosophy recommends that the size of these time buffers be determined by trial and error, and suggests commencing with a total time buffer of approximately one half of the plant's current total manufacturing lead time divided between shipping and the bottleneck resource(s).

6.7.3 THE ROPE

The 'rope' represents a means of coordinating the production on non-bottleneck resources to that of the bottleneck. The philosophy of synchronous manufacturing suggests that this should not depend on the detailed management of all resources but only on a critical few, which clearly would include the bottlenecks.

The effective application of the rope relies on the fact that orders arriving at resources at which no time buffers exist (generally the non-bottleneck resources) will either be on schedule or behind schedule (a direct result of the lack of time buffering). In either of these cases orders should be processed as soon as possible, and because of the lack of time buffer there should be few or no jobs already waiting in a queue. This in turn means that the only job that can actually be processed is the currently arriving job, or at worst jobs can be selected for processing from any queue that might exist simply in order of their due date priority. By ensuring that only the immediately required jobs are available to be processed on the non-bottlenecks, the possibility of over-utilization of non-bottlenecks (i.e. activating them when their output is not required) is greatly reduced, and the scheduling of non-bottlenecks is reduced to simply processing the arriving job, or at most, selecting from a prioritized list.

The fact that the availability of material is being used as the key to controlling product flow means that it becomes critical to regard the points at which material is released into the system (i.e. the gateway operations into the plant) as critical control points for which detailed schedules must be developed. If the release of material to the initial work centres is carefully planned and scheduled, then the remaining work centres should mostly just process the work that becomes available to them as it becomes available.

In a simple linear process, material release points and bottlenecks will be the only points in the process at which a detailed schedule should be developed. However, in cases where items must be assembled from different components, or in implosive industries (V plants) such as oil refineries or the paper industry, where a single material is processed into many products, the situation becomes more complex. The synchronous manufacturing philosophy solves this by means of so-called **scheduled release points** which are points where the activation of a work centre may occur without utilization. This possibility is considered to exist in four places:

- at material release points;
- at bottlenecks;
- at divergence points;
- at convergence points.

The necessity of providing detailed schedules at material release points and bottlenecks has already been discussed.

Divergence points are resources which produce several different items from a single input material. Although the choice of what job to process can be controlled by material availability, it is still necessary to know how much of each item to produce, and this requires the development of a detailed schedule. Also, at convergence points (assembly operations) the availability of a single part is not sufficient to start the process, since all the required parts must be available. Thus detailed schedules are also needed at these points so that how many parts required at what times are known.

The detailed development of a schedule at each release point can then be performed. For the bottleneck resources, process batch sizes and sequences will have already been determined as part of the 'drum beat' (the MPS). The decisions required here are the size of the transfer batch and the required release times of each planned order to the bottleneck. In general smaller transfer batches will improve throughput, although materials handing considerations will impose a lower realistic limit. The schedule performance curves can also provide some guidance in this regard. Scheduling the release times of orders to the bottleneck will depend on the planned manufacturing lead time of the bottleneck. This in turn reflects the size of the planned time buffer to be placed in front of the bottleneck. For the other points at which detailed schedules must be developed, the process batch size must also be determined. However, since there is generally little advantage to be gained in combining batches of similar items, batch sizes can remain equal to the order sizes, unless this results in such a loss of capacity that a new bottleneck appears.

The synchronous manufacturing philosophy provides little further in the way of detailed guidance in constructing schedules on the grounds that individual methods will depend on the specific manufacturing situation. In particular methods will depend on whether the plant is a V, A or T plant. Further details may, however, be found in Umble and Srikanth (1990).

6.7.4 MARKET AND PRODUCTION CONSTRAINED FIRMS

In the synchronous manufacturing philosophy, a distinction is made between market constrained firms and production constrained firms. A market constrained firm is a firm whose total saleable production is limited by the size of the market, which is less than the firm's production capacity. In this type of firm, it is pointless to try to use synchronous manufacturing principles to increase throughput, since this will not be sold. On the other hand, capacity reduction could well lead to new bottlenecks which could disrupt materials flow, reduce delivery performance, and lead to a further drop in sales. The recommended strategy for such a firm is to attempt to use synchronous manufacturing principles to enhance the company's competitive edge by using the excess capacity to improve delivery performance, thereby increasing market share.

On the other hand, production constrained firms can by definition sell at that they can produce, and hence should focus on attempting to improve throughput by such measures as eliminating idle time and reducing set-ups at the bottleneck or purchasing additional capacity, and to compete on the basis of cost by the resulting reduction in operating expenses. We thus see different areas of strategic focus depending on the position of the company within the marketplace, which will have major implications for the ways in which synchronous manufacturing principles are employed.

6.8 CONCLUSION

In this chapter we have discussed the original OPT philosophy, the OPT system itself, and the more general approach of 'synchronous manufacturing' that has evolved from OPT. The OPT system itself, like MRP 2, has limitations. It relies on the existence of a well-defined bottleneck within the plant (even to the extent of recommending the artificial creation of one if it does not already exist). In practical situations this presents problems. Assiduous attention to the bottleneck may well result in it being the bottleneck no longer, and we see what has been termed the 'wandering bottleneck' phenomenon. Also the very tight scheduling of the bottleneck resource can present problems. Since the bottleneck schedule is so critical, any unexpected events at the bottleneck can threaten the integrity of the entire plan and OPT provides little guidance as to how to recover from such events short of a complete re-run of the OPT scheduling system.

You will observe how OPT is similar to MRP 2 in that it is a computer-driven system (although not with such a strong sense of integrated hierarchical planning as MRP 2) and it assumes production will be in discrete batches rather than on a continuous basis. Unlike MRP 2 which provides little guidance on the detailed shopfloor implementation of the plan, OPT provides a very detailed schedule for the bottleneck resource with the schedule for the non-bottleneck being much looser. OPT concentrates also on minimizing the total throughput time of individual orders. This contrasts with MRP in which the throughput times of orders are limited by the planning lead times which are input to the system.

Many of the above criticisms of OPT have been answered in the more general approach of synchronous manufacturing. This provides a set of general guiding principles which, as we shall see in the next chapter, have much in common with the JIT approach, the main difference being the explicit focus on the bottleneck resource. However, difficulties can clearly arise in the technique in plants that are already relatively well balanced, in which case the capacity constraint resources (which can differ from the capacity bottlenecks) may well be rather difficult to find.

The next approach we shall examine – the JIT approach – also rests on an underlying philosophy. Like OPT, one of the objectives of JIT is to minimize the throughput time of materials through the plant. However, unlike both OPT and MRP 2 which attempt to solve the problem using the number crunching power of the computer to develop schedules, JIT relies on an overall simplification and rationalization of the manufacturing facility itself to the point where the scheduling problem becomes so simple that sophisticated computer algorithms are unnecessary.

REFERENCE

Umble, M.M. and Srikanth, M.L. (1990) *Synchronous Manufacturing: Principles for World Class Excellence*. South Western Publishing, Dallas, Texas.

FURTHER READING

Bylinski, G. (1983) An Israeli shakes up US factories. *Fortune*, 5 September, pp. 120–32.

Goldratt, E. (1980) Optimized Production Timetables: a revolutionary program for industry. *APICS 23rd Annual International Conference Proceedings*, pp. 172–6.

Goldratt, E. and Cox, J. (1986) *The Race*. North River Press, New York.

Jacobs, F.R. (1983) The OPT scheduling system: a review of a new production scheduling system. *Production and Inventory Management*, Vol. 24, No. 3, pp. 47–51.

The JIT approach 7

7.1 OVERVIEW

The third method of implementing the master production schedule that we shall consider is the so-called **Just-in-time (JIT) system of production**. The objectives of the JIT system are to maximize the velocity of material flow through the plant (and hence minimize inventory) by arranging materials to arrive at each stage of manufacture **just in time** to be processed and move on to the next stage. In terms of the drum–buffer–rope analogy described in Chapter 6, time buffers in front of each resource (and corresponding inventory levels) would be reduced to very low values (ideally zero) and a given item of material will spend only a very short period of time in the plant between its arrival from the supplier and shipment to the customer as part of the finished product.

The JIT approach to production scheduling was originated by Toyota in the 1970s in their car assembly plants in Japan, and has found most success in repetitive manufacturing environments although some of the principles can also be applied to batch and even, in certain circumstances, to jobbing, one-of-a-kind manufacturers. In reality it is almost impossible to achieve just-in-time production in the literal sense, with zero waiting times and zero interprocess stocks. The term is actually used more to represent an ideal which should be aimed for, in order to foster the culture of **continuous improvement** which is part of the broader view of JIT as an important branch of value adding and total quality management.

The objective of just-in-time production, that of achieving the zero inventory ideal, was originally motivated by the view (with which we should by now be familiar) fostered at Toyota that inventory should be regarded as a significant form of waste which adds no value to the product and should therefore be eliminated. It was also realized that the only way in which inventories could be reduced to zero was to remove the reasons for their existence. These are basically the irregularities in supply and demand at the individual product level, coupled with complex material flow patterns through the plant. With irregularities entirely removed, supply and demand could be perfectly synchronized with no inventory buffers necessary to decouple them and cushion their effects on each other. Simplification of materials flow by reducing the distance in the plant that material needs to travel can then ensure that the material itself spends the minimal possible time inside the plant.

Total smoothing of irregularities and perfect synchronization of supply and demand are only held up as ideals which are unlikely ever to be achieved. Nevertheless the fact that any progress towards these ideals, however slight, will result in simultaneous improvements in both cash flow and responsiveness to the customer gives strong motivation for any company at least to make some attempt to improve itself along these dimensions.

As we shall see during the course of this chapter, the reduction of supply and demand irregularities requires in many companies a fundamental restructuring of the way in which the whole manufacturing operation is conceived. Practically every aspect of the manufacturing process, from product design and facilities layout, through all levels of planning and control, to supplier, maintenance, human resources and financial management will potentially be affected. Thus JIT has emerged as much more than a particular type of production planning and scheduling system, and is more in the nature of a total manufacturing philosophy, having a strong degree of overlap with other so-called philosophies such as value-adding management, total quality management and synchronous manufacturing, with many of the subsidiary types of improvement required to increase material velocity and minimize inventory being themselves the prime improvement objectives of other philosophies. Indeed it may be stated that, whilst all of these philosophies have the common ultimate objective of improving the competitive positioning of the company, their prime sub-objectives, which are the main objects of improvement focus, differ somewhat. Total quality management (TQM), for example, is concerned with improvements in the quality of organizational and production processes. Inventory reductions and increased material 'velocity' will tend to occur automatically as one of the benefits or by-products of this activity. JIT, on the other hand, is concerned with eliminating inventory and increasing material velocity as its primary objective. However, to achieve this, it is necessary to improve the quality of the processes involved in manufacture. TQM and JIT are thus complementary and strongly overlapping philosophies, which both advocate continuous improvement in the direction of a goal that may never be reached. Likewise, value-adding management is concerned with eliminating all forms of waste and wasteful activities, of which inventory and its management is certainly one. JIT from this point of view is a subset of value-adding management.

A further aspect of the JIT philosophy is that it tends to spurn complex planning and control systems, relying instead on restructuring the manufacturing environment in terms of rationalizing products, their designs and the way they are made, so as to simplify materials flow to the point where it can be coordinated using little more than a series of visual signals. The emphasis on simplifying the problem to the extent that it can be solved by simple means contrasts with both the MRP and OPT approaches which take the existing manufacturing environment and attempt to provide complex solutions to a complex problem.

7.2 CHAPTER STRUCTURE

This chapter is divided into the following sections:

* the preconditions for JIT;
* JIT in repetitive production environments;
* JIT in batch manufacturing environments;
* JIT production control – the kanban system;
* group technology and just-in-time production;
* evolution of a company towards JIT;
* matching the approach to the manufacturing situation;
* conclusion.

The chapter commences with a re-examination of why inventories are allowed to develop and how this slows down the speed at which material physically flows through the plant. Consideration is then given to how JIT can be implemented in repetitive manufacturing environments, and how the same techniques can under certain circumstances be adapted to operate in batch production environments. A simple shopfloor control system frequently associated with JIT, the kanban system, is next examined. From here we move on to consider the techniques that can be used by a company to move in the direction of being able to implement JIT and how, in some cases, a mixture of different approaches may be advisable, with JIT techniques being combined with an MRP system or with the principles of synchronous manufacturing.

7.3 THE PRECONDITIONS FOR JIT

As observed in the previous section, JIT involves an examination of the causes of supply and demand irregularities in manufacturing, and their systematic elimination. To analyse the sources of such irregularities, it is convenient to divide supply and demand into:

- **external supply**: supply of purchased raw materials by external vendors;
- **internal supply**: supply of materials to a downstream manufacturing resource or work centre from an upstream one;
- **external demand**: demand by the external customer for the end items produced;
- **internal demand**: demand by a downstream resource or work centre on an upstream one.

Irregularities in external supply tend to occur because of the tendency to order materials in large batches to defray fixed shipping and ordering costs and obtain quantity discounts, and because of late deliveries or quality problems in the materials supplied. Irregularities in internal supply are similarly caused by the tendency to produce items discontinuously in batches rather than on a continuous basis, due to production rates for individual products being generally greater than corresponding demand rates, and also by the occurrence of defective batches and machine breakdowns.

On the demand side, in most companies, irregular external demand arises because customers frequently make orders discontinuously for batches of individual items rather than requiring a steady continuous flow. This occurs both for make to stock companies (where production may be triggered by the inventory level of an item going below its reorder point) and make to order companies where customers may be in the habit of ordering batches of a certain minimal size (again very often for reasons of defrayment of fixed ordering and shipping costs) rather than expecting continuous delivery. Demand uncertainties also occur because of unpredictabilities in the market, particularly where long manufacturing lead times necessitate production planning (and hence forecasting) for some way into the future. Irregular internal demand is generally caused by batch sizing decisions at the finished product end which manifest themselves as a 'lumpy' demand on components processed at upstream resources. Process interruptions caused by machine breakdowns and defective batches can also disrupt internal demands.

From the foregoing, it is interesting to observe in passing that the decision to order or to manufacture in batches at the forward stages of the supply/demand chain has a tendency to propagate backwards to encourage batch production in earlier stages of the chain, often right back to the basic raw material suppliers. This also tends to be encouraged by MRP systems which were designed specifically to plan and control batch production.

Different types of manufacturing company experience the above forms of irregularity to varying degrees. Some companies, because of the nature of their business, experience low degrees of both supply and demand irregularity. For example, where the same product is manufactured continuously on a dedicated series production line to meet a corresponding continuous demand, the achievement of JIT production will be relatively easy and will involve the systematic elimination of residual irregularities such as process disruptions caused by faulty machines, and attempts to negotiate with suppliers to deliver raw materials on a continuous daily or even hourly basis, rather than irregularly in large batches. Companies that make a large variety of relatively complex products with complex material flow patterns will be furthest from the JIT ideal. However, this should not prevent them from taking steps to move in the direction of the ideal, and it is these companies which have the furthest to go which can make the most gains.

7.4 JIT IN REPETITIVE PRODUCTION ENVIRONMENTS

The goals of the JIT production management philosophy can be most closely achieved in highly repetitive manufacturing environments in which a single item or product for which a stable demand exists is manufactured on a continuous basis, in a 'flow shop' environment involving sequential processing of the item at a number of work centres. Materials flow in this situation can be thought of in terms of a rate, rather than in terms of sizes and timings of discrete batches. Implementation of JIT in this environment would be premised on the fact that the demand during one planning period (typically one week) is sufficiently stable that a constant production rate can be maintained in each period. The steps taken in moving to JIT in this type of environment are mainly concerned with:

- eliminating irregularities in production;
- eliminating irregularities in external supply;
- coordination of supply and demand between adjacent work centres;
- minimizing material distance travelled.

A JIT production management system for this simple type of environment would have the following characteristics:

- a master production schedule stated in terms of the required daily or weekly rate of production over a planning horizon sufficiently long to enable capacity changes required to accommodate significant rate variations between periods to be planned;
- a programme of progressive improvement to individual processes to reduce variability, including the development of preventive maintenance programmes to eliminate unplanned interruptions to production;
- a pull system of production control, to ensure very close coupling

between the demand for materials by one work centre and the corresponding production of such materials by the immediately upstream one;

- positioning of sequential work centres in close physical proximity to minimize material transport distances and to allow easy interaction between operating personnel;
- frequent deliveries (possibly several times per day) from suppliers in small batches to coordinate with the rate of consumption of the first process of the line.

The JIT approach as applied in this environment can be envisaged as a simple pull system with small interprocess buffer stocks whose levels are used as triggers to signal to the upstream process (or the external supplier) when production (or delivery of raw material) is required. There is an important difference, however, between a JIT system and a normal production line, to which at first sight it may appear similar.

In the traditional production line, if a particular part of the line slowed down or stopped for some reason, the upstream work centres would nevertheless continue to produce at the same rate in order to maximize their local productivity, and stock would start to accumulate in front of the problematic work centre, which would temporarily be the bottleneck of the process. The traditional production line is thus a push system of production. In the JIT pull system, since production is only triggered at one work centre by the requirements of the downstream work centre, if the latter slows down or stops, the level of the buffer stock in front of it will stay above the point at which production at the upstream work centre is triggered, and the latter will not produce until the downstream work centre has caught up. The idle time can be used by the workforce for such activities as preventive maintenance of production resources (although this obviously requires multi-skilling of the workforce) which will itself minimize the occurrence of disruptions that stop the line.

Problems of faulty unreliable machines that were previously hidden by excess buffer stocks, are now exposed since a faulty machine will now stop the line, Exposure of problems in this manner will result in their rapid correction.

In the original Toyota JIT system, a system of cards and containers were used for visual signalling between work centres to show when production should occur and when it should cease. This type of system is known as a **kanban system**, and will be described in more detail in section 7.6.

Rather than delivering several weeks' or months' supply of raw materials in large batches, small batches of raw materials are 'pulled' from the supplier when needed. This generally requires the cultivation of long-term relations with suppliers, who should be located where possible in close vicinity to the plant. Long-term stability in the relationship can be maintained by issuing the supplier with a 'blanket' order for supply of material over a long timescale (typically a year) which is then called off in small batches as required. The 'blanket ordering' approach is similar to the type of purchasing policy encouraged under MRP. However, in JIT the delivery batches would be 'pulled' as required, rather than planned individually in advance by the MRP system. The emphasis here is very much on **vertical integration** with suppliers and the development of highly synchronized logistics chains.

In a repetitive manufacturing environment in which the production line is dedicated to a single product made continuously, the master production schedule would merely be stated in terms of weekly or daily production rates, and the capacity of the line can be adjusted on a period-by-period basis to match these rates.

7.5 JIT IN BATCH MANUFACTURING ENVIRONMENTS

The JIT approach becomes slightly more complex in situations where different types of product are produced on the same line. This situation is traditionally treated as a batch manufacturing situation, in which the batch sizes are determined by the line changeover costs. Consider the situation of a production line that produces three different products, A, B and C, where the demand for C is double that for A or B. If we assume that each work centre on the line must be set up differently for the different products, then one would normally produce discrete batches of product, in quantities that matched the demand and which were of an economic size in relation to the set-up time. Thus for a production line capable of producing 100 units per day, it might be decided that an economical batch size between set-ups was 1000 units, and the master production schedule shown in Fig. 7.1 might exist for production of the three products in order to meet the demand.

This policy is based on an eight-week production cycle (each product being made once every eight weeks). As can be seen, the policy leads to excessive inventory at the finished product end due to a mismatch between the demand for each item and the economic batch size. Production irregularities for each product have been deliberately introduced into the

Week	1	2	3	4	5	6	7	8
Product A	500	500						
Product B			500	500				
Product C					500	500	500	500

Fig. 7.1 Master production schedule for batch production.

system as a result of the batch sizing policy. Also the arrival of raw materials for each different batch must be coordinated in advance with the production of that batch, which requires an advance planning system such as MRP, and padded lead times to smooth possibly uneven loading of the production line which would also lead to excess inventory at the raw materials end.

Since it is primarily the necessity of producing each item in discrete batches that is causing the problem, the JIT solution to this would be to attempt to reduce each individual work centre's changeover times between products by a combination of redesigning the product and the production methods and possibly making modifications to the machines themselves for more rapid changeover using the emerging techniques of **set-up engineering**. The point would be reached where batch sizes can be sufficiently small that a continuous mix of all three products can be produced rather than alternate batches. In this case, the master production schedule would be stated in terms of a daily or weekly rate for each product as shown in Fig. 7.2.

In this case, a quantity of each of the three products is made every day in a production mix that reflects the relative proportions of each product in the master production schedule. For example, a production sequence of one each of A and B followed by two of C, produced as follows, would produce the correct proportions of A, B and C as required by the MPS:

ABCCABCCABCC . . .

Of course if it is more efficient to produce some minimal quantity of one type before producing the next, due to some irreducible component of changeover time, or the desirability of producing at least one transfer batch of each item before moving it to the next work centre, then the number of consecutive like items in the mix can be increased, provided the overall proportions remain the same. For example, if the minimal number of consecutive like items that should be produced is five, then the following sequence might be produced:

AAAAABBBBBCCCCCCCCCCAAAAABBBBBCCCCCCCCCC . . .

Week	1	2	3	4	5	6	7	8
Product A	125	125	125	125	125	125	125	125
Product B	125	125	125	125	125	125	125	125
Product C	250	250	250	250	250	250	250	250

Fig. 7.2 Mixed model production.

In mixed model production, in the case where the changeover time of a production resource can be reduced virtually to zero, it would be theoretically possible to produce any desired variety or mix of different items at that resource as efficiently as it would be to continuously produce a single item. Practical limits would of course be imposed by the increasing complexity of ensuring the correct item was being produced at the correct time to ensure a smooth flow of items between sequential resources. A means of achieving this coordination is the so-called kanban system, described in the next section. However an upper limit exists on the variety of the product mix that can be handled in this way due to the necessity of maintaining small buffer stocks of each individual item adjacent to the involved work centres.

In practical situations, where the minimum batch size is dictated by some residual irreducible changeover time that remains after all possible methods of further reducing the time have been explored, batch sizes are frequently stated in multiples of the transfer batch. Again, we would use a pull system for controlling the flow of work, with small buffer stocks for each product maintained in front of each work centre (although the available storage space between work centres would again obviously limit the variety of the mix that could be simultaneously produced on one line).

The above sequence is not of course the only way in which the master production schedule may be satisfied. For example, assuming the minimal batch size constraint of five units remains, an alternative sequence would be:

BBBBBCCCCCAAAAACCCCCBBBBBCCCCCAAAAACCCCCBBBBB ...

This would again produce each of the three products in the correct proportions. There are in fact a number of considerations to be taken into account when determining the best production sequence in a JIT situation. For example, if the different items require slightly different processing times then alternative sequences will have implications for the extent to which flow between work centres is balanced (i.e. some sequences will allow better synchronization between successive work centres than others).

A number of heuristics have been developed which attempt to develop sequences that best balance the flow. An important implication that also needs to be considered, particularly where the products are assemblies which require components to be fed into the production line at different stages, is that of levelling out irregularities in material input requirements at each work centre so that these in turn can be more easily produced in a JIT mode. For example, if C requires a particular component E which is not required by A and B, then the alternative sequence in which C is produced in two separate batches per cycle will produce a more even demand on component E than if C had been produced in one large batch. The larger the individual batch sizes within the mix, the more uneven will be the demand on the materials required, emphasizing again the importance of reducing set-up times so that batch sizes can be correspondingly small.

The construction of a master production schedule containing a product mix that as far as possible smooths out the requirements of all items at all levels of the bill of materials into a continuous and uniform set of demands on each item (the opposite tendency to MRP) makes the implicit assumption that set-up times can be made small enough for mixed model production to be possible at all resources. In reality this may not be the case, with set-up times being very low at some resources and substantial at others. Under such circumstances part of the plant might operate in JIT mode, with certain resources having to produce in batches. This is a common situation in manufacturing companies attempting to move towards JIT, and should be regarded as an intermediate state, with effort being undertaken to rationalize product and process plans so that, for example, the problematic resource only processes a range of items having similar set-ups.

Producing a daily product mix in which each of the end items is represented has the advantage that it allows flexibility to respond quickly to changes in customer needs. For example, if the demand for item B suddenly increased from 125 per month to 150 per month and demand for item C reduced from 250 per month to 200 per month, in the batch production approach reflected in the master production schedule of Fig. 7.1, it could take as long as eight weeks (one complete production cycle) for the plant to adapt to the new demands. In the mixed model production case, on the other hand, all that is required to effect this change is an adjustment to the production rate of each item, which can be implemented immediately.

This flexibility is of course a direct result of the much shorter cumulative product lead time associated with the continuous flow nature of mixed model production. It has the added benefit of shortening the length of the required MPS planning horizon (which is directly related to cumulative product lead time) making any necessary forecasts over this reduced period more reliable.

Another advantage stems from the fact that continuous production of a mix of products eliminates the need for much of the transaction processing normally associated with batch environments. In such environments, every time a batch is ordered, produced or moved into or out of stock, the event needs to be recorded in the form of paperwork, computerized data entry or both, so that the status of all ongoing work can be monitored and controlled. This volume of transaction processing can create complex management problems in itself, and has given rise to what some have termed the 'hidden factory'. In continuous production, where the notion of a production batch is virtually eliminated, it is clearly neither practicable nor necessary to record the production of each individual item produced, since production is stated in terms of rates rather than batches. Under these circumstances, what are termed **backflushing systems** may be used for monitoring and controlling production and inventory levels. Instead of creating detailed work-in-progress accounting systems based on shopfloor transactions, backflushing relies on reducing component inventory balances by exploding the bills of materials for whatever has been delivered into finished goods. Quantities of individual components and raw materials consumed are then deduced from the quantities of finished products made.

In cases where only limited set-up times are possible, the question arises as to what is the critical irreducible batch size at which it ceases to be viable to plan and measure production in terms of rates, and it becomes necessary to track batches as discrete entities with all the associated additional information they must carry with them. As a general rule if batch sizes are such that the total cycle time of the normal product mix on a resource exceeds one shift, it will become increasingly difficult to track production purely on the basis of rates, and the recording of discrete batches must be resorted to. It is at this point that simple pull systems of production control start to become inadequate, and finite scheduling systems such as OPT become potentially advantageous.

7.6 JIT PRODUCTION CONTROL – THE KANBAN SYSTEM

Elimination of large batches and the building of small quantities of an item on a daily basis can eliminate the need for sophisticated computerized shopfloor control systems. A very simple shopfloor control system that was developed by Toyota in the 1970s specifically for their just-in-time assembly plant has received considerable attention in the Western world, and is known as the 'kanban' system (literally translated as 'card' system). The kanban is used to reduce inventory to the lowest possible level, and controls the flow of work from one work centre to another using the 'pull' concept.

The philosophy behind the kanban approach is that work should never be pushed on to the next work centre until that work centre is ready for it. When a work centre is ready to receive work, a signal is sent to the work centre involved in the preceding operation, and material is moved on. If the recipient work centre is not ready, the whole production process is stopped. The pressure for movement comes from the end product assembly. Components required for assembly are 'pulled' along by assembly workers who are ready to accept more rather than by workers who, for example, have finished a particular batch of machined parts.

The same is true for the issue of raw materials from stock (usually the only types of item that do have a small stock in a JIT environment).

In the kanban system, materials are stored in standard containers. Each work centre has two small storage areas associated with it – an inbound stockpoint and an outbound stockpoint, and each stockpoint has the capacity for the temporary storage of a limited number of containers. The containers full of parts are 'pulled' through the production system by means of cards, which may be classified into two types:

- **move cards** which authorize the movement of a standard container of parts of a specific type from the outbound stockpoint of one work centre to the inbound stockpoint of another;
- **production cards** which authorize the production of a standard container of parts of a specific type to replace a container just taken from the outbound stockpoint of the producing work centre.

Containers of parts are not kept in stockrooms but only at stockpoints associated with work centres. The maximum amount of inventory of a part stocked at any one time will be limited by the number of standard containers that are allowed to be accommodated at each stockpoint. A single container of each item produced on the line is the minimal 'safety stock' of that item that is required to enable the line, in the assumed absence of any set-up times, to change instantaneously from the production of one item to the production of another, in response to changing 'pulls' from the final process.

Figure 7.3 shows the procedure for using the two types of card. All standard containers of parts at an inbound stockpoint have a move card attached. When a container of parts is selected for use, a worker detaches the move card, and takes it to the outbound stockpoint of the supplying work centre to pick up a replacement full container. At the supplying work centre, the worker removes the production card from the replacement container and attaches the move card. Workers at the supplying work centre pick up the production card, make another container of parts, attach the card to it, and place it in the outbound stockpoint ready for pickup. The rules for the use of these cards are as follows.

1. Always use standard containers filled with the correct number of parts.
2. Never move a standard container forward without getting the authorization of an unattached move card.
3. Never produce a standard container of parts without the authorization of a production card.

The card system allows precise synchronization of the output of one work centre with the input of another. Control is entirely visual. However, the rules have to be very strictly adhered to for the system to be effective.

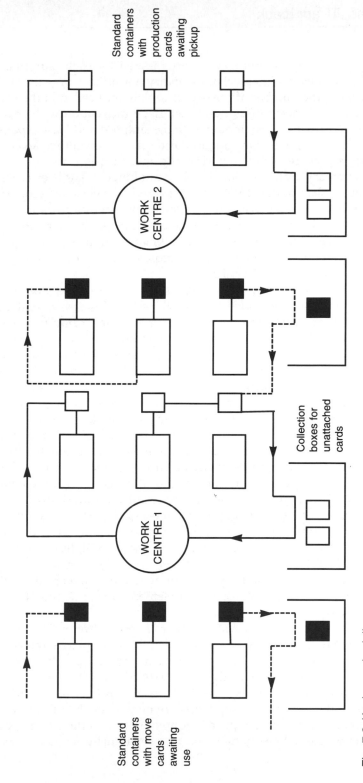

Standard
containers
with
production
cards
awaiting
pickup

WORK
CENTRE 2

WORK
CENTRE 1

Collection
boxes for
unattached
cards

Standard
containers
with move
cards
awaiting
use

Fig. 7.3 Kanban scheduling.

Since there is only one card per container, work-in-progress inventory is always limited by the number of cards issued for each part. Starting with some reasonably high level of inventory (i.e. quite a large number of cards per part), the number of cards is gradually reduced, and the resulting problems and their causes examined. Experimentation with changes in method is carried out, beginning with the simplest and least expensive change, until the system can function at the lower inventory level. The procedure is then repeated, withdrawing more cards until the lowest possible inventory level at which the plant can function has been reached. At this point, when buffer stocks have been reduced close to zero, experimentation is carried out with the automatic transfer of parts from one work centre to the next, as a first stage of complete automation of the process. This can commence with the implementation of some form of electronic signalling device rather than cards, when production or movement is authorized (electric kanban).

A variant on the kanban approach is that of so-called **single-card kanban** in which only the move card is retained. In this case, overall daily production at individual work centres is planned according to a master production schedule for finished product requirements. Containers of parts are produced according to these requirements rather than in response to authorization by the arrival of a production card. Thus there will always be a slight surplus of containers of each type of part at the outbound stockpoint of the supplying work centre. As each container of incoming parts is selected for use by the recipient work centre, the associated move card is withdrawn from the container and placed in a specific location. As containers are consumed, these cards accumulate and are collected at regular intervals. At this time, a full container is removed from the supplying work centre, the move card attached, and the container returned to the inbound stockpoint of the recipient work centre.

In the single-card kanban approach, processed parts are allowed to build up at the supplying work centre. On the other hand, inventory at the incoming stockpoint of the recipient work centre is tightly controlled. Thus single-card kanban may be regarded as a 'push' system for production control, and a 'pull' system for material delivery. It is often regarded as the initial phase of the implementation of a full two-card kanban system.

For control using a kanban system, the number of different items in the product mix must obviously be relatively small, since in general, at least one container full of every item produced in the product mix must be maintained. However, quite a high variety of low volume items (which are not always part of the weekly product mix) can be handled, even to the level of one-offs, provided set-up times are no greater than those for the standard mix. Since their low production volumes and their large potential number would not justify maintaining a separate buffer stock of each, a slight delay would occur in the initiation of production of the item, but this would not matter provided the flow of the standard items was not disrupted. When the work centre involved in the final operation received a request to produce such an item, it would not be able to start immediately as there would be no buffer stock of materials available. A signal to the preceding work centre would mean that production of the relevant materials was required, and this signal would in turn be transmitted back to the first work centre in the chain, which would perform the first operation on the required batch of the 'special' item. This would then be 'pushed' down the production line with the appropriate processing being carried out at each work centre, which in the meantime would have been continuing with the production of standard items using the normal 'pull' signals generated by the kanban cards.

It is possible to extend kanban principles to the 'pulling' of batches of raw materials from suppliers, provided arrangements can be made for many small deliveries to be made (possibly several times a day) rather than infrequent delivery in large batches. However, this obviously implies not only a close relationship with suppliers, but also close physical proximity.

7.7 GROUP TECHNOLOGY AND JUST-IN-TIME PRODUCTION

7.7.1 GENERAL CONCEPTS OF GROUP TECHNOLOGY

The complexity of materials flow has been identified as a major production management problem in batch manufacturing companies, which impedes movement in the direction of JIT modes of production management. If flow can be rationalized and simplified it can, under certain circumstances, be possible to convert batch manufacture into repetitive manufacture, and thus reap the benefits of applying JIT production techniques. This has prompted major efforts in many manufacturing companies to both rationalize and simplify their range and design of products in such a way as to simplify materials flow patterns on the shop floor.

The concept of focused factories or product-based manufacturing cells as a basis for simplifying production flow and thus simplifying the production scheduling problem is becoming increasingly common. A powerful method that can be used to assist in the reorganization of a plant for this purpose is based on concepts of **group technology** which is concerned with the rationalization and grouping together of similar products, parts and processes with a view to achieving simplified work flows.

Group technology (see Gallagher and Knight, 1986; Burbidge, 1990) is concerned with discerning underlying similarities in products, parts, processes and production resources by structuring these entities into clusters based on common attribute values. Through the application of group technology (GT) groups of similar set-up parts can be identified.

Rationalization of product range and design with reference to GT considerations can enhance the degree of standardization and interchangeability of parts which in turn introduces greater simplicity into the manufacturing process. Use of GT coding and classification schemes in conjunction with production flow analysis can assist in the identification of part or product 'families' that flow through, or could flow through, the same clusters of machinery. These clusters of machines can then form the basis for manufacturing cells which are capable of performing all the operations required to produce a given family of parts. Provided the capacity of such cells is reasonably matched to the demand for individual part families, cells can be dedicated to families and hence become self-contained and autonomous in their operation. Thus, the term 'group' in group technology can (and has) been applied not only to groups of similar parts but also to groups of machines that form manufacturing cells, and the groups of people who are responsible for them.

The approach of GT is to solve a large part of the problem of manufacturing coordination by the creation of independent sub-tasks. Since manufacturing cells are autonomous in operation, close coordination between cells is not required, and the activities of each cell can be planned independently of others. The concept has been expressed in a variety of forms by different authors. For example, Skinner (1974) writes of the 'focused factory' concept in which a manufacturing organization is divided into a number of autonomous 'sub-factories' each making their own family of products. The effect of unexpected contingencies within a sub-factory are localized, not through buffer stocks but through autonomy of operation.

Physical grouping of machines into cells devoted to part or product families implies a product rather than a process-oriented factory layout which can drastically reduce the distances travelled by items in their progress from one operation to the next. In the process-oriented layout of the traditional factory, items tend follow to complicated routeings and travel large distances. The paths they follow have frequently been compared to 'bowls of spaghetti' (Fig. 7.4). Long and uncertain throughput times result, with the physical separation of sequential processes increasing the difficulty of interprocess coordination. Items tend to be stored in a central stockroom between processes, which increases coordination problems even further.

A change to a product-oriented layout can result in much simpler material flow patterns, as shown in Fig. 7.5, since sequential processes are performed in physically adjacent locations. Stockhanding costs are reduced, and coordination greatly improved.

A set of steps for plant rationalization and simplification based on group technology is listed below.

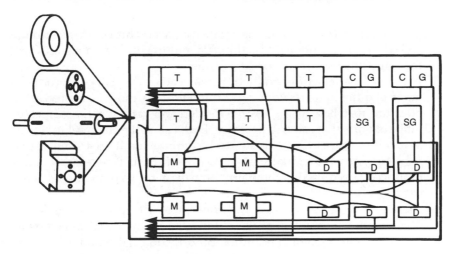

Fig. 7.4 Functional layout.

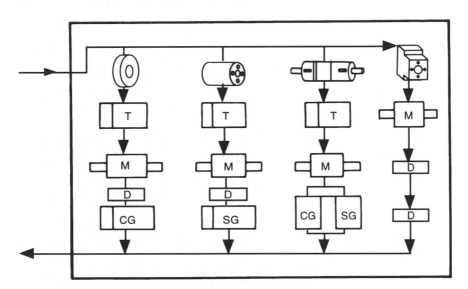

Fig. 7.5 Product oriented layout.

1. Rationalize the range of products made and their engineering design in such a way as to minimize the variety of different types of individual parts used. Group parts into families in such a way that all parts within a particular family can be produced on a common group of machines within a similar machine set-up.
2. Estimate the average demand on each family and divide production facilities (e.g. individual machines) into groups or cells in such a way that each cell can perform all the operations required to produce the

family of parts and the production capacity of the cell is reasonably matched to the demand on the family of parts. This contrasts strongly with the more traditional functional layout in which all machines with the same function are grouped together.

3. We now have a set of production cells each of which can produce a range of different parts within a common set-up and whose production rates are matched to the aggregate demand rates for the respective range of parts that cell will produce. Each cell will remain set up for the family it produces. Since the set-up is common (or at least similar) over the range, any individual part, on a one-off basis if necessary, can be produced as required without any penalty in terms of increased set-up costs.

4. Having virtually eliminated the concept of set-up cost from further consideration, individual parts within a family can be produced by the cell (now effectively a continuous production line) on an as-required basis. A continuous mix of items can now be produced, and a pull system of production employing just-in-time production techniques can be applied.

The elimination of the batch concept through making it as economic to produce a one-off of a particular part as to produce a thousand of the same part invariably has an immediately beneficial effect on load levelling. Large load fluctuations on individual work centres are usually produced by the self-imposed concept of batch production rather than by any fundamental unevenness in demand itself.

A typical physical organization of a factory in which an assembly line is fed by a series of production cells at which various component parts for the assembly are produced is as shown in Fig. 7.6. Here the assembly line produces a continuous mix of different products. The different assembly operations in turn 'pull' the required components from production cells located at the appropriate position along the assembly line, adjacent to the location where the assembly operation will take place. It is assumed that these production cells are dedicated to manufacturing the range of parts required at that assembly point along the assembly line, and that an almost continuous mix of the desired parts (in very small batch sizes, approximating to a standard kanban type container) can be produced at each of the cells, with small buffer stocks of the commonly produced types of part stored adjacent to the assembly point.

7.7.1 PRODUCT RATIONALIZATION AND GROUP TECHNOLOGY

Traditional methods of product design use what might be termed an 'incremental' approach. When a new product is designed, a new set of parts is generated some of which may be very similar to parts used in

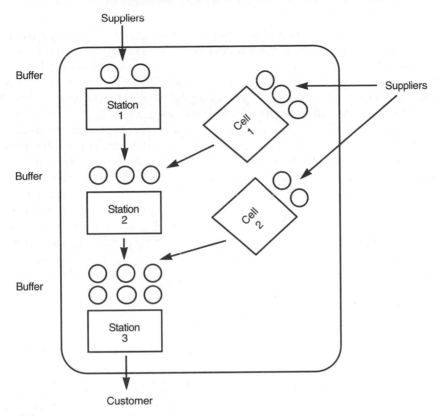

Fig. 7.6 A JIT assembly line.

established products. The new parts will, however, have different part numbers (usually tied to the product in which they appear) with nothing intrinsic in the part number that will indicate any similarity with existing parts. This tends to lead to the familiar 'complexity explosion' of an enormous number of different parts, many of which are almost identical.

New computer-aided design and so-called 'concurrent engineering' techniques (in which manufacturing engineers who are responsible for designing the production process itself have a major input to the product design stage to ensure ease of manufacturability) are allowing a more rationalized approach to be taken to product design. Similar parts can be easily identified, and product designs can be changed in such a way as to allow more parts to be common to a wider range of products. It would not be unusual for such a rationalization process to reduce the number of separate part numbers in manufacturing plant by a factor of 10 or more.

Having produced a rationalized range of products designed in such a way as to increase the degree of commonality of standard parts between products, the next step in the process is to group individual parts into families. A variety of different types of grouping process may be used. Early schemes for this used hierarchical classification schemes in which the initial classification was by type of equipment, the next level by geometric shape, etc. An example of this is shown in Fig. 7.7.

The lowest level of classification is into groups of components produced on the same machine and requiring similar set-ups. In general the target is to match the demand on each group with the capacity of the relevant machine (or a group of similar machines) so that machines can be dedicated to similar set-up groups, and simultaneous and continuous production runs of each group can be made. If this match cannot be achieved with existing product designs and process configurations, consideration might be given as to how this might be achieved by product modification or redesign, or the installation of new or modified machines of the appropriate capacity.

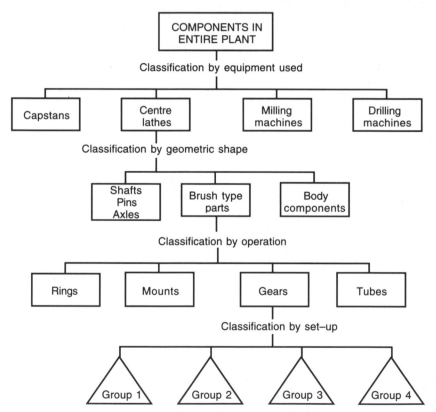

Fig. 7.7 A hierarchicla classification system.

In cases where a very large number of parts exist, it is usually more efficient to use a coding system to assist in classification. Each part is assigned a unique code number, with the coding system having been developed in such a way as to facilitate the identification of groups of similar parts from the code number. Coding systems generally allow the use of computer search algorithms to assist in the grouping process. Two major types of coding proposed for this purpose are the Opitz system and the Miclass system.

The **Opitz** system uses a five-digit code specifying the geometric characteristics of the part, and a four-digit supplementary code giving the diameter or edge length, the type of material and its initial form, and the accuracy to which the component is manufactured. The Opitz classification for a particular component might take the form:

$$11002\ 4301$$

In this code, the first digit (1) specifies we are dealing with a rotational component whose ratio of length to diameter is less than 0.5. The second digit (1) signifies no external shape elements exist. The third digit (0) specifies that no through bore exists. The fourth digit (0) specifies that no surface machining is required. The fifth digit (2) specifies that the component contains axial holes related by a drilling pattern.

Of the supplementary code, the first digit (4) represents a diameter of between 160 and 200 mm, the second digit (3) represents the steel type, the third digit (0) represents the initial shape as a round bar, and the fourth digit (1) represents the requirement for accuracy level 1.

Since the required machining set-up characteristics can be deduced from the code, by searching for components whose code satisfies a particular set of criteria, components that should be machined within the same set-up can be identified and the total demand for this family can be examined in relation to the throughput capacity of the available machines.

The **Miclass** (Metal Institute Classification) system carries information on main shape, shape elements, position of shape elements, main dimensions, ratio of dimensions, auxiliary dimension, form tolerance and machinability of material. These are represented in twelve main fields which can be extended to eighteen for user-defined functions giving information on part functions, lot sizes, major machining operations, etc.

7.7.2 PRODUCTION FLOW ANALYSIS

Identification of groups of similar set-up parts by coding does have a number of disadvantages.

- In cases where parts need to be processed on more than one machine, it does not represent the way in which parts 'flow' through the factory.

- It is laborious and involves starting from scratch.

Production flow analysis (PFA) is based on the assumption that the majority of components in a factory will already belong to clearly defined families or groups, and it is only necessary to identify these in order to provide the basis for reorganization.

PFA involves taking each part in turn and examining its flow through the plant in terms of the machines on which it needs to be processed. Groups of parts can then generally be identified which have common processing characteristics and, within these, sub-groups can be identified having common set-ups. The volume of flow of each group of parts is then established with a view to obtaining groupings of machines in such a way that a machine group or cell can be dedicated to a group of parts with a common set-up, thus enabling a continuous mix of these parts to be produced using JIT principles.

A convenient tool for identifying such groups is to develop a **production flow incidence matrix** in which columns correspond to parts and rows correspond to processes or machines, and an entry in a matrix element indicates that the part corresponding to the column number is processed on the machine corresponding to the row number. An example of such a matrix is shown in Fig. 7.8. The process routeing of each part through individual machines can easily be tracked by referring to the positive entries (identified in the matrix by ticks). The identification of

	K48251A	L48388	L48267B	M44276E	M47693F	L48388M	M48195C	M44276D	E41795	E48596	E34267	E12204	E12288	K47697	E47782	E48586	K34596	E33494	M48265D	K44278C	M45691D	M45691B	M48386H	K34098A	E7392	E46384	E33295	K45199	K43390	M61592	E18694
DMT(3)		√												√	√	√								√		√		√	√		√
DM(3)			√	√			√						√		√		√	√	√					√				√	√	√	√
PG			√		√												√	√	√	√											
OXY(3)	√	√	√														√							√				√	√	√	
P&GR				√																											
PGR													√													√					
PGH																															
PGG																			√	√						√					
P & G					√	√	√	√	√	√	√								√	√						√	√	√	√	√	√
RP																									√						
PGB			√												√	√			√	√						√					
W & P	√					√																		√				√	√		
WG 3												√																			

Fig. 7.8 Production flow matrix.

groups of parts with similar process paths can be performed graphically through rearranging the list of parts or the list of machines in such a way that clusters of entries appear as shown in Fig. 7.9. Once the basic groups have emerged, parts or processes that lie outside any group can be subject to individual scrutiny, and process plans possibly altered to allow them to fit into one of the existing groups.

Manipulation of the matrix to create the groups can be handled by a variety of mathematical techniques concerned with cluster analysis, and be extended to include **similarity coefficients** which indicate the degree of similarity between different parts according to their possession of a set of predefined characteristics.

A highly simplified example of some of the preceding concepts can be seen by referring to Fig. 7.10. Three products A, B and C are assembled from components T, U, V, W, X, Y and Z, with the product structures shown. Machines M1 to M6 are involved in the production of these components. A grouping of components following production flow analysis shows that components X, Y and Z (Group A) are rotational parts which are machined on M1, M2, M3 and M6, as indicated, within a common set-up on each machine.

Similarly, components T, U, V, W and Z (Group B) are non-rotational parts which are machined on M4, M5 and M6. This group of parts can be further subdivided into sub-groups B1 containing T and U, and sub-group

	L48267B	K35496	M48265D	E33494	K44278C	L48388M	E7392	K34098A	K45199	K43390	M61592	M48195C	M44276D	E34267	E12204	E18694	E41795	E48596	M48386H	K48251A	L48388	M45691D	M45691B	M44276E	K47697	E47782	E46384	E12288	E33295	E48586	M47693F
PG	√	√	√	√	√	√																									
DM3/1	√	√	√	√																											
OXY3/1	√	√																													
RP							√																								
DMT3/2																															
P & G								√	√	√	√	√	√	√	√	√	√	√	√	√	√								√		
								√	√	√				√		√		√			√										
DM3/2								√	√	√		√		√			√			√											
OXY3/2								√	√	√	√	√										√	√								
W & P								√	√	√																					
WG 3																	√														
PGG																									√	√			√		
PGB																								√	√	√	√	√	√		
PGR																											√	√			
DMT3/3																										√	√	√		√	
DM3/3																									√	√			√		
P & GR																															√

Annotations on matrix: **Group 1** / **1 Family** (upper-left cluster); **Group 2** / **2 Family** (centre cluster); **Group 3** / **3 Family** (lower-right cluster); "One 'exception'" □√

Fig. 7.9 Production flow matrix rearranged to show families.

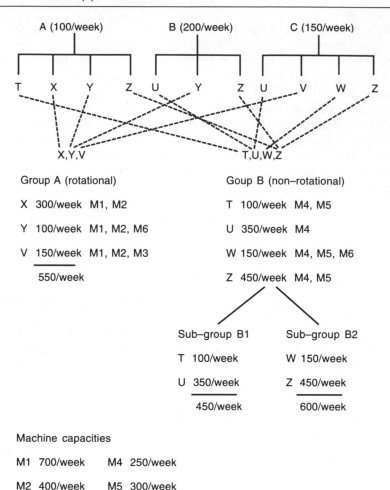

Group A (rotational)

X 300/week M1, M2

Y 100/week M1, M2, M6

V 150/week M1, M2, M3
_____
550/week

Goup B (non–rotational)

T 100/week M4, M5

U 350/week M4

W 150/week M4, M5, M6

Z 450/week M4, M5

Sub–group B1   Sub–group B2

T 100/week   W 150/week

U 350/week   Z 450/week
_____   _____
450/week   600/week

Machine capacities

M1 700/week   M4 250/week

M2 400/week   M5 300/week

M3 100/week   M2 200/week

Fig. 7.10 Dedication of machines to part families.

B2 containing W and Z. Parts within each sub-group can be machined within a common set-up on both machines M4 and M5.

If we now analyse the volume of flow, we observe that, from the expected demand on the end products, the total volume of flow of Group A is 550 per week, and the volumes of flow of sub-groups B1 and B2 are 450 per week and 600 per week respectively.

Checking now on the capacities of the machines that are required, we see that if we dedicate one machine M1, two machines M2, two machines M3 and one machine M6 to Group A, we shall be able to maintain a flow of Group A components with a certain amount of extra capacity available. The machine with the least excess capacity available is M1, and the machine with the most extra capacity is M6 which is only run at 50% utilization. The machines we have identified with Group A will be placed together in close physical proximity and will be known as the machine cell for Group A. The dedicated task of this group of machines is to turn out continuously components belonging to Group A. Components will be moved directly from one machine to the next as they are processed, possibly using a kanban style production control system with minimal buffer stocks. The machine cell will be operated by a group of operators whose job is entirely concerned with components in Group A, and who may organize themselves within their group as they think fit. This forms the basis of a **semi-autonomous work group** in which individuals are assumed motivated as much by their membership of a closely knit, cohesive social unit as they are by any financial reward. As we have previously observed the use of the word 'group' in the term group technology has been taken by some writers to refer to the human groups which can be formed to undertake a logical slice of work (i.e. having complete responsibility for a group of components and a cell of machines) and to avoid some of the dehumanizing effects of individual working at highly specialized, apparently meaningless tasks as in more traditional approaches.

The recommended layout for such a production cell is to arrange machines in a U shape as shown in Fig. 7.11, in order to facilitate communication between operators and minimize materials movement.

Looking now at sub-groups B1 and B2, it will be seen that the flow volumes are 450 per week and 600 per week respectively, and that machines M4, M5 and M6 are required. The required capacity can be achieved by two machine cells. For sub-group B2, we shall require three

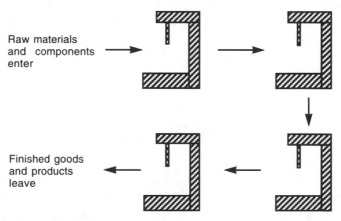

Raw materials
and components
enter

Finished goods
and products
leave

Fig. 7.11 Typical cell layout.

machines M4, two machines M5 (working to capacity limit) and one machine M6.

For sub-groups B1 and B2, we do not have a very good match between workflow and machine capacity on some machines. For example, machine M5 in cell B1 will only be working at one-third capacity, whereas the two M5 machines in cell B2 will be working at 100% capacity and, in the event of scrap or rejects, will be over-extended. In the event of set-ups of M5 not being too different for the two groups of components, it might be feasible to share the M5 machines between both groups without destroying their autonomy too much.

It is important to remember when attempting to design a series of machine cells that the range of products made, the way in which they are designed and the types of machine in the plant will determine the extent to which the whole concept is feasible. The greater the degree of standardization of individual parts, the more likely will one be able to isolate families of common set-up parts whose production volume is sufficient to justify the existence of a cell of machines dedicated to that group. Intelligent CAD packages with rapid transfer of information between sales, design and production departments, and the use of multi-disciplinary design teams consisting of designers, production engineers, production supervisors and marketing personnel, are facilitating the redesign of products for greater commonality of individual components.

7.8 EVOLUTION OF A COMPANY TOWARDS JIT

It has been indicated earlier in this chapter how JIT is easiest to implement in repetitive manufacturing environments, and conversely that batch producers and job shops are likely to be furthest away from the JIT ideal. In this section we summarize the main types of activity that are likely to require attention in non-repetitive manufacturing companies which are trying to move towards JIT. Some of these activities are interrelated and would naturally be performed in conjunction with each other, either in parallel or sequentially.

7.8.1 REDUCE SET-UP TIMES

One of the most important reasons for manufacturing in large batches is the existence of long set-up or changeover times. As we have seen, set-up time reduction is an absolute prerequisite for moving from discrete batch to mixed model production since the latter requires production batches to be sufficiently small that each item is produced at least daily, allowing production to be stated in rates rather than in batches. The economic batch quantity formula discussed in Chapter 3 shows that reduction of a set-up time to $1/f$ of its original value can allow manufacture in batches reduced by a factor of f without any increase in set-up costs. Set-up times are an important form of waste which should be eliminated. A number of standard techniques for reducing set-ups have been documented including the separation of internal set-up (requiring the machine to be inoperative) from external set-up (which can be done when the machine is operating), and the conversion where possible of internal to external set-up. This can involve very detailed analysis of the set-up process including taking videos, and possible minor re-engineering of the machines themselves. A common target to aim for is **single set-up** where the set-up time can be expressed in figures as a single digit.

7.8.2 REDUCE NECESSITY FOR SET-UPS

A powerful means of reducing the necessity for set-ups is the application of the principles of group technology as described in the previous section, such that groups of similar set-up parts are processed on groups of dedicated machines.

7.8.3 ELIMINATE PROCESS VARIABILITY

A high degree of process variability in terms both of rejects, machine breakdowns and fluctuating process times can have a deleterious effect on production flow, and this becomes magnified in a JIT environment. Techniques to tackle this problem vary from statistical process control and condition monitoring through to re-engineering of the process and redesign of the product to eliminate the possibility of defectives and process variability at source. The reduction of inventory associated with JIT programmes has itself a tendency to expose process problems, and provides additional motivation for rectifying them.

7.8.4 REDUCE THE NUMBER OF OPERATIONS PER PART

Since there could be a potential queue of work in front of every discrete operation, the more such operations that exist, the greater the chances that materials flow between operations will get out of synchronization, and the longer their throughput times. Thus a reduction in the number of operations (e.g. by combining several short operations into one long operation) the fewer are the opportunities for the build-up of work in progress, the greater the material velocity and the faster the throughput.

7.8.5 LEVEL CUSTOMER DEMAND

As lumpy customer demand (i.e. the demand from customers for batches of products rather than for a continuous supply) is a principal reason for production in batches, then attempts to encourage customers to place frequent small orders rather than infrequent large ones will tend to level the master production schedule and the resultant loading of the plant, which in turn encourages a more uniform flow of materials. Levelling of customer demand can often be achieved by forging closer and longer-term relationships with individual customers such that better integration is achieved between one's own and one's customers' logistics chains. This is of course entirely consistent with the corresponding activities of integrating with suppliers' logistics chains, and since, from the customers' point of view, one's own plant is acting as a supplier, this might also form a good fit with one's customers' philosophies if they too are in the process of moving towards JIT.

7.8.6 FORM VERTICALLY INTEGRATED FOCUSED FACTORIES

Moving from a single centralized production facility to a number of smaller sub-factories each focused on a specific set of products with similar production characteristics is a means of achieving a tighter degree of coordination between individual production stages. The closer integration of product design and marketing with production that can occur with the smaller scale of operation can facilitate integration with customers' and suppliers' logistics chains, and product and process redesign to facilitate materials flow.

7.8.7 REDESIGN PRODUCTS FOR GREATER COMMONALITY OF INTERMEDIATE COMPONENTS

JIT still implies manufacture of a range of products such that relatively high volume flows of similar items can be maintained. Rationalized product designs which make far greater use of standardized or common parts across a range of products can result in increased volumes of flow of similar items, which in turn can justify the dedication of a group of production resources to a similar set-up item family.

7.8.8 ESTABLISH LONG-TERM SUPPLIER RELATIONSHIPS WITH BLANKET ORDERING AND DAILY DELIVERY

This is the corresponding activity to that of levelling customer demand and implies a much closer degree of integration between one's own logistics chain and that of one's suppliers. The ultimate goal would be to be able to regard one's suppliers as an extension of one's own factory, from which replenishment batches could be called using a system as simple as the kanban approach.

7.9 MATCHING THE APPROACH TO THE MANUFACTURING SITUATION

The approaches that we have been considering so far for translating the master production schedule into detailed operational production requirements are frequently thought of as constituting alternative packaged systems or programmes, and that a manufacturing company must choose which system it is going to adopt. Both MRP and OPT are in fact associated with (often very expensive) computer software and vendors of the software are liable to claim that their system is not only universally applicable to any manufacturing company, but is also superior to the alternatives. Although JIT is not as yet generally associated with computer software, a number of consulting organizations are offering JIT programmes as alternatives to MRP and OPT. The presence of related programmes such as TQM, VAM and kaizen, and the often unclear relationship of these programmes to each other, has resulted in some confusion in many manufacturing companies as regards the direction in which they should go.

Although these programmes are usually offered as alternative solutions with different consulting groups specializing in different alternatives, there is in fact considerable overlap between them, and for many companies the most appropriate path might not necessarily lie in one particular packaged solution but in a composite approach. All the approaches obviously need some form of aggregate production planning down to the level of a master production schedule for the production of individual end items (although in some JIT companies this might be stated as a mix rather than in terms of absolute quantities). Companies who need long lead time purchased materials (for example those shipped from overseas on relatively fixed lead times) will find MRP provides a good method for planning and controlling the procurement of such items, but is less appropriate for the detailed planning of their own internal operations for reasons we have already discussed. Either the approaches of JIT or synchronous manufacturing, or a combination of both, may be more appropriate for reducing internal lead times and inventory levels. The synchronous manufacturing approach, although very expensive if the full OPT scheduling software is purchased, provides some useful concepts for operational planning and control. Its nine principles are very appropriate and most can be implemented in some form with the support of simplified PC-based computer software locally written and maintained. In the same way that OPT can alternatively be regarded as a management philosophy (synchronous manufacturing) or an expensive scheduling system, the JIT approach can also be alternatively regarded as a management philosophy of employee-driven continuous improvement by progressive waste elimination, or as a form of localized very short lead time scheduling using signals such as kanban cards. Perhaps the most important way in which JIT as a philosophy differs from the other two approaches is that it is much broader based, and is less inclined to accept the manufacturing situation (in terms of products, product structures and production processes) as it is, in the way the other two approaches tend to do. JIT is more inclined towards a fundamental restructuring of the manufacturing environment to make it sufficiently simple and predictable that the complexities of the MRP and OPT solutions are not required.

7.10 CONCLUSION

The achievement of a coordinated flow of materials through a manufacturing plant in such a way as to minimize both throughput time and work in progress is one of the most difficult problems of manufacturing management. We can of course accept that the complexity of most manufacturing plants (and hence of the associated production scheduling problems) is a given and design complex systems such as MRP or OPT to solve this complex problem. However, a smarter approach seems to be to try and simplify the problem itself through the progressive redesign of products and processes and the simplification of material flows through the identification of focused factories or production cells, to the point where simplified systems such as JIT/kanban can be used. Indeed this seems to be a general trend that we shall see gathering momentum through the remainder of the 1990s. Not only does this type of approach provide a potential solution to the scheduling problem, it also provides possibilities for greater employee satisfaction and involvement and a greater degree of fit between strategies for managing individual focused factories and the competitive posture that the company is attempting to adopt in the market.

REFERENCES

Burbidge, J.L. (1989) *Production Flow Analysis for Planning Group Technology.* Clarendon Press, Oxford.
Gallagher, C.C. and Knight, W.A. (1986) *Group Technology Production Methods in Manufacture.* Ellis Horwood, Chichester.
Skinner, W. (1974) Manufacturing and Corporate Strategy. John Wiley, New York.

FURTHER READING

Hall, R.W. (1983) *Zero Inventories.* Dow Jones-Irwin, Homewood, Illinois.
Schonberger, R.J. (1982) *Japanese Manufacturing Techniques – Nine Hidden Lessons in Simplicity.* The Free Press, New York.

Total productive maintenance   8

8.1 OVERVIEW

Maintenance is becoming a crucially important aspect of manufacturing and service industries, especially where there is a high degree of technology dependence. In modern manufacturing and service involving complex automated machinery, it is essential that maintenance is properly planned and controlled. Under the OPT system of production management, for example, effective maintenance of the bottleneck resources is essential to keep them running. In just-in-time production we can clearly see that it is impossible to produce 'just in time' if unscheduled breakdowns occur. The costs involved in unscheduled breakdowns can not only be extremly high but also can make production 'just too late'. Not only is production lost, but the cost of resources, including capital, labour and materials, can be crippling in a competitive environment. Often in these situations there are also conflicts which must be resolved successfully. For example, a careful maintenance plan may be under attack from the need for continuous running to meet production requirements and shift/labour efficiencies which management sometimes (rather short-sightedly) allow to take precedence. Attitudes like these are one of the major causes of poor maintenance performance. The result, all too often, is that plant and equipment is not available when it should be.

Maintenance has always been considered necessary, but until recently, it was not regarded as an important function of plant or industrial organization. However, due to increased international competition, increased plant and unit sizes, and the greater complexity of machinery, the maintenance function has become vital for an organization's profitability and survival. This chapter therefore has been designed to serve as an introduction to the need to:

- establish plans for maintenance management and control;

- show the importance of maintenance for enhancing the profitability and competitiveness of industry;
- access information on what the Western world might investigate from the newly developed Japanese system of total productive maintenance;
- improve condition-based maintenance through the reliability, availability, safety and profitability of plant and equipment.

8.2 CHAPTER STRUCTURE

This chapter is structured in four sections:

- maintenance management and control;
- condition monitoring;
- total productive maintenance;
- TPM and JIT.

Each section explains one aspect of maintenance management and the importance of that aspect to an overall picture. There are several steps towards attaining sound maintenance planning and control. Firstly, we must ensure that our equipment and methods are designed correctly. Design is undoubtedly the source of reliable plant and equipment. We must therefore ensure that maximum attention is paid to this activity and that techniques aimed at assessing and improving the reliability of designs are utilized to their maximum benefit.

Condition monitoring is a fast developing area. Developments in sensor applications and technology together with computer analysis are becoming an essential technique to enable the condition of machinery to be assessed whilst it is running, and more importantly, to predict the need for attention, allowing failures to be avoided before production is lost. Condition monitoring will also help avoid excessive expenditure on unnecessary maintenance. This is becoming an increasingly important area for consideration in our attempts to improve the reliability of our equipment.

To bring the whole of maintenance management together in a totally integrated way, the Japanese have evolved the technique of total productive maintenance (TPM). TPM reflects many of the ideals of TQM (total quality management) and has been proved to be an effective means of encouraging personnel at all levels to be aware of their role in monitoring equipment and the activities they must undertake to ensure that plant and machinery remain effective and reliable. In the West we may well have much to learn from this philosophy in attempting to improve reliability and availability in our manufacturing systems.

Availability of plant and equipment through efficient maintenance is becoming even more important for the survival of many industries in the wake of fierce international competition. Huge financial resources are

Table 8.1 Estimates of maintenance costs in various industrial areas as a percentage of sales value in the USA and Japan

	USA	Japan
Steel	15.0	4.0
Paper	10.0	1.7
Chemical	6.0	2.7

often spent on the maintenance and upkeep of machinery, in the hope that we can improve its availability for adding value and creating profit. Table 8.1 highlights the importance of maintenance and the potential savings which can be effected if maintenance is efficiently carried out. It shows an estimate of the effect of different maintenance policies in the USA and Japan, and tends to suggest that we must reconsider the way we allocate expenditure on the maintenance function as a whole to sharpen our competitive edge.

In addition to the direct costs, inadequate maintenance can result in:

- production losses (often several times greater than the maintenance costs);
- loss of market share because of unreliable deliveries;
- poor quality;
- increased replacement costs because of the reduced lifespan of equipment.

Although several maintenance strategies and tools have been developed, there are many compelling factors which indicate that more developments in the area of maintenance management are required.

8.3 MAINTENANCE MANAGEMENT AND CONTROL

Maintenance management is the application of general management principles of planning, organizing and controlling the maintenance function in an industrial organization. Using inputs such as finance and information, maintenance management endeavours to make the best use of the workforce, spares, tools and information to provide outputs in the form of plant availability, performance and safety. Firstly, we should examine the responsibilities and duties of a traditional maintenance department which can be listed as follows:

- maintenance of existing plant and equipment;
- rebuilding or reconditioning plant and equipment;
- installation and alterations to plant equipment, buildings and other factory services;

- maintenance of buildings and factory services;
- operation and supervision of factory services including steam, air, power, heating and ventilation;
- waste and effluent disposal.

The maintenance function of the manufacturing organization must ensure the availability, reliability and efficiency of plant, equipment and buildings in a way required by the manufacturing system at a reasonable cost.

8.3.1 ORGANIZATION AND ADMINISTRATION OF THE MAINTENANCE FUNCTION

The position of the maintenance function in the organization structure can have a large impact on the effectiveness of the maintenance function. Depending on its position in the organization structure, the maintenance function may be able to attract more cooperation and technical assistance and in particular greater attention from top management. For this reason, cultural aspects of an organization may have a critical influence on the success of maintenance, which depends on everyone seeing maintenance as an important part of their function. Organization structure must be reviewed at regular intervals to ensure that it is relevant to present organizational needs. Modern, flatter structures are beginning to recognize maintenance as an integrated function across the main divisions of an organization.

In effective maintenance management, we must not underestimate the influence of human attitudes on the successful operation of the function. Production requirements, the need for continuous running and a lack of interest in equipment condition on the part of operators are key issues which must be addressed when maintenance planning takes place.

The maintenance function within an organization can be structured in several ways:

- based on service;
- based on trades;
- based on areas of equipment;
- based on maintenance policy.

A structure based on a single method would have boundaries which are too rigid. Therefore, the maintenance function is normally structured using a combination of methods.

8.3.2 PRODUCTION MAINTENANCE INTERFACE

The maintenance role of an organization should be played by the management at a level which allows the availability of the equipment to suit the required production levels. In other words, production targets and safety requirements should set the levels of the maintenance required for plant and equipment.

There is now an increasing trend towards:

- maintenance to come under the control of a manufacturing manager who can no longer simply be responsible for 'work out of the door' but must now also take a responsible attitude to the condition and availability of equipment;
- greater responsibility on the operators for maintaining the equipment which they operate (towards TPM);
- communication of commonly required maintenance information (via computer) to whoever is required to act upon it;
- more and more maintenance personnel reporting to a manufacturing department.

This trend, however, clearly indicates the strategic importance of the maintenance function which must be employed to maximize equipment availability and effectiveness.

Equipment uptime depends upon many aspects, but theoretically equipment reliability is controlled by the designer and manufacturer. However, maintenance time is also largely influenced by the equipment user. Maintenance managers must adopt strategies to enhance equipment availability and reliability. **Fault tree analysis (FTA)** and **failure mode and effects analysis (FMEA)** are typical techniques used in attempting to balance and optimize these factors. These are widely used tools which allow maintenance requirements to be analysed and objectively evaluated.

8.3.3 MAINTENANCE CONTROL

Maintenance control is employed to ensure that maintenance resources and their application are monitored and properly directed towards the achievement of the maintenance objective.

A practical maintenance control system employs three principle mechanisms of maintenance control:

- **Availability and cost control** – ensures that the budgeted levels of maintenance effort are sustained and availability targets are achieved.
- **Plant reliability control** – monitors the reliability of the equipment in terms of mean time to failure and mean time to repair.
- **Tradeforce performance** – monitors the usage of maintenance personnel. This means feedback information via work orders for updating and modifying the maintenance schedules concerning equipment.

A maintenance control system must be clearly understood and have full cooperation of the personnel involved in it. Therefore whenever a maintenance control system is designed it is worthwhile to ask the following questions:

- What is being controlled?
- What information is required for control?
- In what form and how frequently should the information be collected?
- Who requires the control information?
- What information needs to be collected for providing effective control?
- How should the collected information be stored and analysed?
- Will the control system be cost effective?

8.3.4 MAINTENANCE DOCUMENTATION SYSTEMS

A **maintenance documentation system** contains information that might be required to facilitate maintenance work. A good documentation system can significantly reduce the maintenance time and enhance the productivity of the maintenance function. Therefore a documentation system which provides a formal system for collection storage, analysis, interrogation and reporting of the maintenance information is a necessity for any industrial organization.

Two types of maintenance documentation systems are in use in industry:

- **Manually operated maintenance documentation system**. This system requires a large effort for data storage, retrieval and analysis. In many instances the cost restrictions of such an effort have resulted in the absence of any historical records.
- **Computerized maintenance documentation system**. A computerized documentation system can act as an efficient database for plant history records, ongoing work planning and control, resource availability, planned shutdowns of machinery and their maintenance

The replacement of a manually operated documentation system by a computerized maintenance documentation system has been observed to greatly increase the productivity of the maintenance function.

8.3.5 RELIABILITY

So far in this chapter, we have considered the need for plant and equipment to be available and the way in which we might think about organizing people to meet these needs. However, there are many areas of conflict to be resolved. Not least of these is the need to balance maintenance policies against shift, labour and machine efficiencies, requirements for continuous running and the effects of human awareness and attitudes.

One factor which can make the balance a little less sensitive is that of the reliability of equipment. If equipment is inherently reliable and in need of minimal maintenance, the nature of some of the conflicts becomes less critical. However, greater reliability inevitably incurs greater cost and hence we then find a further conflict to balance.

In some ways, the reliability issue tends to be a 'red herring'. Management often attempts to overcome fundamental defects in maintenance strategies by pursuing more reliable equipment. In fact this can be very costly when there is no change in the maintenance culture. No matter how theoretically reliable equipment is, if it is not cared for appropriately then availability will not be maximized. Hence the need for cultural changes involving total productive maintenance (TPM) (see section 8.5).

8.4 CONDITION MONITORING

8.4.1 MAINTENANCE STRATEGIES

Industrial plant and machinery can be maintained in several ways as follows:

- operate to failure or breakdown maintenance;
- fixed-time or preventive maintenance;
- opportunity maintenance;
- design out maintenance;
- condition-based or predictive maintenance.

Breakdown maintenance is the oldest and simplest method where a machine is run until it breaks down and is then repaired. There are, however, several problems associated with this method:

- breakdowns can occur at very inconvenient times;
- failure of critical components can cause large consequential damage;
- safety risk for operators.

Because of these problems we should only use this strategy as a last resort.

Fixed-time maintenance is based on the assumption that identical or similar machines behave in a similar way with respect to failure. However, this is not true. Moreover fixed-time maintenance requires stopping machinery at regular intervals to replace critical parts which have short lives and to carry out any adjustments required to keep the machine running satisfactorily. Although an improvement on the breakdown maintenance approach, this procedure has its own drawbacks:

- costs are high;
- there are large demands on manpower at periodic intervals;
- unexpected failures causing large financial losses still occur.

Condition-based maintenance overcomes many problems faced in breakdown or fixed-time maintenance strategies. However, it only offers real advantages if the condition of the machine can be monitored in such a way that impending failure of the machine can be detected. Faulty components can be replaced and thus a possible major breakdown of the machine can be avoided. However, it should be noted that condition-based maintenance will only be satisfactory if the right type of condition monitoring techniques are used to assess the condition of the machine.

8.4.2 WHAT IS CONDITION MONITORING?

Condition monitoring can be defined as the process of using systematically collected data for the evaluation of system performance, reliability and maintenance requirements and planning. More specifically condition monitoring is used for:

- keeping the plant running and avoiding any catastrophic failure;
- indicating areas of deterioration and anticipation of necessary maintenance activities;
- prediction of a level of fault conditions so that a machine can be run until a convenient time is found for repair.

When an industrial organization plans to introduce condition monitoring, the additional costs incurred due to equipment and staff training etc. should be weighed against the savings effected. Therefore, organizations must consider the issue carefully in terms of costs and savings. Costs can include:

- initial investigations, selection of monitoring locations and establishment of warning limits;
- selection and purchase of condition monitoring instrumentation;
- training of staff for taking routine measurements;
- evaluation of measurements by engineers.

Savings include:

- increased time interval between machinery overhauls and therefore greater productivity and reduced maintenance costs;
- virtual elimination of unexpected breakdowns resulting in greater reliability;
- elimination of secondary damage due to component failures;
- elimination of replacement of good components;
- reduction of spare parts inventory due to forewarning of part requirements;
- reduced maintenance and repair times due to advanced planning.

A relative comparison of maintenance costs for breakdown, preventive and predictive or condition-based maintenance clearly indicates that condition-based maintenance carried out by using condition monitoring is significantly more economical when compared to the other two strategies.

During the recent past, several techniques of condition monitoring have been developed. Many of these techniques can be used in on-line, off-line or in-line monitoring of equipment depending on the maintenance policy or strategy of the organization. The various condition monitoring techniques which are presently in use are as follows:

- direct and assisted visual monitoring;
- automated vision monitoring;
- thermal monitoring;
- vibration and noise monitoring;
- acoustic emission monitoring;
- performance monitoring;
- wear debris and contaminant monitoring;
- environmental pollution monitoring;
- corrosion monitoring;
- optical flow monitoring;
- condition checking.

It is beyond the scope of this chapter to examine each and every technique listed above in detail. Therefore, only a few important ones will be considered in the following sections.

(a) Visual inspection

Visual inspection can be achieved directly or assisted by aids such as mirrors, baroscopes, etc. Inspection with the naked eye can reveal wear, scoring, pitting, distortion, oxidation and fouling. Visual aids such as baroscopes, stroboscopes, closed circuit television, etc., can reveal cracks, erosion, corrosion. Non-destructive testing, such as radiography, ultrasonic testing and other crack detection methods also fall under this category.

(b) Performance monitoring

Poor performance of equipment is an indication that there is some malfunction. Usually, plant performance is monitored through permanent instrumentation and readily visible on meters fixed in a control room. Performance monitoring usually relies on the measurement of one or more of the following basic parameters:

- temperature;
- pressure;

Symptoms Abnormal performance parameters	Compressor	Blower	Fan	Pump	Motor
Change in efficiency	•		•		
No delivery		•	•		•
Insufficient capacity		•		•	
Excessive leakage		•	•		

Fig. 8.1 Process machine performance deficiencies.

- displacement;
- flow;
- speed;
- power input/output (when both are monitored machine efficiency can be calculated and indicated.)

The matrix diagram shown in Fig. 8.1 gives typical process machinery performance deficiencies. Whenever the performance and symptoms look abnormal, the cause should be investigated and rectified. Computerization offers clear advantages in this area.

(c) Wear debris and evaluation of contaminants

The evaluation of wear debris from lubricated components is a powerful method of condition monitoring machinery. Care should, however, be taken to obtain repeatable oil samples without contamination by external sources. Sample frequencies can range from 10–500 hours.

After thorough mixing of oil, the following techniques can be employed for analysis:

- filtering and inspection;
- particle counting;
- spectrometric oil analysis programme (SOAP);
- ferrography.

These are either physical or chemical techniques used in the diagnostic analysis of lubricants which allow a great deal of information to be obtained about the condition of machinery. They are widely used in assessing the condition of aero engines.

(d) Vibration analysis

This is by far the most popular method of monitoring rotating machines. A good design will produce low levels of inherent vibration. As the machine wears and parts deform, subtle changes in the dynamic properties of the machine begin to occur. These changes result in vibrations which put considerable extra loads on the bearings. Such vibrations therefore can not only reduce the equipment life but can also decrease the quality of components produced on such machinery.

The methodology for taking vibration measurements should be systematic and well documented. The measurements should be taken regularly and compared with previously established reference values to highlight any deviation or trend in the observations.

In this chapter so far we have addressed a few issues which should indicate that modern maintenance ideas are clearly about to overhaul traditional views. It should also be appreciated that traditional maintenance management will come under severe pressure if we attempt to implement many of these ideas in current environments. Total productive maintenance brings about a change in the management environment which will readily foster modern maintenance ideas.

8.5 TOTAL PRODUCTIVE MAINTENANCE

Total productive maintenance (TPM) is widely known in Japanese industry as productive maintenance which involves all employees in the organization, from shopfloor personnel to top management. It has enhanced maintenance standards in the same way as total quality management (TQM) has raised quality standards in Japanese industries.

TPM is, in fact, an American concept of preventive maintenance which has been modified and enhanced to suit the Japanese industrial environment. The modifications in TPM are based on the Japanese kaizen approach which is best translated as gradual, unending, people-based improvement (see Chapter 11 on total quality management).

8.5.1 EVOLUTION OF TPM

After the Second World War, increased competition in industries resulted in the idea of preventive maintenance in the USA. The Japanese introduced this idea into their manufacturing industries in 1951. Preventive maintenance was further improved and evolved into productive maintenance in both the USA and Japan in the 1950s and 1960s. In the productive maintenance approach the machine operators were solely devoted to production and a maintenance crew was responsible for maintenance.

When	What	Where
Post WWII	Preventive maintenance	USA
1951	Preventive maintenance	Japan
1950s 1960s	Productive maintenance	USA (GE) Japan (Toyota)
1969 to 1971	TPM	Japan (Nippondenso)
1980s	TPM	Japan (Toyota) USA (GE) Korea Taiwan Brazil China Thailand Australia UK Europe

Fig. 8.2 Evolution of TPM strategies.

Companies using increasing automation in the manufacture and assembly of components started to realize that it was becoming impossible to maintain their plant by using conventional maintenance crews. In 1969, the management of Nippondenso decided to develop TPM. By 1980 the TPM concept was becoming highly developed.

Today in Japan over 20% of the companies use TPM. Included among those are automotive, steel, chemical, household appliance and a variety of other industries. Figure 8.2 shows the evolution of TPM in various stages.

8.5.2 BENEFITS OF TPM

The introduction of TPM in Japanese industries has enhanced maintenance standards in the same way as TQM has raised the quality levels of their products. In fact TPM has a dual goal of zero breakdowns and zero defects. Obviously, when breakdowns and defects are eliminated, equipment utilization improves and production costs are reduced. The benefits of TPM are summarized in Table 8.2.

Table 8.2 Possible examples of the benefits of TPM

Category	Examples of TPM effectiveness
P (Productivity)	• Labour productivity increased: 140% (Company M) 150% (Company F) • Value added per person increased: 147% (Company A) 117% increase (Company AS) • Rate of operation increased: 17% (68%–85%) (Company T) • Breakdowns reduced: 98% (1000–20 cases/month) (Company TK)
Q (Quality)	• Defects in process reduced: 90% (1.0%–0.1%) (Company MS) • Defects reduced: 70% (0.23%–0.08%) (Company T) • Claims from clients reduced: 50% (Company MS) 50% (Company F) 25% (Company NZ)
C (Cost)	• Reduction in manpower: 30% (Company TS) 30% (Company C) • Reduction in maintenance costs: 15% (Company TK) 30% (Company F) 30% (Company NZ) • Energy conserved: 30% (Company C)
D (Delivery)	• Stock reduced (by days): 50% (11 days–5 days) (Company T) • Inventory turnover increased: 200% (3–6 times/month) (Company C)
S (Safety/Environment)	• Zero accidents (Company M) • Zero pollution (every company)
M (Morale)	• Increase in improvement ideas submitted: 230% increase (36.8–83.6/person per year) (Company N) • Small group meetings increased: 200% (2–4 meetings/month) (Company C)

*The company designation letters are simply to differentiate between organizations.
Source: Nakajima (1988).

The benefit of zero pollution or cleaner plant and equipment is worth noting in the context of a comment made by a sales executive of a Japanese plant that had recently won the PM (Preventive Maintenance) prize. The comment is as follows:

> When we show the plant to clients, they think that if maintenance is so good then the quality of our products must be good too, and their trust in us heightens and we are flooded with orders.

8.5.3 TPM IMPLEMENTATION

It will be noticed that much of the above TPM implementation strategy is aimed at creating a culture which invites a Japanese workforce to become part of the system. In a Western environment, this particular strategy to motivate the workforce may be found unattractive. For example, there is no mention of union involvement or empowerment of individual operators. These are just two aspects which must be addressed in a cultural change to TPM in the West. It should be stressed that careful consideration of these and many other aspects is essential if an effective cultural change is to be achieved.

Key performance indicators can be employed to calculate overall equipment effectiveness as follows:

> Overall equipment effectiveness = Availability × Performance efficiency × Rate of quality products × 100

Using some typical figures for Western manufacturing industry:

> Overall equipment effectiveness = $0.82 \times 0.78 \times 0.58 \times 100 = 62.7\%$

Such a figure of equipment effectiveness does not look good in comparison to Japanese results of 85% and above (see below). TPM aims to enhance equipment effectiveness by upgrading the performance and skills of all personnel, particularly the personnel who operate the machinery. This requires a radical shift of maintenance responsibility from maintenance staff to operators if and when TPM is introduced into Western industries. It should be noted that allocating authority and accountability to lower levels will be a useful vehicle for the implementation of TPM. Flatter organizational structures can only be successful by utilizing ideas like TPM. However, we must not underestimate the enormousness of the changes in organization structure and culture which are required.

Total productive maintenance promotes the reduction and eventual elimination of the six big losses to raise the three key performance indicators of availability, efficiency and quality. The six big losses, according to Nakajima (1988), are:

- downtime:
  1. breakdowns due to equipment failure;
  2. set-up and adjustment;
- speed losses:
  3. idling and minor stoppages;
  4. reduced speed;
- defects:
  5. defects in process and rework;
  6. reduced yield between machine start-up and stable production.

Overall equipment effectiveness of 85% and above has been achieved in Japanese industries by the elimination of the six big losses. This, when compared with the overall equipment effectiveness of typical Western manufacturing industries of 40–70%, tells part of the story of why Japanese products are very cost competitive.

8.5.4 DEVELOPMENT OF TPM

The development of TPM should be carried out in stages. The Japanese Institute of Plant Maintenance divides a programme for developing TPM into twelve steps from a preparatory stage to a point where it is firmly established.

On average, implementation of TPM may take about three and a half to four years. However, the organizations which implement TPM start obtaining benefits within a few months after introduction.

One method of changing the organizational culture to TPM is described by Nakajima (1988) who presents the stages involved in implementing TPM as in Table 8.3.

8.6 TPM AND JIT

8.6.1 THE RELATIONSHIP OF TPM WITH JIT

Elsewhere in this text we have discussed the importance of JIT production in modern manufacturing systems. JIT progressively works towards the removal of all slack (or buffers) in a manufacturing system. The 'pull' nature of JIT means that waste is reduced because no operation is started until the latest possible time to allow on-time delivery to the customer. In this type of environment, equipment must perform reliably and predictably. If it does not, we are left with a situation where the manufacturing system cannot deliver good product on time. In fact, many organizations will find that their delivery and quality performance will deteriorate after implementing JIT. This is simply because JIT will highlight deficiencies in the performance of plant and equipment. If equipment fails due to

Table 8.3 Stages in TPM implementation

Stage	Step	Details
Preparation	1. Announce top management decision to introduce TPM.	Statement at TPM lecture in company; articles in company newspaper.
	2. Launch education and campaign to introduce TPM.	Managers: seminars/retreats according to level. General: slide presentations.
	3. Create organizations to promote TPM.	From special committees at every level to promote TPM; establish central headquarters and assign staff.
	4. Establish basic TPM policies and goals.	Analyse existing conditions; set goals; predict results.
	5. Formulate master plan for TPM development.	Prepare detailed implementation plans for the five foundational activities.
Preliminary implementation	6. Hold TPM kick-off.	Invite clients, affiliated and subcontracting companies.
TPM implementation	7. Improve effectiveness of each piece of equipment.	Select model equipment; form project teams.
	8. Develop an autonomous maintenance programme.	Promote the Seven Steps; build diagnosis skills and establish worker certification procedure.
	9. Develop a scheduled maintenance programme for the maintenance department.	Include periodic and predictive maintenance and management of spare parts, tools, blueprints and schedules.
	10. Conduct training to improve operation and maintenance skills.	Train leaders together; leaders share information with group members.
	11. Develop early equipment management programme.	MP design (maintenance prevention); commissioning control.
Stabilization	12. Perfect TPM implementation and raise TPM levels.	Evaluate for PM (Preventive Maintenance) prize; set higher goals.

Source: Nakajima (1988).

unpredictable patterns in its availability then clearly attempts to operate JIT will yield catastrophic results. In a JIT system there are no buffer stocks or contingency time allowances. Elimination of these elements is the essence of the economic viability of JIT.

We can understand from this that effective maintenance policies are essential to efficient JIT. Every machine must be available and it must produce the quantity and quality specified. It can in fact be argued that JIT cannot exist without TPM.

TPM attempts to shift much of the accountability and authority for maintenance to 'the source' (i.e. the operator). By performing maintenance at the source, the real causes of problems are discovered and eliminated, rather than being repeatedly corrected. The ultimate aim of TPM is to detect potential problems in their infancy and eliminate them before downtime and quality variations result. For example, operators could be using **statistical process control (SPC)** (in the form of common control charting techniques) to monitor the process capability of a machine. SPC can give advanced warning that the capability of a process is deteriorating. In a situation where SPC charts (e.g. average and range) indicate an unsatisfactory trend an operator would have the authority to stop the process to prevent defective production. It has been widely suggested that 15% of the causes of variation are controllable by operators. Therefore, when a deterioration in process capability is detected the operator can deal with this 15%. However, the question remains as to what happens to the other 85%?

This 85% is said to be controllable by management actions. More realistically, it would be sensible to consider 85% of the causes to account for the normal, random variation of a process when everything is functioning normally (i.e. the causes of variation which are inherent in the system). It is this 85% which we must control and improve if we are to be successful with JIT. TPM can provide an answer because it becomes the responsibility of operators and maintenance specialists to work together in teams to reduce variations in the capability of a process. The teams must become fully conscious of the six big losses and motivated towards reducing the variation in process capability which causes these losses. This work may involve equipment modification or changes to procedures. In many cases (for example, in setting up machinery) standard procedures often do not exist with the result that massive uncontrolled variations can occur which are highly detrimental to JIT. TPM teams are often first set the task of developing standardized maintenance procedures which form a basis for ongoing improvements which are implemented by operators themselves.

Taking the issue of set-up times further, the success of JIT depends on predictable, fast changeovers. The faster a TPM team can develop a changeover from one product to another on the same machine, the more effective JIT will be. This is because the aim of JIT is to have very small batch sizes – something which cannot be achieved when set-up times are long and uncontrolled. TPM teams can have a major impact in this area. We can see the effect of process capability improvement achievable by TPM in the process capability distributions shown in Fig. 8.3.

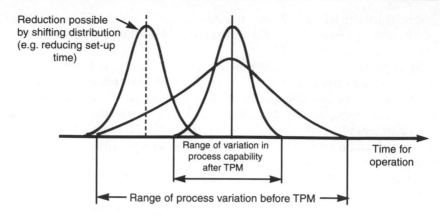

Fig. 8.3 Process capability distributions.

8.6.2 EFFECT OF TPM ON PROCESS CAPABILITY

There is little doubt that TPM can have a very critical influence on the success of JIT. King (1990) elaborates further on the advantages which will support JIT by giving the following examples from winners of the PM prize:

- breakdowns reduced by 90%;
- equipment effectiveness up 50%;
- defects reduced from 1% to 0.1%;
- maintenance costs down 30%;
- stock on hand reduced 50%;
- labour productivity increased 50%;
- improved employee morale;
- safer, more pleasant working environment;
- cleaner plant/equipment.

8.7. CONCLUSION

Maintenance management and TPM are very important aspects in the management of a manufacturing system. There is little doubt that efficient maintenance management can increase the availability of plant and equipment and in so doing result in an improved competitive edge in the marketplace. If Western industry does not take advantage of new ideas and technologies but merely continues with present practices and current levels of poor performance in plant and equipment it will be in a very poor position in relation to Japanese competitors. There can be no doubt that the maintenance function cannot be ignored in the never-ending search to improve the health of the manufacturing economy. It should also be remembered that improved maintenance can also result in indirect benefits, not least of which are improved quality and safety.

Whenever we consider maintenance management and its success (or lack of it), we must not forget the problems of current manufacturing performance measures which lead to pressures for continuous running as a result of production requirements and the need for high labour and machine efficiencies. We could argue that these issues have more to do with outdated management by objectives philosophies where the aim is to maximize product shipments (and hopefully profit), rather than to 'delight' the customer. More modern thinking, especially TPM, pays less credence to these numbers and puts customer satisfaction and quality at the top of the list of priorities. In the West, changing to this thinking will involve a very painful transition period where day-to-day management issues such as labour and machine performances will inevitably conflict with new ideas. Dealing with conflicts of this type will undoubtedly be one of the biggest challenges for a manufacturing systems manager.

The previous chapters have examined detailed management techniques to ensure a coordinated flow of materials within the manufacturing organization. In the next two chapters we shall look at the two main interfaces between the organization and the outside world as far as materials flow is concerned: purchasing and physical distribution.

REFERENCES

King, C. (1990) *Achieving Total Productivity Maintenance.* Proceedings of the 7th National Maintenance Management Conference, Melbourne/Sydney, pp. 55–75.

Nakajima, S. (1988) *Introduction to TPM.* Productivity Press, Cambridge, Mass., pp. 1–19.

PART THREE
Managing the Logistics Interface

Purchasing – achieving quality and value

9

9.1 OVERVIEW

This chapter addresses the subject of purchasing in its own right, but also introduces the subject as an overall concept which could be known in various organizations either as supply or materials management and which is basically concerned with managing the flow of material inputs to the manufacturing operation. A suitable definition of purchasing might be: 'the acquisition of goods and services required by an organization at the lowest possible overall cost, taking into account quality, quantity, delivery and price'. Organizations range from trading or manufacturing companies and government bodies to hospitals, educational establishments and restaurants. This chapter will concentrate on manufacturing systems but we should note that many of the principles and techniques we discuss are broadly applicable to a wide range of organization types.

In manufacturing industry, it is not unusual for purchased goods and services to amount to the largest single cost factor. The purchasing function can therefore have a critical influence on the profitability of an organization. As an example, consider a company with a sales figure of £50 000 000, making a profit of £5 000 000. It would not be unusual for such a company to purchase goods and services to the value of £30 000 000. If a 5% saving could be made in purchasing (that is a typical possible saving) this would be the same as a 36% increase in profits! This could be compared with the amount sales would need to be dramatically increased to generate 36% more profit under the existing scenario. This simple example serves to illustrate the importance of purchasing and why it is essential that it is efficiently managed.

This chapter should provide an insight into:

- the influence the purchasing function has on the profitability of an organization;

- how purchasing can be viewed in a fairly narrow context or as part of a wide function within an organization;
- the importance of purchaser–supplier relationships and the factors which influence these relationships;
- different methods of measuring supplier performance and selection of an appropriate method for a specified organization;
- differentiation between various purchasing methods and identification of the appropriateness for different situations;
- international strategies to assure quality of purchased supplies.

9.2 CHAPTER STRUCTURE

The chapter is structured as follows:

- introduction to the purchasing function;
- supplier management and monitoring;
- purchasing methods;
- assuring the quality of purchasing;
- purchasing and total quality management.

The introduction to the purchasing function attempts to illustrate the way purchasing should be considered as part of a wider function which could include planning, inventory control, purchasing, follow-up and expediting, transport and materials handling. In some larger organizations, these activities are handled by one specialist department which could be known as the materials department. This leads us to discuss and formulate some ideas on one way we could perhaps view the role of purchasing as a function within a function within a manufacturing system.

Supplier management and monitoring is discussed in the next section. Here, ideas are developed on purchaser/supplier partnerships and it is stressed how making the purchasing decision involves far more than simply locating the cheapest supplies. Objective methods for monitoring suppliers' performance are introduced, and the usefulness and application of these techniques discussed.

In the next section purchasing methods are discussed. There are many techniques available for particular situations and the variations available are examined. This is an important area where procedures are established by the purchasing function. For business success, it is essential that the most efficient procedures are adopted whilst ensuring that purchasing remains under control.

We finally discuss quality assurance (QA) in the purchasing function. We first define what we mean by QA and refer to international trends in quality systems. The cost of purchasing from organizations whose quality cannot be assured is discussed. A case study is next introduced to highlight the way in which quality systems standards are implemented. Finally we review the quality systems standards and discuss the manner in which these could be developed.

Throughout this chapter, we emphasize the view that the purchaser should establish a partnership with a supplier rather than an adverse relationship. Purchasing should encourage suppliers to become an integrated and continuously improving part of their organization so that both parties feel an ever strengthening healthy bond between them.

9.3 INTRODUCTION TO THE PURCHASING FUNCTION

The aim of the purchasing function within a company is to provide the products and services that are essential to the company's operations, but which in most cases are not available within the company. The responsibility of the purchasing department is to procure these products and services at the lowest total cost (Institute of Purchasing and Supply Management, 1985).

The objectives of the purchasing department can be defined as follows (Institute of Purchasing and Supply Management, 1985):

1. To purchase the raw materials, parts, components, services, etc., at a level of quality suitable for their purpose, being neither higher nor lower than required.
2. To purchase the quantities required to ensure uninterrupted production, consistent with the company's guidelines for delivery and inventory cost minimization.
3. To minimize the cost of parts supplies and services purchased to predetermined levels of quality and service.
4. To advise other departments within the company of information obtained from outside sources regarding market conditions, materials and processes.

9.3.1 ARGUMENTS FOR AND AGAINST A CENTRALIZED FUNCTION

In many organizations, responsibility for most functions is distributed between many departments, e.g. marketing, design, manufacturing, finance and research and development. The arguments for a centralized function suggest that if these departments are also responsible for purchasing their raw materials and supplies, then the organization will probably be compromised in some way because they will not possess the resources to search out the most economic supplies and suppliers. However, on the other hand, it can be argued that in large organizations, long chains of communication may result in very slow and rigid procedures which tend to inhibit the efficiency of the purchasing function. Decentralization results in efficient communication and fast reactions. From this, we can therefore see that there is a need for a compromise between centralization and decentralization. Blanket orders where a department may requisition directly from a supplier are one way of working towards this. Very specific purchases, which the user is most qualified to judge (for example, a plant maintenance department may be the best department to decide to whom a specialist plumbing job should be contracted) may also be decentralized. There have been trends in both directions in recent times. Unfortunately, we can only conclude that there are no simple solutions to the centralization/decentralization issue, but that the trend towards centralization has been damaging to responsiveness, quality and competitiveness.

9.3.2 THE ELEMENTS OF THE PURCHASING FUNCTION

Purchasing can be considered from a number of points of view. The centralization/decentralization question is only one issue. We might also ask: what does purchasing involve? There are many answers to this question which depend on how wide we see the purchasing activity. The department to which purchasing is assigned is often called the materials department. Within the department, using an industrial company as an example, the tasks can be divided into the following main areas (Institute of Purchasing and Supply Management, 1985):

- planning;
- inventory control;
- purchasing;
- follow-up and expediting;
- transport;
- materials handling.

Under each of the headings, two elements of that activity are given below.

(a) Planning

- Issuing of purchasing requisitions.
- Breaking down production plans into requirements, bought-out raw materials and components.

(b) Inventory control

- Stocktaking checks against stock balances and initiation of action as a result of deviations.
- Budgeting and cost control of stock levels.

(c) Purchasing

- Buying plant, machinery and equipment.
- Processing requests for purchased goods and services.

(d) Follow-up and expediting

- Following up deliveries from suppliers.
- Expediting late deliveries.

(e) Transport

- Assessing the need for and arranging transport.
- Review and control of transport invoices and costs.

(f) Materials handling and stores

- Receipt and inspection of supplies.
- Storage and issuing of raw materials parts and sub-assemblies.

At this point it should be apparent that purchasing could be defined in either a fairly narrow or broad context. Taken in a broad context, purchasing implies much more than the relatively simple buying procedure. It might also be considered whether the broad context known as materials management is broadly applicable to a wide variety of organizations. In practice, it probably is not. We could well see advantages in engineering or manufacturing businesses where there is often a very large quantity of expensive supplies contributing to a very significant proportion of the organization's sales. Improved control could reduce large amounts of capital tied up in stores, work in progress and finished goods. However, in organizations where supplies take up a relatively low proportion of sales value (e.g. in labour intensive activities) it is unlikely that a broad materials management concept would be applicable or advantageous.

9.4 SUPPLIER MANAGEMENT AND MONITORING

9.4.1 THE IMPORTANCE OF SUPPLIER RELATIONSHIPS

If we are to ensure that we obtain superior supplies at the lowest possible overall cost (i.e. not just the lowest possible purchase price) great care must be taken with supplier relationships. A typical policy might be to discard suppliers who do not perform. Another typical policy might be not to invite vulnerability by being tied to a single supplier. In Australia, for example, these attitudes have resulted in some manufacturing industries expressing preferences for supplies from overseas, with all the unfortunate consequences that has for the domestic economy. This situation is further exacerbated by the fact that Australian suppliers are not fully alert to the threat of possible extinction. A frequent response is the 'quick fix' to what is in fact a very difficult and complex problem. Single solutions such as automation, quality circles or robotics are frequently applied. Some companies focus on more correct objectives of value added management cost reduction and continuous quality improvement but then often lose their way by concentrating on activities which involve direct labour (which might only account for 5–10% of total sales) whilst almost completely neglecting purchased materials, which perhaps contribute to 50% of total sales.

It is clearly necessary to make a critical examination of supplier–customer relationships if competitiveness is to be systematically improved. However, it is also necessary to ask whether policy plans for supplier management can be developed with universal scope which are applicable to widely differing organizations. The supplier–customer relationship is one of the keys to success in achieving these aims. Suppliers should be seen as partners rather than an adversaries who must be 'beaten into submission'. The emphasis of this partnership must be on helping the supplier to improve in terms of cost, delivery quality and order cycle times. This emphasis must equally apply to the customer organization for the partnership to be meaningful. In fact, no customer organization should attempt to reform a supplier without putting its own house in order first. The image of a customer as dictator rather than practitioner will erode the credibility of a partnership very rapidly (Bhote, 1987).

9.4.2 SINGLE-SOURCE SUPPLIERS

Many buying organizations today are attempting to set up **single-source supply agreements**. That is they deliberately develop an arrangement whereby they only use one supplier and agree not to induce competition between suppliers. This encourages a close working relationship which can minimize the total cost of using a supplier as together they strive towards continuous improvement of supplied service or material. This clearly depends on a commitment to build a customer–supplier partnership based on trust. The Japanese have used this idea very effectively. In the West, results have been less spectacular and questions have even been asked about the legality of single-source agreements as they have been described as corrupt practice. Clearly, the mistrust which is common in Western supply agreements makes many managers feel very uncomfortable about the benefits of single sourcing and a great deal of work remains to be done if the benefits of this concept are to be fully reaped. However, it must be recognized that this is where partnership building will ultimately lead and that the journey will be in stages. Many organizations have already taken steps to reduce the number of suppliers and this has yielded significant benefits in supplier economies simply as a result of reducing the variation in what is built into products or services.

The 'Well-Being Test' shown in Fig. 9.1 is adapted from an idea by Bhote (1987) and shows an example of a way in which the overall well-being of an organization may be assessed. Each test element of an organization is considered and given a score. The resulting score indicates the 'health' of a supplier. In many cases, the results of applying this test indicate much greater effort is required in the establishment of customer–supplier partnerships.

9.4.3 CUSTOMER WORSHIP

Bhote (1987) goes on to consider the concept of not just customer satisfaction, but the 'worship' of customers. According to Bhote, if we ask the question 'What is the purpose of business?' the first answer that may come to hand is 'profit'. Many management writers are suggesting that the purpose of business is not profit but customer satisfaction which may run totally counter to the basic philosophy of traditional Western managers. Nevertheless, the Japanese practise these beliefs. Worship of the customer has taken the place of emperor worship. Engineering graduates are not put on the bench but sent first to the field to learn about customers. The needs of the customer are assiduously pursued through the latest Japanese discipline, **quality deployment**, which combines many techniques ranging from value engineering to market research. Even their final measure of success, market share, is a direct reflection of customer satisfaction. They say that if the customer is truly satisfied, profits will follow. In the West, management tends to be so obsessed by profits that the customer is not intensively served. This is true of customer and supplier companies alike.

9.4.4 SUPPLIER MONITORING

Although the above philosophy may seem intuitively reasonable, in practice it will always be necessary to have objective information on which to base conclusions about the success of supplier management. To provide this, suppliers will need to be monitored in some way – although if it is possible to foster the type of partnership described above, then it should also be possible to place the responsibility for monitoring supplier performance with the suppliers themselves.

In order to successfully monitor performance, it is clear that it will be necessary to carry out audits. These are usually of two types:

- product/service audits;
- system audits.

Test element	Not in exis– tence (1)	Basics only present (2)	Urgently needs upgrading (3)	OK (4)	Excellent (5)
A. Management of supplier–customer partnership: 1. Management commitment to partnership 2. Minimum number of suppliers 3. Attitude to sub–suppliers 4. Role of materials management					
B. Partnership in design: 1. Value analysis carried out 2. Cost agreement rather than imposition 3. Supplier involvement in product design 4. Technology and cost information exchange					
C. Supplier evaluation: 1. Customer evaluation of supplier by survey 2. Full 2nd and 3rd party supplier audits 3. Critical component control 4. Delivery/quality/service incentives and penalties					
D. Quality improvement programme: 1. Incoming product assessment 2. Supplier statistical process control (SPC) 3. Supplier employee involvement in continual improvement 4. Next operation as 'customer' 5. Use of quality function deployment (QFD)					
E. Inventory control: 1. Supplier lead time reduction 2. Supplied stock level reduction programme 3. Supplier and sub–supplier stock level reduction programme					

Total score assessment:

The following shows a way of rating the result:

00 – 24	Terminally ill
25 – 49	Intensive care
50 – 64	Hospitalized
65 – 84	Fit
85 – 100	Fit and healthy

Fig. 9.1 Supplier 'Well-Being Test'.

The objective of a **product/service audit** is to measure the effectiveness of product/service control whilst that of a system audit is to provide objective information about the effectiveness of the management system which is supposed to assure the quality of the supplier's manufacturing operation.

(a) Product/service audit

Product/service audits may consist of the following steps:

1. Evaluation of a relatively small sample of a product/service, upon which all operations, tests and inspections have taken place.
2. All characteristics which should have been previously assessed in some way are re-evaluated under customer-centred use conditions.
3. Additional tests (for example corrosion, reliability) that are not carried out in manufacture may also be performed.

These types of audits may be carried out in:

* facilities whose purpose is performing audits;
* at the end of a production line;
* in the case of sub-assemblies, in some assigned areas.

How often should exhaustive product audits be performed? Clearly it would not be sensible to conduct daily in-depth product audits on aero engines (less than one product may be made per day). The frequency of audits should in fact be matched to the production rate, as indicated in Table 9.1. If we turn our minds to service industries, a hospital, for example, may wish to audit the results of a routine surgical procedure on a weekly basis, or less frequently for, say, heart transplants.

A major international motor manufacturer may use a system called PAS (Product Assurance System). A product is given a score out of 1000, which is a measure of the number of defects in 1000 units of product. The corporate headquarters of the organization is able to compare the performance of various branches throughout the world when making purchasing decisions. Products are assessed from customer use perspectives and a defect may take the form of, for example, a paint blemish, a poorly fitting trim panel or an engine vibration. A full defect point is scored when a defect is detected which it is believed that 100% of customers would be

Table 9.1 Product audit frequency

	Daily	Weekly	Monthly
1. High production rate (e.g. TVs)	√		
2. Medium production rate (e.g. cars)		√	
3. Low production rate (e.g. aero engines)			√

conscious of. If, for example, a defect would only be noticed by 10% of customers, it is given a score of 0.1. Typical results might be as shown in Table 9.2.

The organization has a policy of not supplying cars at a level in excess of 600. However, this type of product audit information should not be utilized by customers in a way that simply eliminates inferior suppliers. A more positive approach would be to choose a level (say 250) where suppliers are identified who require special attention to nurture the purchase/supplier partnership.

(b) System audit

System audits vary a great deal. In their simplest form they could be used merely to assess the supplier's reputation. At best, use of reputation is vague, imprecise and unreliable. Reputations are not guarantees, and they also assure nothing. Nonetheless, they are used widely when organizations make purchasing decisions.

Using data from other buyers is a way of determining a supplier's previous performance. However, other buyers are often competitors and usually unwilling to divulge directly useful information. Moreover, if they are not purchasing the same supplies, the information is irrelevant. Agreements where several purchasing organizations provide information to a confidential data bank may be more useful. Lists of approved suppliers can then be created.

(c) Full quality audit

Full quality audits of suppliers evaluate the suppliers' ability to meet requirements. These vary from simple questionnaires to a visit from a team of specialists. These types of audits can be carried out on a first-, second- or third-party basis. First-party audits are when the suppliers are responsible for providing the information themselves. Second-party assessments take place when the supplier is assessed directly by the purchaser. This often leads to multiple assessments because many customers may wish to assess the same supplier. Third-party assessments are carried out by independent assessing bodies on their assessed supplier list. In

Table 9.2 Product assurance scores

The best European branch	130
A newly acquired specialist European branch	300
A smaller, more remote, branch in the southern hemisphere (!)	600–700

most Western countries, the trend is for large purchasing organizations (for example, government bodies and large companies) to demand that their suppliers have obtained accreditation to one of the independent third-party assessing bodies (for example, Lloyds). Supplier companies must be assessed against one of the international standards for quality systems (i.e. ISO 9000 series). These standards are widely implemented internationally and it has been postulated that for any company to compete in international markets (particularly Europe) it will be essential to obtain accreditation to an organization who uses one of these standards. We will take a further look at assuring the quality of suppliers using third-party accreditation in section 9.7 of this chapter.

In quality system audits, practically every aspect of a supplier's system will usually be assessed. Examples are:

- quality policies and practices (for example, is the supplier working to ISO 9000);
- facilities (for example, sufficient inspection and testing carried out);
- procedures (for example, corrective action procedure);
- personnel (for example, training programmes).

A survey should allow predictions of the ability of a particular supplier to provide the quality, price and delivery which the purchasing department requires. This is referred to as a second-party audit when carried out by the purchaser.

9.4.5 RATING OF SUPPLIERS

One of the problems with system audits is that they often concentrate on subjective aspects of the supplier's organization. Some purchasers feel that this type of information must be supplemented by more quantitative data. One way of achieving this is to give a supplier a rating. Consider the following example.

A purchasing department wishes to compare the performance of suppliers for quality, price, delivery and service. They use a base of 100% to establish ratings using a rating formula. Over a period of time, they have obtained the data shown in Table 9.3.

Table 9.3 Supplier rating data

Supplier	A % acceptable units	B Price*	C % units delivered on time	D % satisfactory service
Butler Engineering	97	97	97	98
Arnold Products	96	100	95	95
Fletchers Concepts	98	98.5	97	96

1. A standard of 100% is set for the cheapest supplier. The figures for more expensive suppliers are obtained by reducing the 100% standard by the percentage the price is higher.
2. The supplier rating $= 0.6A + 0.2B + 0.1C + 0.1D$ (or whatever weightings are deemed appropriate).

A rating can then be calculated for each supplier and expressed in the form of a table, of which an example is shown in Table 9.4. From this we can easily see who offers the best overall service as a supplier. However, care must be taken only to allow **supplier ratings** (also known as **vendor ratings**) to assist in making decisions – other information also needs to be taken into account. Supplier ratings vary in sophistication and application. However, the aim is usually to obtain a total picture of the supplier's ability to meet the requirements of the purchaser and in so doing to identify the lowest possible overall cost of using particular suppliers (that is not just the lowest purchase price). Much more sophisticated computerized versions are available than the simple example shown above.

9.4.6 SINGLE-SOURCE SUPPLIERS REVISITED

One way of improving well-being test (see Fig. 9.1) results is to move towards single-source suppliers. This does not make the test less relevant, but it then becomes a means of assessing the success of building a partnership.

In establishing a supplier–customer partnership, many organizations have tended to favour a policy of working with a few selected suppliers, rather than carrying out business on the open market. This is a clear trend in Japan and has given remarkable results in improving the quality and efficiency of the supply function. However, some organizations in the West have tended to resist this idea because they feel that limiting supply to one source may make them very vulnerable to the vagaries of that supplier. If the partnership is established on a sound basis this should not be a problem. There may, however, be ethical issues in this practice. Favouring particular suppliers may be seen as corrupt practice in certain quarters. This problem is a very strong example of the cultural issues which must be resolved before we can take advantage of much of the modern management practice outlined in this book.

Table 9.4 Supplier rating table

Supplier	Rating
Butler Engineering	97.1
Arnold Products	96.6
Fletchers Concepts	97.8

9.5 PURCHASING METHODS

Having located appropriate suppliers and established a relationship with them, it is then necessary to consider the way in which an order will be placed. This is a very important consideration because there are a very large number of opportunities for error in the mechanism between the decision to place an order and the supplies arriving on site. It must also ensure that inflexible, bureaucratic and time consuming procedures are not encouraged. It can be extremely frustrating for the operations department to decide that they must place an order and then be left waiting for the purchasing function to carry out its paperwork.

The following purchasing methods exist.

(a) Quota agreements

The customer reserves supplier production capacity. For example, assume over the last six months the customer has averaged 150 tonnes per month of a certain type of steel. Customer and supplier may then agree to establish a quota agreement whereby the the supplier reserves capacity of 150 tonnes per month for the next twelve months.

(b) Annual agreements

These are usually arranged where the customer orders quantities of standard products (i.e. not designed by the customer). Products may be of low value and required irregularly. Annual agreements are useful in minimizing the cost of placing an order. Delivery, payment, approximate annual quantities, prices, invoicing procedures, etc., are specified. The customer may obtain quotes from a number of suppliers for this type of agreement, choosing the most appropriate.

(c) Fixed period blanket order

These are designed to simplify administrative procedures. They are becoming increasingly popular because goods can be reordered over a period by specifying delivery requirements in separate delivery schedules. Specifications and descriptions are initially agreed but do not require repetition on delivery schedules, thus avoiding the need for separate contracts each time an order is placed.

(d) Continuous blanket order

This method is similar to the fixed period blanket order but reduces paperwork for supplier and customer. It is applicable to companies where continuous production will require the same supplies for the foreseeable future. It is particularly useful in the automotive industry but all requirements must be specified, including terms for the termination of the agreement. Single-source supply agreements are able to take maximum economic advantage of this purchasing method.

(e) Options

This allows the customer to buy not only what is specified in the order but also to extend the contract for further options. They are commonly used by airlines who may be buying a number of new aircraft but are unable to predict what market conditions will be like by the time the aircraft are deliverable due to extended lead times on delivery.

(f) Pricing formulae

This involves the inclusion of price variation clauses in supply contracts and can allow unforeseen changes in inflation or variations in raw material prices to be taken into account. These protect both customer and supplier.

Further details of purchasing methods can be found in Institute of Purchasing and Supply Management (1985).

9.6 ASSURING THE QUALITY OF PURCHASING

There are many factors which are likely to contribute to good quality in the purchasing function. Quality is a very important issue in purchasing because it has been shown that many manufacturers may well be in a situation where their quality problems are not simply the result of their own activities but can be traced back to faulty or inadequate bought-in material. For example, in the late 1970s a major European prestige car company was in great danger of going out of business, and quality was cited as one of the main reasons for its problems, particularly in the all-important US market. The management decided to categorize all faults customers found in their cars. The result was that the majority of problems were found to be caused not by what happened in the car plant, but were the result of poor quality purchased material. They were simply building other people's problems into their products. This demonstrates how purchasing quality can have a massive influence on the success of a manufacturing organization. Extra costs can appear in many ways, and the example above shows that whilst some costs are clearly visible (e.g. warranty costs), we must look much deeper for the fundamental reasons for extra cost. We can clearly see that many of these extra costs are directly related to deficient purchasing in some way or other. Avoiding and reacting to the obvious costs will probably not reach the fundamental causes.

Quality assurance, as it relates to purchasing, encompasses the following:

1. a satisfactory design of product, thoroughly proven by testing to establish its reliability under service conditions;
2. specification of requirements, which must be understood by everyone concerned with manufacturing the product;
3. confirmation that outside suppliers and in-company manufacturing processes are capable of meeting the specified requirements;
4. motivation of all those concerned with manufacturing the product inside and outside the company to achieve the standards set by the specification;
5. verification that products conform to specification;
6. accurate and reliable means of inspection;
7. feedback of inspection results and the user experience to prove that all the above stages are effective.

The above raises some interesting questions:

- How do we verify that the above seven requirements are met?
- Who will carry out the verification?
- Does this imply that we should only purchase from suppliers who operate total quality management?

Addressing the third question first, we should not confuse quality assurance (QA) with total quality management (TQM) which is introduced in Chapter 11 of this book. The essence of TQM is total involvement in continuous improvement. Whilst QA contains aspects of this, true TQM is a considerably more broad concept. For our purposes, we will concentrate on QA in relation to the purchasing function, where the emphasis is on prevention rather than improvement.

The answer to the first question is that some type of standard must be utilized. In recent times a number of international QA standards have evolved. The most prominent of these is the ISO 9001 series for Quality Systems (AS/NZS 9001: 1994).

The second question is answered by the concept of third-party certification. A purchasing department does not need to assess a particular supplier before they can be assured that that supplier is capable of providing the supplies they require. Many large purchasing organizations are now insisting that suppliers obtain certification of a third-party organization which will independently assess the supplier to one of the above standards. The supplier then becomes **quality endorsed** and appears on a list provided by the certifying organization. As a result, there is no need for a purchasing organization to carry out its own assessments, although it must be acknowledged that some do, using the above standard or some other standard of their own. (This is known as second-party certification and is widely used in the motor industry.) If an organization is involved in purchasing or selling, it is highly likely that they will meet these documents sooner rather than later. Therefore, as these are becoming a national (and international) standard, before a supplier can be considered for purchasing from, it is essential that we know something about them from the purchasing point of view. The twenty requirements of ISO 9001 are:

1. Policy and responsibility
2. Quality system
3. Contract review
4. Design control
5. Document control
6. Purchasing
7. Purchaser supplied product
8. Product identification and traceability
9. Process control
10. Inspection and testing
11. Inspection and test equipment
12. Inspection and test status
13. Control of non-conforming product
14. Corrective action
15. Handling, storage, packaging and delivery
16. Quality records
17. Internal quality audits
18. Training
19. Servicing
20. Statistical techniques.

The supplier must establish policies and procedures for each of the above requirements, which must be documented in a quality policy manual and procedure manuals. The aim is to ensure that defects are prevented and the activities of the supplier are carried out consistently every time an order is placed. The supplier can be audited by a third-party certifying body (e.g. Lloyds) and then appear on a list of registered suppliers, providing the supplier is found to meet each of the requirements adequately. In this way, the need for customers to audit each of their suppliers (on a second-party basis) is lessened.

The above gives some idea of what is required for a supplier to meet the requirements of one of the quality systems standards. However, it should also be understood that although these standards have been widely (and even enthusiastically) accepted, they have also been criticized for encouraging too much inspection and verification. There are also reservations about whether implementing the standards is really cost-effective. In general, the standards are considered to be a positive contribution to quality. However, it should be remembered that there is always a need for continuous improvement in quality management. Chapter 11 on total quality management will develop this theme further.

9.7 PURCHASING AND TOTAL QUALITY MANAGEMENT

As will have become apparent from previous sections, QA is critically important in purchasing activities. The ISO 9000 standards, which are rapidly becoming the world norm for QA in supplier organizations, prescribe a system whereby a supplier must establish an organizational structure and accountability/authority relationships which meet the requirements of the standard. This usually leads to a clearly defined mode of operation which is designed to minimize variation both in the purchasing procedures and the delivered products or services. However, this also means the QA approach may lead to a situation where goods and/or services are procured in a way which assures minimal variation but this level of quality may not provide the quality which totally satisfies the customer. Suppliers with flexible organizational structures and procedures may be able to offer improved goods or services which may offer a higher degree of satisfaction to the customer. However, if a highly prescriptive QA is operated by the customer's purchasing function, it will insist on rigid policies and procedures.

The key to making the very best possible purchasing decisions lies within a communication link established between the end user of the supplies and the supplier. However, communication on its own will do little to improve the situation. Decisions must also take place at that interface. The effect of regulated purchasing procedures, and to some extent QA, has been to remove decision-making from the end-user/supplier interface and as such has resulted in less than satisfactory purchasing decisions in many instances. In reality the situation is probably even worse because centralized QA system purchasing functions are encouraging control to be removed from the customer interface by giving authority and responsibility to a remote purchasing department to make purchasing decisions. Many such decisions are made with insufficient regard for the appropriateness of supplies and delivery with the result that operations departments are often struggling to complete their duties with barely adequate and untimely supplies. However, QA systems will assure the customer that this performance will remain consistent and that supplies are exactly as ordered. Problems arise when what is ordered is not what is required. A classic, rather tongue-in-cheek example could be that of a quality assured supplier who supplies concrete lifejackets. The customer can be assured that they will be in receipt of very high quality concrete lifejackets!

It should be realized that although this is a pessimistic view, it is possible for QA systems to be designed which will overcome these problems. The key to doing so is to ensure that QA is entwined with total quality management as explained in Chapter 11 of this book. This does, however, involve empowering people at the customer–supplier interface to take an active and, more importantly, controlling role in the procurement of supplies. Most importantly of all, these people must be able to initiate improvement which will be made with the customers' needs closest to heart. This will maximize value to the customer.

9.8 CONCLUSION

In this chapter we have studied the role of the purchasing function in managing the material inputs to a manufacturing organization. We have shown that purchasing raw material components could quite well amount to the largest single expenditure in many organizations and therefore concluded that we must make sure that the function is optimized to minimize cost and hence maximize profit. However, it is also essential that the customer is satisfied. It must be recognized not only that the customer is at the centre of purchasing activity but also that customer satisfaction can only result if a partnership is established and nurtured.

The need to assure quality in purchased product or service is paramount. Building other people's quality problems into one's own products or services can be very expensive indeed, and so international strategies have been developed aimed at alleviating this problem. There could well be benefits in developing current strategies in the context of total quality management approaches. An appropriate ending to this chapter is a quotation by A.W. Shaw in his 1915 work, reported by Bhote (1987):

> The relations between the activities of demand, creation and physical supply . . . illustrate the existence of the two principles of interdependence and balance. Failure to coordinate any of these activities . . . or to place undue emphasis or outlay upon any one of these activities is certain to upset the equilibrium of forces.

REFERENCES

Australian/New Zealand Standard AS/NZS 9001: 1994. *Quality Systems – Model for quality assurance in design/development, production, installation and servicing.* Standards Australia, Hombush, NSW 2140, Australia.

Bhote, K.R. (1987) *Supply Management – How to Make US Suppliers Competitive.* American Management Association, New York.

Institute of Purchasing and Supply Management (1985) *Purchasing and Supply Management for Australia.* Hargreen Publishing, North Melbourne.

Physical distribution 10

10.1 OVERVIEW

This chapter is not intended as a comprehensive study of physical distribution. However, to achieve an understanding of manufacturing systems management it is necessary to understand the important systems within the distribution function and how they relate to other systems within manufacturing. The aim of this chapter is to provide an overview of the elements of distribution so that the potential application of systems is identifiable. On completion of this chapter readers should be able to:

- understand the terms physical distribution and logistics;
- appreciate the major information technologies relevant to distribution;
- understand the concept of customer service;
- understand the major warehouse location factors;
- be able to apply the major ideas concerning warehouse systems, including storage systems;
- understand the impact of distribution centres on cost and service;
- appreciate the capabilities and limitations of the chief modes of transport;
- appreciate the nature of strategy in distribution.

10.2 CHAPTER STRUCTURE

This chapter is divided into the following sections:

- distribution and logistics;
- information technology and distribution;
- customer service and distribution;
- warehousing;
- transport;
- distribution strategy.

The first section on distribution and logistics essentially concerns definitions that have been employed in the past and how they have changed over time. This section is necessary because there is still confusion as to what these terms mean. Information technology (IT) has increasingly important applications to distribution, particularly in view of the linkages that can be fostered in the value chain, which is not only concerned with production but also extends to physical distribution. We thus provide a brief overview of the major IT applications in distribution. Customer service and distribution reviews the concept of customer service and some of the common practical problems encountered in industry. The section on warehousing reviews four key areas of importance and serves as a review of the terminology and current practices. The section on transport is a practical review of the chief modes of transport, their characteristics and limitations. The final section on distribution strategy reviews the key factors which need to be considered in developing a distribution strategy.

10.3 DISTRIBUTION AND LOGISTICS

Physical distribution management was defined by the Australian Physical Distribution Management Association as:

> Generally considered to be the flow of products from the production plant to the user. It describes the wide range of activities needed for the efficient movement of materials, components and finished articles from production to consumer. The key elements of a physical distribution system are transportation, warehousing, inventory control, materials handling, packaging and order processing. Economies generated by a unified, integrated PD system increase corporate profits.

A similar concept was adopted by the National Council of Physical Distribution Management in the United States until the late 1970s when the definition was revised to include movement of raw materials, components and sub-assemblies from the source of supply into the manufacturing facility:

> Physical distribution management is the term describing the integration of two or more activities for the purpose of planning, implementing and controlling the efficient flow of raw materials, in-process inventory and finished goods from point of origin to point of consumption. These activities may include, but are not limited to, customer service, demand forecasting, distribution communications, inventory control, materials handling, order processing, parts and service support, plant and warehouse site selection, procurement, packaging, return goods handling, salvage and scrap disposal, traffic and transportation and warehousing and storage.

In the mid-1980s, both professional associations changed their names: the Australian Physical Distribution Management Association became the Logistics Management Association of Australia and the National Council of Physical Distribution Management changed its name to the Council of Logistics Management. Both adopted the following definition of **logistics management**:

> Logistics management is the process of planning, implementing and controlling the efficient, cost-effective flow and storage of raw materials, in-process inventory and finished goods, and the related information from point of origin to point of consumption for the purpose of providing cost-effective customer service.

The logistics concept is based on a total systems view of the materials and goods flow activity from the source of supply through to the final point of consumption. It recognizes the interconnections and inter-relationships between the multitude of functions involved in this movement from source to user and in so doing forces management to think in terms of managing the total system rather than just one part of it.

The logistics management task is concerned with the integration and coordination of these activities in such a way that end markets are served in the most cost-effective manner.

Since the task of managing the flow of material inputs to the organization (purchasing) was covered in Chapter 9 this chapter will be restricted to physical distribution.

10.4 INFORMATION TECHNOLOGY AND DISTRIBUTION

For any sizeable business, **information technology** (IT) is potentially important because it can create powerful information links between different parts of the organization. In distribution the most important links are between transport, warehousing, sales, marketing, supplier and customer. It is sometimes helpful to regard these links as **information channels** and the resulting network as a **delivery control system**.

The eight major IT applications in distribution are:

- **Sales order processing**, where orders for goods are relayed from the sales office to the distribution department for dispatch. Some of the more common methods of order capture include:
  - telesales;
  - customer phone calls;
  - postal orders;
  - representatives taking orders;
  - van sales;

  - dedicated computer-to-computer link;
  - stock replenishment using electronic point-of-sale;
  - direct on-line viewdata.
- **Dispatch goods invoicing**, where information on goods delivered to customers is relayed to the accounts department for invoices to be prepared and sent to customers.
- **Stock control**, where demand for stocked products is monitored and new stock ordered in line with forecast demand. The systems used here vary considerably in sophistication and function and include:
  - stock file only;
  - stock file linked to order processing;
  - picking sheets;
  - portable data entry terminals;
  - bar coding to record inter-depot stock movements.
- **Stock location**, where particular product lines are allocated to defined locations within the warehouse. Random stock location systems are also used.
- **Depot location**, where the optimum location of depots are determined according to the volumes and destinations of goods dispatched to customers (and possibly the volumes and origins of goods from suppliers).
- **Fleet management**, where the fleet vehicles are monitored according to maintenance (e.g. frequency of component repair) and administrative needs (e.g. reminder of payment date for vehicle taxation).
- **Vehicle scheduling and routeing**, where vehicles are assigned delivery work and routes are designed for the vehicles to follow.
- **Tachograph analysis**, where tachograph discs are analysed to give management information on, for example, vehicle speeds and the time of deliveries.

10.5 CUSTOMER SERVICE AND DISTRIBUTION

Customer service problems in industry are seldom what they superficially seem to be. They are almost invariably symptoms of deeper more basic problems in a company's logistical coordination. The key to effective customer service policies lies in the extent to which the total logistical activities of a company – from raw material and plant location decisions through to delivery modes and credit policy – are brought together and viewed as an interrelated system.

Many companies have no clearly defined policy toward customer service. Indeed, in many cases, customer service is only narrowly perceived in a technical or after-sales sense. The wider view of customer service, adopted by a handful of innovative companies, brings together all the points of contact with the customer in terms of delivery frequency and lead time, back-up inventory, responsiveness to complaints, technical service and a host of other aspects. Obviously creating an integrated and cohesive service involving all these elements is a task requiring careful analysis and planning.

A systems approach to physical distribution management must operate in a continual interrelationship with customer service. It makes no sense to minimize total distribution costs if at the same time customer relations are being eroded. On the other hand, customer service levels can be excessive and wasteful of resources. For example, it is not uncommon to find firms with a central warehouse in Sydney and depots with additional stocks in cities as close as Newcastle and Wollongong. Given that same day delivery and next day delivery is available to these areas, the need for stock in these locations is questionable. The difficult task is to find the balance between these extremes.

This task is made even more difficult because there is no clear definition of customer service. The concept of customer service often means different things to different industries – and even to different companies within the same industry. It can mean:

- the elapsed time between the receipt of an order at the supplier's warehouse and the shipment of the order from the warehouse;
- the minimum size of an order, or the limits of the assortment of items in an order which a supplier will accept from the customer;
- the percentage of items in a supplier's warehouse which are out of stock at any given time;
- the proportion of customer orders filled accurately;
- the percentage of customers, or volume of customer orders, which are served (whose orders are delivered) within a certain time period from the receipt at the supplier's warehouse;
- the percentage of customer orders which can be filled completely upon receipt at the supplier's warehouse;
- the proportion of goods which arrive at a customer's place of business in saleable condition;
- the elapsed time between the placement of an order by a customer and the delivery of goods ordered to the customer's place of business;
- the ease and flexibility with which a customer can place an order;
- availability of stock;
- order cycle time;
- frequency of delivery;
- on-schedule delivery;
- reliability of delivery.

Distributors often sell their services on the basis of a customer service promise that includes, say, '95% of all orders delivered from stock'. Also, contracts are often negotiated on the basis of stock availability measures, with a given percentage of orders or items to be met from stock. Penalty clauses may be introduced whereby a failure to reach or maintain a given level of service will result in the distributor being effectively fined for poor performance.

Order cycle time is the elapsed time between a customer conveying a need and that need being satisfied. It is wrong to regard order cycle time simply in terms of the time interval over which the supplying company chooses to exercise direct control. A mail-order warehouse, for example, may claim to be offering a 24-hour service if it dispatches goods the day after receiving the order for those goods. However, the customer would almost certainly see the order cycle time as being longer than 24 hours.

It follows that order cycle time should be defined as the sum of three time intervals, which are:

- the inbound order communication;
- the order processing as well as the preparation and dispatch of goods;
- the outbound transportation of the goods.

While the timing of deliveries is important to many retail customers, the frequency of delivery can also be a key consideration in customer service. Many retail outlets now have little or no stockroom capacity and large consignments cannot, therefore, be readily accommodated. Smaller, more frequent, consignments are more usual.

As distribution has become increasingly retailer-driven, meeting the delivery requirements of retailers has become of paramount importance. In particular, on-schedule delivery is now an integral part of many distribution operations serving the retail sector.

In order to avoid queues and in an effort to smooth their workload, many grocery retailers have instituted delivery control systems. These require that deliveries are made at specific times determined by the retailers. All deliveries must be booked in. Any vehicle that arrives without a predetermined delivery time, or any vehicle that is late may well be refused access to the unloading bay. Meeting the exact delivery requirements of a customer is therefore an important facet of customer service.

Regular delivery not only satisfies customer service requirements, but it can benefit the distributor, since distribution planning becomes relatively simple. In particular, there is scope for grouping calls on a geographical basis with all deliveries to a particular area being made on a specified day. The simplicity of the arrangement has a certain appeal for the distributor and will help reduce some costs. Vehicle routeing and scheduling, for example, will be less complex and therefore less costly.

10.6 WAREHOUSING

In this section we consider four issues related to the warehousing function, namely:

- location factors;
- warehouse systems;
- storage systems for unit loads;
- mechanical handling.

10.6.1 LOCATION FACTORS

There are many factors which will affect the choice of a location for a warehouse. Some of these factors are broad in their effect; that is to say their consideration will indicate only a general area in which a site should be found. Other factors are detailed; they will point to specific sites. In addition, many of the factors are closely related to the purpose for which the warehouse will be used. This is an area which often deserves close scrutiny in the light of possible alternatives. Some of the most important factors are detailed below.

(a) Market orientation

It is sensible to locate warehouses close to customers in order to provide a good service to those customers. There are often sound economic reasons as well. Customer orders are frequently smaller than a lorry load and are delivered in smaller vehicles which are often more expensive per tonne-kilometre to operate than trunk vehicles. It pays, then, to minimize the workload of those small vehicles by bringing the warehouse closer to the customers.

(b) Production orientation

A warehouse with this type of orientation usually ships in bulk, i.e. in lorry or container loads, to retailers, wholesalers or break bulk depots as well as to their own distribution depots. This type of warehouse should be located as close to the end of the production line as possible to minimize the cost movement between the two points.

(c) The nature of the product

The type of products being handled will have a profound effect on the number of warehouses required. If the product is, for example, perishable, then it is important to deliver to the customers as quickly as possible, perhaps within a day. Warehouses facing that sort of delivery constraint will need to be small and many in number. Warehouses serving as common stockrooms for several high street shops are also of this kind. By contrast, warehouses handling consumer durables, where a fast delivery service is unnecessary, can be larger and fewer in number.

(d) Communications

Present and planned road and rail networks can have a strong locational influence on the warehouse. In particular the speed with which goods can be delivered in bulk will have a direct bearing on stockholding. This factor may be critical in just-in-time operations.

(e) Financial considerations

Development incentives or rate 'holidays' can also influence where a warehouse is sited. However, this type of incentive may only influence the choice of site in a quite localized way.

(f) The type of warehouse

In many cases it may be possible to operate the distribution system using either conventional warehouses or highly automated warehouses. The latter are very expensive which means there must be fewer of them.

(g) Local considerations

The above six points will influence companies in their choice of area when looking for a suitable site. There are, of course, many other factors which will determine the choice of the actual site to be used. These include:

- availability of buildings;
- local site values and the attitude of local government towards building development and use;
- labour availability;
- ease of access and traffic congestion;
- expense of building including drainage, access to power supplies, etc.;
- ancillary services including the availability of facilities for vehicle repair or the repair of specialized equipment;
- local communications, e.g. travel facilities for employees.

10.6.2 WAREHOUSE SYSTEMS

When considering efficiency, it is worth noting that warehousing makes use of considerable resources in terms of people and building space. In a conventional warehouse, for example, the cost of direct labour can be up to 35–40% of the total warehouse costs, and half of the direct labour costs can be associated with order picking. Building and building services, expressed on an annual basis, can account for a further 40% of the total costs. Consequently, anything which enables better use to be made of people's time, or allows building space to be used more effectively, can have a beneficial and significant effect on warehouse efficiency.

(a) Order processing

Order processing is often combined with stock control and location systems. Computer systems, handling large amounts of data with speed and accuracy, give a reduction in lead times over manual systems and provide better control over stock levels. They also provide an early warning of low stocks, replenishment requirements and abnormal demands. From a strategic point of view it is possible to identify patterns and trends in ordering and sales.

(b) Stock control and stock location

There are numerous stock control packages, which record receipts and issues, calculate stock balances and display stock reorder warnings. For warehousing, however, it is often useful to have stock control combined with stock location. Apart from maintaining accurate stock balances and location records, such systems can also lead to:

- much tighter warehouse control;
- better use of warehouse space through immediacy of information;
- savings in clerical effort and removal of duplicated tasks;
- shelf lives not being exceeded and stock being used in correct sequences;
- tracing faulty batches of material;
- reduction in stock replenishment travel distances by locating reserve stock close to picking faces, while maintaining the high space utilization of a random location system.

It should be noted that stock location checks are often incorporated into location systems (manual or computer). To ensure that a forklift truck driver has gone to the correct location to put a pallet into stock, he records a random check code which is printed on to the location, and this code is correlated by the computer (or manually) to the location code in the data files, and if the two match, the correct location has been used.

(c) Order picking

Product line items on orders are often listed in catalogue sequence, resulting in fast and slow movers being grouped together, but this is not the most efficient sequence for picking. There are systems to sort orders into any chosen sequence, normally by location code, to minimize travel time and to check for zero or previously allocated stock to save the picker visiting locations where no stock is available. Furthermore, systems can be designed for different picking methods, such as batch or zone picking or other applications.

An interesting variant of the conventional picking list, which minimizes the clerical effort required of the picker, is for the picking list to be printed, in correct picking sequence, on sticky labels. As the picker selects each item from stock, the appropriate label is stuck to it and the picker then moves on to the next item, and so on. When all labels are finished, the pick is complete, and any unused labels give automatic indication of shortages, that is items not picked.

Even with computerized order processing packages, it is still common for the order picker to require a paper picking list. However, over the last few years, there have been developments towards 'paperless' picking. Systems include:

- truck mounted terminals (on-line);
- portable data entry terminals;
- picking by lights;
- automatic systems.

(d) Unit loads

There are interesting computer packages available for optimizing the use and utilization of unit loads. The two examples below illustrate this.

- **Pallet stacking patterns**. This type of computer package determines the near optimal number of a given size of package that can be fitted into a pallet of given plan and height dimensions. It also applies weight constraints if this is appropriate.
- **Pallet control**. Pallet control can now be put on to a computer package designed to control the return of pallets from delivery points, keep pallet stocks to a minimum and reduce pallet losses. Clearly such a system can be applied to any unit load – wooden pallets, roll cage pallets, beer kegs and so on.

10.6.3 STORAGE SYSTEMS FOR UNIT LOADS

Unit load storage systems may be categorized as either **selective** (where all loads are directly accessible from the aisles) or **non-selective** (where access is limited to a proportion of the loads in order to achieve better space utilization). Selective systems are used where there is a wide variety of product lines but very few pallets of each line item. Conversely, non-selective systems are most suitable where there is a limited range of product lines and a large number of unit loads or pallets per line. In practice, the choice of system is often a compromise between selectivity and space utilization efficiency. A range of unit load storage systems are commonly used:

- Block stacking:
  - minimal equipment cost;
  - poor selectivity and space utilization;
  - labour intensive.
- Selective racking:
  - relatively inexpensive;
  - 100% selectivity;
  - reasonable space utilization.
- Double-deep racking:
  - special truck required;
  - 50% selectivity;
  - good space utilization.
- Drive-in/drive-through racking:
  - high space utilization;
  - poor selectivity;
  - moderately expensive.
- Cantilever racking:
  - ideal for long loads;
  - good selectivity;
  - may need special truck.
- High-bay turret truck:
  - high equipment costs;
  - 100% selectivity;
  - lift heights to 12 m.
- High-bay stacker crane:
  - very high equipment costs;
  - 100% selectivity;
  - lift heights to 24 m or more.
- Pallet live storage:
  - high racking costs;
  - high space utilization;
  - ideal for stock rotation.
- Mobile pallet racking:
  - very high racking costs;
  - moderate selectivity;
  - good space utilization.
- Remote entry module (REM):
  - very high equipment costs;

– poor selectivity;
– high space utilization.

10.6.4 SMALL PARTS STORAGE

The storage of small parts is more usually a requirement of warehouses in the manufacturing and service industries (for example, motor vehicle spare parts) rather than in wholesale distribution centres. In the latter case, the storage systems are generally geared to handle goods in carton or pallet lots, or small items may be order picked from opened cartons (or 'split cases'). Some examples of storage systems for small parts are:

- standard steel shelving;
- tote boxes clipped on to louvred backing plate;
- horizontal carousel;
- vertical carousel.

10.6.5 MECHANICAL HANDLING

(a) Trucks

Today there is a wide variety of industrial trucks available for warehousing and distribution-related materials handling activities. They include pallet trucks, tow tractors, counterbalanced forklift trucks, reach trucks, turret trucks, order-picking trucks and combined forklift order pickers – to name just a few. Many of the simpler and low capacity machines are available in pedestrian as well as rider-operated versions. Pedestrian-operated machines are relatively inexpensive and simple to operate. Rider-operated forklift trucks (and their derivatives) generally require operators to be trained and licensed by the appropriate authority. In smaller organizations, therefore, the pedestrian-operated machines are often preferred because of their low cost and flexibility of operation.

Perhaps the most significant development in unit load handling during the last twenty or more years has been the development of **automatic guided vehicles (AGVs)**. During the last five years advances in the design and application of AGVs have accelerated with the availability of relatively low-cost microprocessors and customized electronic chips. Initially AGVs were used for simple horizontal transportation tasks and this is still the dominant application today. Today machines are also available which can perform a variety of tasks, including, for example, duplicating the lifting and positioning capabilities of forklift trucks.

(b) Conveyors

Conveyors have been used in the manufacturing industry for the last 80 or more years. Probably the major thrust for conveyor development and application has come from the motor vehicle and other mass production industries. The application of conveyors to warehousing tasks has mainly occurred during the last 20 years. Conveyors are ideally suited to the high throughput of palletized and carton stock associated with modern distribution centres. Advances in conveyor design and, more recently, the application of PLCs (programmable logic controllers) and microprocessors to conveyor systems has widened the scope of applications.

Powered pallet conveyors are mainly used in conjunction with high-density storage installations for the transport of palletized goods to and from the system. The input conveyor typically incorporates stations which automatically check the load weight and dimensions and reject those out of tolerance. Bar code scanners may be used on the output conveyors to automatically monitor stock movement and update computerized stock records. As previously stated, AGVs rather than pallet conveyors are frequently used in overseas installations for the movement of palletized goods from receiving docks as AS/RS (automatic storage/retrieval systems) and from the AS/RS to order-picking zones or dispatch.

The principal applications for conveyors in warehouses and distribution centres are in the transportation, accumulation, merging, sorting and storage of cartons and tote boxes. Various types of conveyors may be used, including gravity roller and wheel, belt, powered roller and wheel, and accumulation conveyors. The choice of conveyor is largely governed by the function to be performed, constraints on cost and installation, and the dimensions, weight, orientation, stability and fragility of the objects to be carried. If a diverse range of items are to be conveyed, it is necessary to determine the maximum and minimum size and weights of the units and identify any special handling requirements.

(c) Cranes and hoists

In general, cranes and hoists are predominantly used in manufacturing and construction environments rather than in warehousing and distribution-related activities where unit load handling by forklift trucks, and their derivatives, is dominant. Nonetheless, there are many applications where cranes and hoists are used in distribution activities, such as the handling associated with the storage and transport of timber, steel and non-ferrous plate and sheet, pipes, construction materials and, of course, the handling of large freight containers. In a number of these applications, specialized industrial trucks are being used as an alternative to cranes.

(d) Robots

Robots are essentially programmable single-arm machines with servo-mechanisms at each joint, enabling an operating head to perform tasks in various planes. The reprogrammable feature of a robot distinguishes it from special-purpose automatic handling or manipulating machines.

Today increasing attention is being focused on the application of robots to warehousing-related activities, such as palletizing and order picking. There are probably two main reasons for this trend: first, to handle loads which are heavier than the regulatory and union-imposed weight limits on manual lifting of materials; and second, to avoid potential injuries to personnel in lifting operations and the consequential heavy cost to the employees and employers.

Many warehousing tasks, although seemingly simple, are in fact highly variable and complex for robotic application. For example, the task of palletizing cartons of varying size arriving in random sequence would require a robot with some form of vision and considerable 'intelligence'. On the other hand, some current robots are capable of dealing with a limited range of packages and can palletize them efficiently, providing, of course, the machine has been programmed with information for that batch of packages. The complexity of these operations, coupled with the current high cost and relatively slow operating speed of robots, will tend to inhibit their wide use for such applications for the next five or more years.

10.7 TRANSPORT

Transport costs for many companies form a large part of total distribution costs and the effective management of the transport function can lead to enhanced profitability both through cost reduction and service improvements. One of the key questions facing transport managers is what modes of transport are available and how should the choice be made? Each transport mode has its own specific characteristics in terms of cost, flexibility, speed and so on, and the transport decision must be based upon a careful assessment of relative costs and benefits. The chief modes of transport are:

- road;
- rail;
- water;
- pipeline;
- air.

(a) Road

The chief reason for the predominance of road transport is its flexibility – the sort of flexibility not normally available by rail, for example. The shipper has the ability to schedule shipments from where he has the goods to where he wants them at the time he wants them. In comparison

to rail, motor carriers have relatively small investments in terminal facilities and in general operate on public roads. The variable cost per
kilometre is high for motor carriers because a separate power unit is
required for each trailer or combination of trailers. Labour requirements
are high because of the need for substantial dock labour. The net result is
a structure of low fixed costs and high variable costs. In comparison to
railways motor carriers are economically adapted to handle small shipments moving short distances.

(b) Rail

The capability of railways to transport very large tonnages efficiently over
long distances is the main reason they continue to command significant
inter-city tonnage and revenue. Railway operations experience high fixed
costs because of expensive equipment, right-of-way, switching yards and
terminals. This fixed capacity, coupled with the nature of rail power,
results in a relatively low variable operating cost. The replacement of
steam by diesel power reduced the railway's variable cost per tonne-mile,
and electrification offers a potential for even greater reductions. A minimal use of power, combined with limited labour, allows a large volume of
traffic to be transported considerable distances at low variable cost per
tonne-mile.

(c) Air

The newest, most attractive and by far the least utilized mode of transport
is air freight. The attraction of air freight lies in the speed with which a
shipment can be transported. A coast-to-coast shipment via air may require only a few hours, in contrast to days via other modes of transport.
The tradeoff of speed for cost associated with other elements in the
logistical system, such as field warehousing, has attracted considerable
attention to the potential of air freight.

Air transport still remains more of a potential than a reality. Air transport capability is limited by lift capacity and availability of aircraft. Traditionally, most inter-city air freight has been transported on scheduled
passenger flights. While this practice was economically justified, it caused
a subsequent reduction in both capacity and flexibility of freight
operations.

No particular commodity dominates the traffic carried by air freight
operations. Perhaps the best distinction is that most freight handled is on
an emergency, rather than a routine, basis. Most firms utilize scheduled or
non-scheduled air cargo movements when the situation justifies the high
cost. Products with the greatest potential for regular air movement are
those having high value or extreme perishability.

(d) Water

The main advantage of water transport is the capacity to move extremely large shipments. Deep-water vessels are restricted in operation. In contrast, diesel-towed barges have considerable flexibility. Water transport ranks between rail and motor carrier with respect to fixed cost. The fixed cost of operations is greater than that of motor carriers but less than that of railways. The main disadvantage of water is the limited degree of flexibility and the low speeds of transport. Unless the source and destination of the movement are adjacent to a waterway, supplemental haul by rail or truck is required. The capability of water to transport large tonnage at low variable cost places this mode of transport in demand when low freight rates are desired and speed of transit is a secondary consideration.

10.8 DISTRIBUTION STRATEGY

Until recently few firms conceived of such a thing as a physical distribution strategy. Of course the marketing and selling aspects of distribution strategy have long been a part of business life, but the fusion of marketing thinking and physical distribution thinking rarely occurred. The physical distribution concept and, later, the logistics concept confined their strategic approach to including customer requirements and then putting into effect a network designed to meet those requirements. The other important aspects of strategy which are outlined below were only included in the strategic process by way of the experience of the managers involved. Today, the advanced companies have fused marketing and logistics thinking to achieve well thought-out strategies capable of enhancing both short-term and longer-term business performance.

The primary factors which influence distribution strategy are:

- product characteristics;
- market segment characteristics;
- buying behaviour of intermediaries;
- buying behaviour of end users;
- distribution costs.

Product characteristics will be familiar to those working in distribution. They include the value of the product and its margin, the weight to value ratio, whether the product is a stock item or made to order, the need for after-sales service, and the quantity and complexity of information exchanged between buyer and seller.

Market segment characteristics include the level of demand, the concentration of buyers, buyer purchasing power, the number of applications the product is designed for and service characteristics.

Buyer behaviour includes whether buying is centralized or decentralized, the frequency of ordering and order characteristics, and the level of uncertainty in demand.

Distribution costs include freight, inventory, warehouse operations, and transaction and communication costs.

The physical distribution strategy is essentially concerned with the design and management of a network, including the concept of channels, which deliver products and associated services from the manufacturing facility to the end users via intermediaries. The aim is to determine the most cost-effective network to deliver those products and services.

10.9 CONCLUSION

Physical distribution of product is an essential (but often neglected) part of the value chain in many manufacturing organizations. As such, the distribution system of an organization can be as critical to its competitive survival as its manufacturing system. Close integration of manufacturing and distribution systems are essential if value which is potentially added at the manufacturing stage is not to be subsequently lost by failures in the distribution system. Materials flow considerations need to be extended beyond the final work centre (often conventionally regarded as the packaging and finishing section) to the channels by which the customer receives the product. This requires attention not only to the details of the distribution system, but to its relationship within the wider context of the supplier/customer network as a whole. In this chapter, we have essentially fleshed out the details of what needs to happen at the interfaces between two manufacturing organizations in terms of management of the physical flow of materials.

FURTHER READING

Bowersox, D.J., Closs, D.J. and Helferich, O.K. (1986) *Logistical Management.* Macmillan, New York.

Christopher, M. (1990) *The Strategy of Distribution Management.* Heinemann Professional, Oxford.

Cooper, J. (ed.) (1988) *Logistics and Distribution Planning.* Kogan Page, London.

Gilmour, P. (ed.) (1987) *Logistics Management in Australia.* Longman Cheshire P/L, Melbourne.

PART FOUR
Global Issues

Total quality management – tools and techniques

11

11.1 OVERVIEW

We have now completed our examination of the individual manufacturing management functions, and turn our attention back to a number of very important issues and concepts which are all-pervasive and have a profound impact on manufacturing management as a whole. In this chapter we look at the subject of **total quality management**. Total quality management (TQM) ideas – which we have already briefly introduced in Chapter 2 – had their origins in Japan. The West has attempted to implement many of these ideas in response to the economic dominance of Japan in the modern trading community, and TQM has now been widely accepted and implemented in the West. However, if we look around, we can see that there are many different versions which have been implemented with varying degrees of success. TQM in some companies has amounted to no more than 'cheer-leading' apparently in the hope that some mystical reaction will take place among employees which will result in the complete elimination of defective products and services and the evolution of never ending improvement in everything the company does. In other cases, more perceptive managements have realized the enormousness of the task of implementing successful TQM.

In general, Western companies have evolved from a tradition of an autocratic management style which dates back to the ideas of Frederick Taylor, the inventor of **scientific management**. Taylor's ideas were widely adopted in American and European manufacturing industry and have resulted in much of the organizational strategy we have in industry today. Taylor believed that there was only one best method of work, which should be defined by experts. In this way planning and problem-solving were completely separate from doing. Operators were expected to do as instructed and it was believed that no improvements to work practice were possible because experts had optimized the work strategy.

TQM can be considered to be diametrically opposed to this view. If we consider the totality aspects of TQM, we are really implying that it is applicable to the total organization. In other words, all employees are not just involved in quality control, but also in the never ending search for improvement. This also means that vertical functional barriers between departments and narrowly skilled workforces are replaced by a team structure which attempts to foster a spirit of cooperation across the very functional barriers which were a feature of scientific management. TQM is creating a trend which is encouraging workforces to become multi-skilled and hence much more flexible. For example, a welder might be happy to do much more than weld. In a TQM environment, a welder would be part of a team and could drive a forklift, operate a crane, carry out maintenance, check company accounts and deal with customers. Far from Taylor's ideas that operators (and others) should simply be passive recipients of instructions on how a job should be performed, they are now encouraged to actively participate in improving their work methods. Improvement in this way is probably why Japan has transformed its manufacturing economy from a situation where it was infamous for producing cheap, often poorly copied goods, to the point where it is now renowned for offering some of the best manufactured products in the world. Clearly, there has been a massive rate of improvement which has outstripped Western manufacturing companies. J.M. Juran, one of the world's leading quality management specialists, warned that the Japanese were heading for world quality leadership and would attain it in the next two decades because no one else was moving there at the same pace. The date was June 1966 at the Conference of the European Organization or Quality Control in Stockholm.

Juran often illustrates how the Japanese have overtaken the West using the graph in Fig. 11.1. In the 1950s, Japan's manufactured products had a very inferior reputation compared to those from the West. The graph shows that both the West and Japan have improved from that time. For example, if we compare cars, Japanese vehicles of 1950 had a very poor reputation in comparison with Western cars. Since that time, both have improved. However, the Japanese have improved at a much faster rate, to the point where Juran suggests that they actually overtook the West in the 1970s. For the West to catch up, it can be seen that they will have to improve at an even faster rate than Japan. To do this, it is clear that the West will need to follow the path of continuous improvement and move away from the idea that no improvements to the best method are necessary.

Success in the implementation of TQM in the West has at best been patchy and many explanations have been put forward for this result. For example, the unique Japanese culture has been cited as a reason for their workforces readily accepting the need to work in teams and become

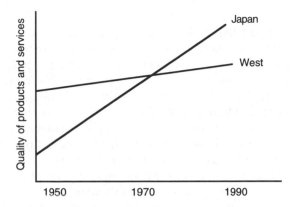

Fig. 11.1 Rates of quality improvement.

involved in continuous improvement. However, there are many counter-arguments to this belief. For example, Japanese management has been successful in turning around quite a few struggling Western manufacturing companies. TQM may have been less successful so far in the West than it could have been because of the way it has been promoted. We have heard a great deal of what TQM can achieve but comparatively little of how this can be achieved. There has been a lack of coordinated TQM education and training, where the emphasis has been on the organization, its culture, and use of tools and techniques. Many organizations have tended to neglect or ignore the massive overhaul in management style and the flatter organizational structure which has been a characteristic of successful Western TQM. This cannot be achieved without radical and difficult changes in organizational culture.

Whilst it would be impossible to take an in-depth view of TQM in this chapter, the TQM philosophy and the way in which a company could be organized to take advantage of it will be described. A coherent set of tools and techniques which are commonly used in the continuing search for improvement are then presented and their usage explained.

11.2 CHAPTER STRUCTURE

This chapter is structured in sections as follows:

- total quality Management – the 'continual improvement way';
- the seven statistical tools (the basic 7);
- the new seven tools;
- case study.

Previous chapters have stressed the need to be competitive in the modern world manufacturing community. We have realized that a competitive advantage means meeting customer requirements by offering value and not necessarily the lowest initial cost. In Chapter 3 on the 'dynamics of materials flow' and Chapter 4 on tactical planning, we studied a number of strategies which we should use to the best of our abilities to meet our customers' requirements by managing value-adding activities in such a way that the organization remains profitable. In Chapter 8 on purchasing, we examined the potential for a competitive advantage by use of an effective purchasing strategy and should have noted that much of the potential advantage was related to sound quality management. Chapter 9 on distribution showed how optimization of distribution networks can also have a major influence on competitive position.

All these activities are linked by an underlying philosophy which espouses a refusal to accept that any particular solution cannot be improved upon. Total quality management is a philosophy which can help us achieve this. The tools and techniques provided in this chapter give some insight into how this philosphy might be put to good practical use in improving the solutions studied so far in this book.

11.3 TOTAL QUALITY MANAGEMENT – THE 'CONTINUAL IMPROVEMENT WAY'

11.3.1 THE KAIZEN CONCEPT

In his text 'Kaizen – The Key to Japan's Competitive Success, Imai (1986) develops a number of key concepts.

- Continual improvement, in essence, means never accepting that there is not an improvement which can be made. Improvement takes place in small incremental steps which involve a never ending climb. A further important factor is that the improvements involve the efforts of the whole workforce and not just a group of 'experts'.
- Imai talks of a concept of 'maintenance'. This means maintaining the system as it is (i.e. without looking for improvement or allowing it to deteriorate).
- Imai also talks of 'innovation'. This refers to 'big step' improvements, in contrast to the small steps outlined in 'continual improvement' (which Imai terms **kaizen**).

The West is often seen as being 'innovative' (i.e. prepared for a big one-off investment, rather than slow continuous improvement). This was recently illustrated very strongly by comparing a major Western motor manufacturer with a similar Japanese manufacturer operating a plant in the same Western country. The Western manufacturer spent £1.9 billion on a highly 'innovative' new plant. During the same period, the Japanese spent £2 billion on slowly, but continuously, improving their existing plant. The result was that both had an excellent plant capable of producing very high quality products. The only difference was that the Japanese operated plant had twice the capacity.

Continuous improvement clearly cannot be achieved without the total involvement of the workforce. One mechanism Imai describes for achieving this is the **quality circle**. A quality circle involves a group of workers who voluntarily meet to discuss and improve their own work-related problems. There are often problems in attempting to change Western work cultures to accept this type of activity. The reasons for this should be considered.

A view which might be expressed on this point alludes to Taylorism. Taylor really thought that there are only two main motivational forces which are likely to stimulate a response in a worker: fear and greed. Fear is used to make a worker believe that they will probably not remain in employment if they do not meet the required performance level. Greed is used to encourage workers to perform to the required level by offering cash incentives. However, it should be clear that continual improvement cannot be successful without the 'moral' involvement of employees. This entails employees working together as a cohesive unit and becoming morally responsible for the quality of their products and the smooth, efficient running of 'their' manufacturing unit. Motivation for this type of moral involvement cannot come from Taylorist philosophies. People will only become 'totally' involved if they thoroughly believe in what they are attempting to achieve and continue to see the usefulness of this.

When we hear about job redesign, multi-skilling, etc., we also often hear that this is part of a restructuring arrangement which puts the onus on employees to carry out extra functions for extra money. However, careful thought is required about theories of motivation and particularly about the appropriateness of Taylorist theories when utilizing job redesign or multi-skilling in attempts to implement total quality management. Total moral involvement of all employees must function from sound foundations. TQM has in fact gone much further than quality circles. Quality circles became popular in the 1980s but met with limited success in the West. They were often little more than a group of workers who met occasionally to discuss work-related problems and make suggestions to management for improvements. They usually had little authority and were limited in the types of problems they were allowed to discuss. Pay and conditions were not usually subjects that were discussed, and thus management found it difficult to provide incentives for involvement and maintaining commitment. However, a new development of the quality circle is the **self-directed work team**. In their most progressive form, these teams have authority and accountability for a much greater number of tasks. They can become accountable for hiring and firing, determining rates of pay and conditions of work, scheduling, rostering, customer liaison, purchasing, maintenance and many other functions relevant to their team. Although Taylorism has created a hierarchy to take care of many of these types of decisions, an empowered self-directed work team structure within an organization can lessen the need for this hierarchy and make possible the flatter structures which are increasingly becoming a characteristic of successful organizations. Peters (1992) gives examples of progressive organizations, including Asea Brown Boveri and the Union Pacific Railroad, which have obtained spectacular results from this type of organizational structure. However, this goes somewhat further than the common expectation from TQM at the current time. If we look beyond TQM it is likely that teams will develop into small, virtually autonomous businesses which reflect much more than the utilization of TQM tools. Peters (1992) claims that teaching teams tools and techniques is not enough and introduces a concept involving teams adopting an entrepreneurial attitude which he terms 'businessing' as a means of meeting the primary objective of TQM – delighting the customer.

We are now developing ideas related to one of the prerequisites for total quality management. The questions of 'involvement' and 'commitment' are the two major problems in making TQM successful in the West in general. In the following section we will investigate the way in which one Western motor manufacturing facility made continual improvement ideas work.

11.3.2 CULTURE AND KAIZEN

What role does the Japanese culture play in success with TQM? Many explanations are offered as ways of explaining Japanese success. Of these, culture and national character are very controversial.

Arguments in favour of these explanatory factors are:

- tradition of Japanese fine craftsmanship, for example bonsai and netsuke (intricate carved toggles);
- attention to detail;
- fastidiousness, perfectionism and cleanliness;
- customers unwilling to accept defects;
- personal honour in work activities;
- society built upon social groups and group processes.

Arguments against are as follows.

- If quality comes so naturally to the Japanese, how is Japan's pre-improvement period explained when their reputation for manufactured goods was anything but good?
- Why are subsidiaries of Japanese companies successful outside Japan? There are many examples of Western companies staffed by local workers and small teams of Japanese managers which have excellent quality records that equal or surpass their Japanese counterparts.

Clearly, the Japanese culture is unique and very different to the somewhat more 'laid back' attitudes often seen in the West. However, there are no guarantees that the Japanese culture creates certainty that TQM in Japan will be successful or that TQM in another culture will fail. However, there is increasing evidence to suggest that even greater benefits than those obtained from TQM in Japan are possible utilizing Western talents for creativity and entrepreneurism by breaking large organizations into small team-orientated businesses to foster creativity and curiosity in the way described by Peters (1992). The following case study adapted from Wickens (1988) describes a typical approach to quality management in a Japanese manufacturing organization which was transplanted to the West. It should be noted that whilst the Japanese approach described here represents differences to established Western work practices, it does not reflect the radical 'disorganization' described by Peters, where hierarchy becomes negligible and 'management' responsibilities are carried out within small teams of multi-skilled, empowered workers.

11.3.3 CASE STUDY: NMUK

Nissan Motors UK is committed to a policy of team-working and development of the team members. The key to success is seen as the integration of the quality circle activity into jobs and not viewing it as a separate activity. To give substance to quality circle activity as a means of achieving employee commitment to continuous improvement throughout the company, a formal framework has been established which consists of a steering committee under the chairmanship of the director of production. Problem-solving and continuous improvement are integral parts of everyone's job and therefore no financial recognition is given for achievement. The steering committee decides on the nature of rewards for good work.

The title used for quality circles is kaizen teams. Kaizen workshops are areas of the plant where manufacturing staff go to make or improve tooling or fabricate aids to ease manufacturing.

NMUK see kaizen (or continual improvement) as part of team responsibilities and also see it as important that supervisors in all areas are an integral part of that responsibility. The supervisor becomes the leader of the kaizen team, but as experience develops other team members are expected to assume leadership of problem-solving groups. There is a strong commitment to team-work. The aim is to build a company with which people can identify and to which they feel commitment.

A five-minute meeting at the start of the day is very important in building teams and commitment. This was learned directly from other Nissan plants and in Japan may involve an exercise period. However, to Nissan Motors UK, this is a time when the team starts to do something together when, each day, the supervisor talks with his people. This talk is often about quality but can also be used to discuss changes to work processes. Meeting areas have been constructed for each team. These are spacious, well lit areas where there are recreational and refreshment facilities. There is only one union in the plant.

The results are an establishment where there is an egalitarian culture and mutual trust and cooperation are fostered. This has been translated into world-class production rates and quality. There is a belief that improvement ideas will be encouraged by minimizing bureaucratic time-consuming procedures, but for some issues, a formal process to resolve problems may be necessary. That process uses analytical techniques which have to be learned by the workforce. Therefore, training in the tools and techniques of TQM is an important consideration for all the teams.

The NMUK exercise is a fairly typical example of transplanting a Japanese company to the West. Such transplants and their results, in comparison to their Western counterparts, are discussed in detail by Womack, Jones and Roos (1990). This definitive work outlines the Japanese concept of **lean production** which is put forward as the philosophy behind the spectacular success of the Japanese motor industry, both in Japan and elsewhere. Lean production really means doing more with less (less inventory, less space, less time, less people, etc.). A key characteristic of lean production is that multi-skilled teams are required to become involved in TQM-style improvement activities. Womack, Jones and Roos (1990) put forward a scenario which suggests that there is little alternative for the West than to quickly adopt these ideas. However, major reservations to lean production have been expressed by prominent Western authors (e.g. Jurgens (1993)). There is little doubt that Japanese-style quality management will not encourage the expression of the 'creativity and curiosity' which is so important in the futuristic organizations discussed by Peters (1992). Peters describes the need for 'necessary disorganization' which does not seem to align with the uniformity and elimination of variation which characterizes Japanese quality management.

Whichever way we see the achievement of customer delight in the twenty-first century, there is little doubt that the future is going to be exciting with radical changes to the organization of work, the magnitude of which has not been seen since the industrial revolution.

11.4 THE SEVEN STATISTICAL TOOLS (THE BASIC 7)

We have discussed the fundamentals of TQM, especially in terms of human involvement and organization. The question may now perhaps be asked what the precise activities of such groups will be. According to Imai (1986) tools are used extensively at all levels of the improvement process. Tools fall into two main categories in continual improvement. Whilst an in-depth analysis of all of the tools available is far beyond the scope of this book, we will attempt in this section to introduce the idea of the **seven statistical tools** (basic 7) and then go on to briefly discuss the **new seven tools** (new 7).

The seven statistical tools are:

- Pareto diagrams;
- cause and effect diagrams;
- histograms;
- control charts;
- scatter diagrams;
- graphs;
- checksheets.

11.4.1 PARETO DIAGRAMS

Pareto diagrams are drawn as shown in Fig. 11.2 which uses the failure cost data supplied by a beverage manufacturer over a three-month period.

Failure	£	Cumulative £
Faulty seal/cap	45 000	45 000
Off colour	16 500	61 500
Off taste	12 000	73 500
Out of date	9 000	82 500
Leaking container	2 000	84 500
Faulty packaging	1 000	85 500

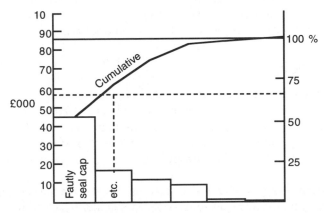

Fig. 11.2 Failure cost data and Pareto diagram for a beverage manufacturer.

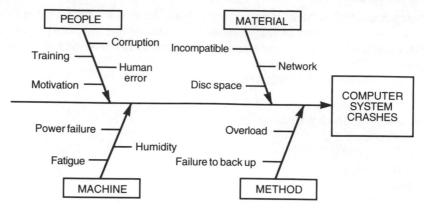

Fig. 11.3 A cause and effect diagram.

Pareto diagrams are useful for illustrating the 'significant few' causes of defects and provide a view of where the most significant gains can be made. The cumulative line is useful to illustrate the percentage of defects which respective groups contribute to, e.g. it should be noted that 'Faulty seal cap' and 'Off colour' make up the major percentage of defects (about 58% of all problems).

11.4.2 CAUSE AND EFFECT DIAGRAMS

This type of diagram (of which an example is shown in Fig. 11.3) enables a continuous improvement team to brainstorm and categorize the various 'causes' which could contribute to an 'effect'. The effect is shown in the box on the right of the diagram. The four cause categories shown are often employed, but the user may define other more applicable categories for other situations. After determining the causes of a particular problem, the users may decide to collect data relating to the relative severity of each cause. This data may then be used for Pareto analysis.

11.4.3 HISTOGRAMS

The following example illustrates the use of a histogram. A motor manufacturer uses a high-pressure water test to check whether door seals are effective. The design specification states that the seal should effectively seal the gap as long as the gap between the door and its frame remains between 15 and 17 mm. A histogram (Fig. 11.5) is drawn from the data in Fig. 11.4.

If the company asked why they occasionally get seals that leak although the average gap size from samples of 26 cars is always close to the centre of the specification, the histogram in Fig. 11.5 can easily illustrate whether

15	16	15	17	16	16	14	17	17	15	16	16	15	
16	17	16	15	18	16	16	16	15	17	15	15	16	mm

No.	Section boundary values	Check	Frequency
1	14	1	1
2	15	11111111	8
3	16	11111111111	11
4	17	11111	5
5	18	1	1
Total			26

Fig. 11.4 Histogram data.

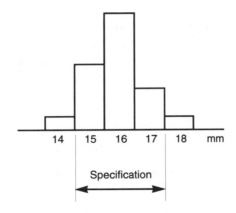

Fig. 11.5 Histogram.

the process is capable by showing whether the tails of the distribution are within the specification limits. If a large proportion of the distribution is outside the specification limits, it is clear to a continuous improvement team that the process is not capable of producing substantially correct work, as shown in this example.

11.4.4 CONTROL CHARTS

Control charts are available in many various types. Some are very complicated, others relatively simple. A few types are

- $\bar{X}$ charts;
- R chart;
- pre-control charts;
- cusum charts;
- P charts;

- s charts;
- u charts;
- C charts.

It is not within the scope of this text to take an in-depth look at control charts and so we will investigate one of the relatively simple types with the aim of showing how processes can be controlled by their use. It should be understood that control charts fall into two groups: **variable charts** and **attribute charts**. Variable charts are applicable where we are working to a variable specification between two limits, for example a hole size with upper and lower limits. Attribute charts are usually more simple (but less powerful) and refer only to specifications which can be right or wrong, or good or bad. In the example below, we will investigate the C chart which is a simple aid to controlling the number of defects in a product (an attribute chart).

The number of defects on successive sheets of rolled steel was counted and the following data obtained:

Sheet no.	1	2	3	4	5	6	7	8	9	10	11	12	13	14	15
No. of defects (C)	3	2	1	0	2	3	5	4	6	3	1	3	2	8	1

First, the average number of defects ($\bar{C}$) is calculated:

$$\bar{C} = 44/15 = 3 \text{ (approx.)}$$

Then the control limit (CL) is calculated (this corresponds to roughly three standard deviations of the distribution):

$$CL = \bar{C} + 3 \times \sqrt{\bar{C}}$$

$$CL = 8.196$$

It is not possible to have 8.196 defects and so we say that CL = 8. The control chart is then drawn as in Fig. 11.6. The CL indicates a situation which should only occur with a very low probability (in other words an

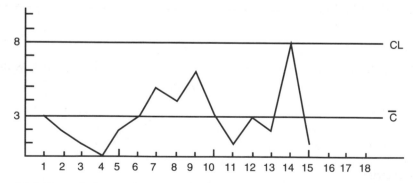

Fig. 11.6 Control chart.

abnormal trend). Therefore, if the operatives continue to plot the number of defects on each subsequent sheet, they can see very quickly that the process is going out of control if more than eight defects occur per sheet.

A great deal of information can be determined from control charts. For example, a trend, sequence or bias can be quickly and easily seen. Control charts also play a very important role in providing data for process improvement.

11.4.5 SCATTER DIAGRAMS

A scatter diagram may be illustrated using the following data. A manufacturer of a toiletry product consisting of layers of tightly wound cloth is finding that complaints of underweight product are resulting from the production of one particular machine. The machine is situated close to a large door and the quality circle wishes to investigate whether humidity may have some effect. Complaints are graded in terms of severity on a scale 1–10 and humidity is graded on a scale 1–5:

No.	Humidity	Complaints	No.	Humidity	Complaints
1	3	7	11	4	7
2	2	4	12	1	3
3	1	3	13	2	5
4	5	8	14	3	7
5	4	8	15	5	10
6	1	2	16	2	4
7	3	5	17	1	0
8	2	6	18	3	4
9	1	2	19	2	3
10	4	6	20	1	1

Humidity is then plotted against complaints as shown in Fig. 11.7. The users can quickly see if there is any correlation between the two factors. A purely random pattern indicates that there is no correlation. In this case

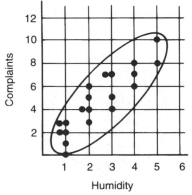

Fig. 11.7 Scatter diagram.

there is a positive correlation as illustrated by a positive slope in the collective positions of the plotted points shown in the diagram.

11.4.6 GRAPHS

Each of the following graphs can be used to present data for use in improvement activities. There are many types of graphs, and those illustrated here are only a small selection:

- bar graph – Fig. 11.8;
- line graph – Fig. 11.9;
- pie chart – Fig. 11.10;
- band chart – Fig. 11.11;
- gantt chart – Fig. 11.12;
- Z diagram – Fig. 11.13.

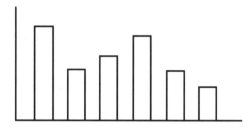

Fig. 11.8 Bar graph.

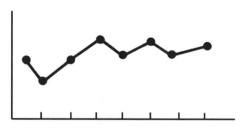

Fig. 11.9 Line graph.

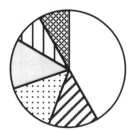

Fig. 11.10 Pie chart.

Fig. 11.11 Band chart.

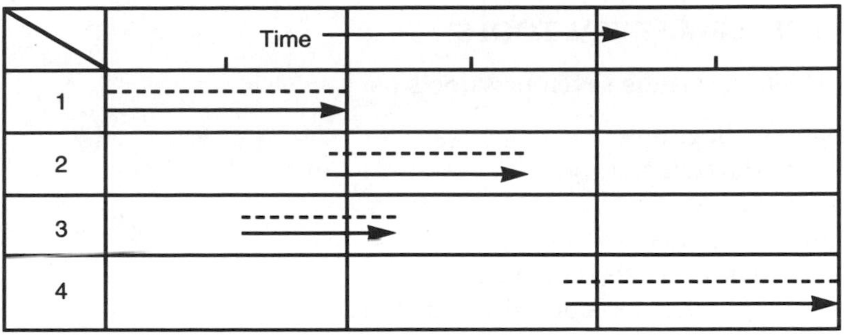

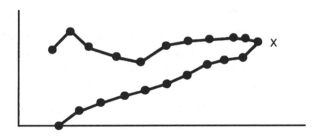

Fig. 11.12 Gantt chart.

Fig. 11.13 Z diagram.

11.4.7 CHECKSHEETS

Checksheets are a fairly simple means of gathering data. Figure 11.14 shows the format of a checksheet which could be used at the final inspection stage at the end of a motor vehicle assembly line.

	M	T	W	T	F
A	III	I	III	JHf	I
B	I	JHf I	IIII	II	IIII
C	I	III	JHf	I	III
D	JHf	I	I	III	JHf
E	I	II	III	II	III

Fig. 11.14 Checksheet.

From the seven statistical tools we have seen so far, it is clear that utilizing them would almost revolutionize shopfloor practices in the West. It is also apparent that the culture in many organizations would need to change in order to implement these seven statistical tools.

11.5 THE NEW SEVEN TOOLS

Imai (1986) terms the seven new tools as:

- relations diagrams;
- affinity diagrams;
- tree diagrams;
- matrix diagrams;
- matrix data analysis diagrams;
- PDPCs (process decision program chart);
- arrow diagrams.

The following quote from Imai probably summarizes the rewards for using the new seven tools:

> . . . what data are available are often only available in the minds of the people concerned, and expressed in language and not mathematical figures. Such verbal data must be rearranged into meaningful form so that a reasonable decision can be made . . .

The seven new tools could be described as management and planning or design tools. Design is the source of good quality (e.g. it could be said that manufacturing rarely makes scrap – but design often makes manufacturing make scrap). If we do not get the design correct, we have little hope of getting manufacture, service and price correct. However, when we address the question of design, we must remember that design does not only apply to products but also equally to methods, materials, management and even people. We can therefore see that the list of the new seven applications could be almost endless.

To complete this introduction to the new seven tools consider the following quotation from Brassard (1991):

> The Seven Management and Planning Tools finally provide every manager with the tools needed to make planning an effective and satisfying process. They also break down Taylor-type barriers by giving more individuals the ability to contribute to the planning step.

11.6 CASE STUDY

The following case study is based on a company which is a subsidiary of one of Australia's largest manufacturing organizations. The case study reports on the final session of an in-house course on quality improvement and implementation which had consisted of 14 three-hour seminars. The participants consisted of 24 supervisory/middle/senior managers from a broad cross-section of departments of the company. The group had been exposed to various TQM techniques and philosophies including continual improvement and the 14 tools. They came from a background where their organization had been attempting to implement TQM for almost nine years but the company was unprofitable and delivery performance was poor. They were also going through very difficult labour relations where the company was attempting to shed 2000 of its 10 000 workforce. The group was divided into four smaller groups. Each of the smaller groups was asked to prepare a presentation answering two questions:

1. What would they do to reorganize quality improvement activities if they had a clean piece of paper?
2. What could be achieved in practice?

A few responses are summarized below.

The first group to report suggested that they would implement continual improvement groups, who would be well trained in the use of the basic seven tools. However, they felt that in practice, their success with TQM had been limited because they had not had commitment from shopfloor workers. They suggested that none of the TQM ideas could be at all successful unless they got total employee involvement. They therefore proposed a very structured training plan to try to nurture a committed attitude to improvement and suggested that this could be achieved through current job redesign negotiations so that people would begin to realize that there would be a requirement for their jobs to be enlarged to include TQM activities.

Another group reiterated similar views but further emphasized the employee involvement problem. They consisted largely of supervisors and middle managers who felt so perplexed with their current predicament that they suggested the company should close down for three months and then re-employ only the employees who were judged to be receptive to non-Taylorist types of motivation. They also suggested that only one union should be allowed on the site. They expressed reservations about current job redesign negotiations because there was no mention of TQM activities. The group conceded that closing the factory might not be practical but re-emphasized that total employee involvement must become a policy priority for the company and management by objectives was not helping their problems.

The next group again expressed the view that lack of total employee involvement was the major reason for limited success so far with the company's approach to TQM. They also were uncomfortable with job redesign negotiations, suggesting that even if TQM had been included in the negotiations it may not be appropriate to motivate people by use of fear and money to be committed to TQM. They were very concerned that senior management should demonstrate commitment to TQM but not attempt to motivate by fear and greed.

This case study shows that TQM cannot be introduced without carefully considering the 'behaviour' of the workforce and the management. In fact this is probably the most difficult area to be considered. The conclusion should not be drawn that TQM is no more than a set of principles and techniques. This is only 'the tip of the iceberg'. Perhaps it could be argued that the real reason why Japan has been so successful with TQM is because they have changed the behaviour of their workforce to a point where the total workforce is concerned about quality and is effectively working as a cooperative team to continuously improve organizational performance. The sum of the parts of a workforce is much greater than the individuals working separately.

11.7 CONCLUSION

We have seen that TQM is heralding a new dawn in the way work is organized. The Japanese approach to TQM has had great success but we must treat the Japanese strategy to implementation with some caution in the West. The view that TQM is a fad which will soon be replaced by some other acronym is misleading (Niven, 1993), although there are already signs of this happening, for example with 're-engineering' (Stewart, 1993). The TQM acronym probably will disappear but the involvement of workforces in customer delight and Peters' style of 'disorganization' are undoubtedly pointing the way to the future. We must recognize the contribution of the TQM era and remain enthused about the way forward that this has shown. The changes in ways of work which are continuing to result from TQM will indeed be radical.

REFERENCES

Brassard, M. (1991) *The Memory Jogger Plus*. GOAL/QPC, Methuen, Massachusetts.

Imai, M. (1986) *KAIZEN – The Key to Japan's Competitive Success*. McGraw-Hill, New York.

Jurgens, U. (1993) *Lean Production and Co-determination: the German Experience*. Proceedings of the Conference on Lean Production and Labor: Critical and Comparative Perspectives, Wayne State University, Detroit, Michigan, USA, May.

Niven, D. (1993) When times get tough, what happens to TQM? *Harvard Business Review*, May–June, pp. 20–34.

Peters, T. (1992) *Liberation Management – Necessary Disorganisation for the Nanosecond Nineties*. Macmillan, London.

Stewart, T.A. (1993) Re-engineering – the hot new management tool. *Fortune*, 23 August, pp. 3–9.

Wickens, P. (1988) Total quality: the Nissan experience. *Automotive Engineer*, December, pp. 16–20.

Womack, J.P., Jones, D.T. and Roos, D. (1990) *The Machine that Changed the World*. McGraw-Hill, New York.

Manufacturing strategy 12

12.1 OVERVIEW

The purpose of **manufacturing strategy** is to align manufacturing with the needs of the business and to help the business compete over the longer term. A well thought through manufacturing strategy will translate the business strategy, the firm's competitive posture and the key factors for success for the industry into issues for manufacturing to resolve. The aim of this chapter is to provide an overview of manufacturing strategy in order that the systems issue is placed in its proper perspective.

Specifically, on completion of the chapter readers should be able to:

- understand the characteristics of strategic business units (SBUs);
- understand the nature of manufacturing strategy;
- understand and use the elements of a manufacturing strategy document;
- appreciate the need for an analytical approach to strategy development and be able to use selected mapping techniques;
- be able to apply the concepts of strategic design principles and positioning framework;
- understand the need for a change management approach to major change projects;
- understand the place of systems in manufacturing strategy;
- appreciate current developments in manufacturing strategy thinking.

12.2 CHAPTER STRUCTURE

This chapter is made up of the following sections:

- strategic business units;
- the strategy document;

- analytical approaches to strategy development;
- implementation issues;
- generic strategies.

The first section on strategic business units (SBUs) is concerned with the nature of SBUs and the need to understand whether a particular business is a single business or a combination of businesses. SBUs have implications for manufacturing strategy. The section on the strategy document explains the elements which make up such a document and provides examples of each. The need for processes to uncover issues motivates the section on analytical approaches to strategy development. The mapping approach, together with design principles and positioning architecture, are explained as a method to develop the strategy document in a disciplined way.

The discussion of implementation issues which follows is designed to highlight the problems surrounding the management of change. The final section on generic strategies attempts to resolve two prominent misconceptions about the nature of manufacturing strategy.

12.3 STRATEGIC BUSINESS UNITS

Many organizations are made up of more than one business. For example, until recently many pharmaceutical manufacturing companies consisted of:

- an OTC (over-the-counter) business made up of, for example, cough and cold medicines;
- a prescription products business;
- a hospital products business;
- an animal health care business.

Although all were lumped under the heading of pharmaceuticals they were in fact separate businesses. These separate businesses are termed **strategic business units or SBUs**.

Another example may be taken from an organization in the food industry. The major section of the factory produced canned meats and vegetables. A smaller section produced bottled sauces while another section contained an orange juice plant. Although the products went to similar markets the characteristics of those market segments had distinct differences which needed to be reflected in manufacturing activities. For example, in the orange juice market sales fluctuated to a much greater extent compared with the other market segments. This meant that manufacturing had to be considerably more responsive with regard to producing orange juice than with producing canned vegetables.

The general characteristics of SBUs are as follows:

- each has a unique mission statement;
- each has visible and obvious competitors;
- each has identifiable key factors for success;
- each requires senior management attention;
- each has unique requirements for the primary operating functions, namely marketing and manufacturing.

Two important issues need to be considered when a manufacturing strategy is being developed for a facility which produces products for two or more SBUs. First, when developing a manufacturing strategy, the head of manufacturing may assume the company has a complete understanding of the nature of the markets being served. It is unlikely that this is the case and it is important that manufacturing executives consult other functions to satisfy themselves that all relevant industry, market, customer and competitor information is available.

The second issue concerns the capability of the manufacturing operations. There are limits as to the number of markets a single facility can serve. Where the markets have different requirements and the basis for competing is very different then for all practical purposes it is not usually possible for a single facility to have the proper focus – even when the 'factory within a factory' concept is applied. The principle applied here is that a given manufacturing facility is capable of doing only a few things very well because of the constraints imposed by product and process technology and infrastructure. A factory tailored to meet the specific demands of one market is hardly likely to be able to do a proper job of serving a totally different market.

12.4 THE STRATEGY DOCUMENT

It is beyond the scope of this single chapter to provide a comprehensive coverage of manufacturing strategy. However, an understanding of the components of a **manufacturing strategy document**, an appreciation of how it is derived and a knowledge of some generic strategies will allow you to place production management in its proper perspective. In particular, you should be able to relate systems issues to other issues within manufacturing.

The actual structure of the manufacturing strategy document will vary from organization to organization. Practical and useful documents, however, have similarities and it is these similarities which we will now briefly discuss.

A manufacturing strategy document will usually consist of the following sections:

- background;
- competitive base;

- key issues;
- goals;
- strategy.

Background is a brief (one page) section summarizing what has occurred over the last few years and thus provides the reader with a sensible perspective with regard to the present strategy. It usually includes a statement on the results of initiatives taken in recent years.

Competitive base consists of a simple matrix showing for each major market segment how the organization will compete. This is particularly useful for manufacturing facilities which must service more than one significant market. For example, in the paint industry it was not uncommon for a single factory to produce products for two or more of the following:

- the architectural market;
- the industrial market;
- the automotive market;
- the refinish market.

When developing a manufacturing strategy it is important to recognize that the basis for competing may be different for the different markets. As an example, one paint company competed on the basis of the following:

- architectural market: product availability;
- industrial market: superior product consistency;
- refinish market: short delivery time.

The resulting strategy must respond specifically to these bases of competing.

Key issues are events, trends, facts or realities which may have a significant impact (either positive or negative) on manufacturing performance. These issues are those things that must be addressed when considering the longer-term well-being and effectiveness of the manufacturing function. It is important to understand that manufacturing goals and strategy address directly the key issues. As such the key issues must reflect the basis for competing and the relevant key success factors for the industry. In the context of manufacturing systems and the bases for competing stated above examples of key issues might include:

- poor responsiveness by manufacturing to changes in market demand;
- inadequate order status information for customers;
- poor management information on key non-financial performance factors, for example product quality.

Goals are broad qualitative or quantitative but results-orientated statements of what must be achieved over the time horizon of the strategy.

Goals provide direction and are a direct response to the key issues, but not necessarily on a one-to-one basis. Examples of goals consistent with the above issues include:

- to improve significantly our response to changing market requirements;
- to life significantly the effectiveness of our performance system;
- to become the recognized market leader in product quality.

Strategies are the set of initiatives which will achieve the above goals. Whereas the key issues and goals are written as single statements (or at most a couple of sentences) the strategies require a paragraph or two because it is necessary to explain how the goals will be achieved. A strategy related to the need to improve the response to changing market requirements might be written as follows:

An improvement in our response to changing market demand has a number of components, namely:

- systems, particularly:
  - materials management;
  - production scheduling methods;
  - customer information and sales order processing;
  - distribution management;
  - production lead times;
  - communications with marketing.

At the present time the systems associated with materials management, sales order processing and distribution management are considered to be more than adequate. In addition working relations at both senior and operating level between manufacturing and marketing are considered to be very good. Priority areas to improve responsiveness now must address:

- scheduling methods which are cumbersome, time-consuming and manual;
- the need for sales order entry staff and account managers to access information from the distribution system;
- inadequate internal lead times for production.

Given the above the following initiatives will be put into action:

- Suitable PC-based finite scheduling software will be sourced and installed as a matter of urgency. The package will have the facility to connect to the materials management processes.
- As an interim measure sales order entry staff, account managers and all relevant employees will be able to access modules of the distribution management information system regarding customer

information. A further initiative will integrate electronically all major customers with company systems. The plans for this integration will be complete within 12 months. The implementation process should be complete within 18 months.

- The vehicle to collapse internal lead times will be an in-house programme (already developed) combining the (similar) concepts of value-adding management and just-in-time (JIT) including total quality control (TQC) and total preventive maintenance (TPM). For non-seasonal make-to-stock repetitive manufactured products the kanban approach will link the market and the factory. Make-to-order products will be incorporated into the production schedule.

12.5 ANALYTICAL APPROACHES TO STRATEGY DEVELOPMENT

The manufacturing strategy document consisting of background, competitive base, key issues, goals and strategy is, or should be, derived from a comprehensive analytical process. This process should provide the opportunity for all significant issues to be uncovered. In theory as well as in practice it is the correct identification of the key issues which is most important since the goals and strategies are a direct reflection of them.

Although it is beyond the scope of this book to cover the complete analytical approach to strategy development it is useful to show briefly some important aspects. Figure 12.1 is an outline of an analytical approach for the development of a manufacturing strategy.

The organization's basis for competing and business strategy will have been derived from a study of the industry (industry dynamics) and other influences, either global or local, for example the political situation. For manufacturing there is then the need to carry out an analysis that is specific for that function.

One approach now being used by some organizations to document the present shape of the business is that of **mapping**. The term mapping refers to a method of relating the various components being considered. In some cases, for example the customer map and supply chain map, the map will be geographic. Others, for example the systems map, will be diagrammatic representations of reality. In practice each map should take up a single page. When complete the maps provide a new and different view of the organization to enhance group discussion on issues. The number of different maps may vary but will usually include the following.

- **Customer/market map**. This map shows the physical and geographic relationship between the manufacturing facility and customers or groups of customers.
- **Supply chain map**. A physical map showing locations and flow dynamics of suppliers, plants, stock points and customers.

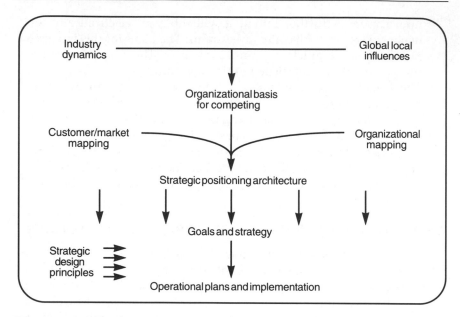

Fig. 12.1 An analytic approach for the development of a manufacturing strategy.

- **Financial map**. A series of maps the first being a simple overlay on the supply chain map showing financial figures of assets, materials, transport, sales, etc. The more important maps involve activity-based costing and Du Pont analysis. Figure 12.2 is an example of a Du Pont chart. It shows the breakdown of return on assets (ROA) into its components profit before interest and tax (PBIT) and net assets and then a further break down into subcomponents. The various subcomponents of the Du Pont may be modified or broken down further depending on the nature of the business. For example, the divisions of large companies often omit long-term liabilities because these are taken up at the corporate level. Other firms break down the overhead component into sub-components. The Du Pont chart is very useful to demonstrate the sensitivity of the business to small changes in the values of sub-components. It is not meant to focus management on short-term results on an ongoing basis.
- **Operations and systems map**. A diagram or series of diagrams showing work patterns, material flows and the major systems involved.
- **Technology map**. Similar to the supply chain map in outline but showing significant product, process, transport, communications and information technology.
- **Support map**. A diagram showing the physical parameters and interactions between typical support functions such as engineering and maintenance and the remainder of the organization.

Financial results – year to date

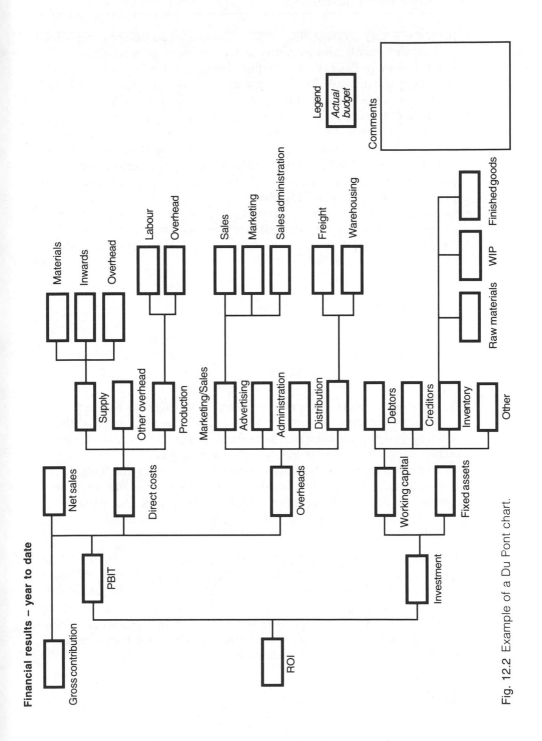

Fig. 12.2 Example of a Du Pont chart.

- **Job design map**. A map of the organization's locations showing levels of decision-making and authority as well as management style.
- **Historical map**. Basically a time line showing turning points in goals, strategy, performance, management style, systems, competitor activity, industry changes, etc., over the previous five to eight years.
- **Time map**. This map makes use of the physical map but in place of physical quantities, the lead times for the various activities are shown. In many instances a time range will be required together with the most common time. Activities on the time map include the various aspects of materials supply, manufacturing processes, sales order entry and processing, transport and distribution.
- **Competitive map**. Essentially a combination of all other maps showing as much information on competitor activity as possible.
- **Complexity map**. Within manufacturing industry complexity is related to such things as number of:
  - raw materials;
  - suppliers;
  - components;
  - processes;
  - systems;
  - products;
  - markets;
  - customers.

  As complexity rises more time is required to manage the elements of it. Modern computer systems are often purchased to manage the seemingly ever-increasing number of activities required to make the business function effectively. Much management time, however, goes into managing the system as opposed to managing the business. A key activity in strategy development is to reduce the level of complexity by identifying those activities which might be managed in a much simpler manner. An example from industry of a complexity map is shown in Fig. 12.3.

By itself the mapping of the organization and its environment is of little value. It is just a method for viewing the organization from different perspectives. To develop the issues from which the goals and strategy will be derived the mapping needs to be put to use. This is achieved by critically examining the maps within the combined framework of the **strategic design principles** and the **strategic positioning framework**.

The strategic design principles consist of:

- simplicity;
- quality;
- flexibility;

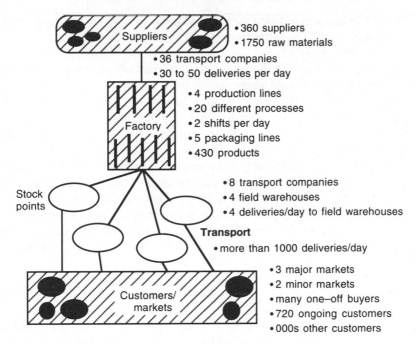

Fig. 12.3 Complexity map for manufacturing industry.

- value added;
- time.

Considerable effort should be spent in devising options to:

- remove the non-value-adding operations, assets and activities;
- simplify the remaining operations, assets and activities;
- collapse the time required for all operations and activities;
- apply the principles of 'quality at source' and 'right first time';
- increase flexibility and speed of response to changes in market demand.

Having carried out the exercise with the strategic design principles the strategy may then be developed. This, however, is not as easy as it might seem. Strategies which are both comprehensive and able to act as a driving competitive force require considerable depth of thought and creativity. In short it is not just a matter of finding ways to improve current operations but rather to find superior and different ways of competing.

To assist the process the strategic positioning framework (SPF) may be used. This framework acts to correctly position manufacturing relative to the business strategy. The elements of the framework represent the significant issues around which the final goals and strategy will be written. The nine elements of the framework are as follows.

- **Customer service**. Whatever form customer requirements take, the organization must meet them. Long-term business success is heavily dependent on identifying customer needs and then orientating the entire organization to service those needs. True customer service requires an understanding of the organization's focus and that a given factory is only able to do a few things very well.
- **Cash generation**. In the new accounting, historical measures such as return on investment are not seen as reliable indicators of shareholder value. In their place are measures of forward cash flow and cash generation. Increasingly cash flow is being seen as a prime determinant of business success. In Australia in recent years we have seen a number of high-profile organizations fail primarily because of their inability to service high levels of debt.
- **Competitive impact**. The question here concerns how the manufacturing function will help the business compete or (preferably) drive the competitiveness of the business. For example, in the confectionery business two of the key success factors are product consistency and product availability. Both have obvious implications for various manufacturing activities. One test of the strategy would be the impact on these two key success factors.
- **Manufacturing/logistics network**. The configuration of the network is a prime determinant of competitive strength. It requires close attention since the network consumes considerable organizational resources, for example assets, management time, people and expenditure, and simultaneously is the prime operational function servicing the market.
- **Information systems and control**. Today, responsive and decisive organizations design management and operational systems to enable them to monitor market servicing and the internal levers which drive business performance.
- **Product and process technology**. Here product technology refers not only to design to meet customer needs but also to design for manufacture which means material cost-effectiveness and minimum processing and handling. In the area of processes, organizations should be identifying proprietary technology which will provide some form of business advantage.
- **Culture and job design**. Clearly it is not possible to compete successfully over extended periods of time without skilled people in key areas. A major issue for senior management is how to harness the potential power of all individuals and create a culture which drives the competitiveness of the organization.

- **Capital management**. The issues here concern first the identification of the real capital needs of the organization and how they relate to competitiveness, and secondly the timing of the capital injection.
- **Total cost of operations**. Regardless of the chosen basis for competing, all organizations must continually reduce their operating costs. To reduce costs in real terms on an ongoing basis means finding new and different ways of doing business.

12.6 IMPLEMENTATION ISSUES

For many organizations the implementation of strategy is a major issue. More correctly the issue concerns how to maintain sufficient stability to continue to service customers while carrying out the desired changes. It is not uncommon to find organizations with well thought through strategies but with little to show after a few years of attempted implementation. Some of the symptoms of poor implementation include:

- changes not achieving expected benefits;
- extensive delays;
- significant disruption to ongoing operating activities;
- conflict between functional groups.

There is a need for senior management to recognize that line management and change management require different skills. Further, there is a need to recognize that line managers with heavy operating loads cannot be expected to carry out major change programmes without extra assistance. Additional structures are required to ensure that the change process is managed correctly. Figure 12.4 attempts to demonstrate that separate and distinct management processes are required for change to take place. This does not mean that line managers are external to the process. The relevant line managers are accountable for the change processes that take place within their area of accountability. However, these line managers

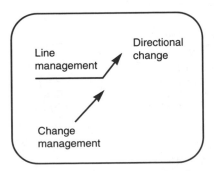

Fig. 12.4 Relationship between line management and change management.

must have additional resources specifically focused on the implementation of the change. Line managers must not be expected to continue to manage the business while simultaneously implementing complex change.

12.7 'GENERIC' STRATEGIES

There are two important misconceptions regarding manufacturing strategy. First there are those who think that because they have implemented a programme of, say, just-in-time (JIT) or manufacturing resources planning (MRP 2) then that is 'strategy'. Secondly there are those who believe there is no such thing as a unique manufacturing strategy for a particular business.

The response to these two misconceptions is helped if we consider Table 12.1 which shows a number of different strategies. With a little thought it should be clear that the implementation of, say, MRP 2 or JIT in isolation from any sensible strategic process cannot be called 'strategy'. The companies cited in Table 12.1 did not become successful by blindly following a programme which had generalized benefits. In other words the MRP 2 or JIT implementation is not a strategy unless it is designed to

Table 12.1 Possible strategies to follow

Strategy	Example
Product based:	
• Product variety	Toyota
• Product quality	Mercedes Benz
Times based:	
• Delivery time	Caterpillar
• Rapid response	Ice cream
• New product introduction	Electronics
Market based:	
• Niche	Apple
Technology based:	
• Advanced	BMW
Service based:	
• Stock availability	Hospital drugs
• Delivery reliability	Steel
• Technical backup	Industrial coatings
Cost based:	
• Price	Commodities
Industry dynamics based:	
• Flexible response	Electrolux-Europe

achieve a specific goal that has been distilled from some form of strategic process. It is unfortunate that so many organizations have installed MRP 2 or initiated a JIT programme after having been sold on the generic benefits. In doing so they have ignored the specific requirements of the business and the possibility that additional programmes may be necessary to resolve other business issues.

For example, a company with a quality reputation for the manufacture of security products decided that to dominate the industry they needed to introduce more new products more quickly than their competitors and to make the plant much more responsive to market demand. To do this they added resources to their product development group and introduced a kanban system to link production to the market. Although on the surface these decisions appeared sensible they were not the product of a comprehensive strategic management process and significant problems were encountered.

- The standard kanban approach did not suit a number of 'fashion' security products which had violently fluctuating sales during promotional periods. An important aspect of 'fashion' products is stock availability and the result was a significant level of lost sales.
- The function of forecasting the future demand for all products was downgraded by the marketing manager in the mistaken belief that with kanban it was not necessary. Manufacturing had no forward vision of expected demand and had to fall back on inadequate extrapolations of historical sales.
- The production planning and control, and purchasing and supply systems had been designed some years prior for a fixed number of products using (as far as possible) common parts. The directive for new products resulted in a proliferation of new and different products with new and different parts. The old systems could not cope with the increased volume of different parts, necessitating the addition of a PC-based stand-alone system. The lack of integration resulted in parts and material shortages in the factory. Further, the supply function did not have the resources to go through the usual procedures to ensure quality materials from suppliers. Within a few months the growing level of consumer complaints resulted in some new products being taken off the market.
- All of the above gradually increased the level of confusion on the factory floor. Schedules were changed frequently with the result being poor reliability and high levels of work in progress which eventually placed a heavy load on the company's financial resources.

This example shows the need to think through the ramifications of strategic decisions. This is best carried out using a predetermined methodology which involves all functions of the company.

The second misconception concerns the idea there is no such thing as a unique manufacturing strategy for a particular business. Under this thinking if the modern principles of manufacturing are followed and implemented correctly all benefits are available. If this were true every strategy in Table 12.1 would be implemented in exactly the same way. It would also mean that each organization would be able to move from one strategy to another at will without making any changes to any aspect of any function. This is clearly not likely to be the case with the vast majority of organizations. Over time the characteristics of markets change and organizational responses also must change. Although there are valid principles upon which to manage manufacturing, long-term business success is not guaranteed by following a simple formula.

12.8 CONCLUSION

This chapter has addressed some of the key issues in the development of a manufacturing strategy that ensures the manufacturing division of an organization is responsive in the most effective possible way to the organization's business needs. This is not easy. Some tools and techniques for facilitating the process have been presented, together with some common misconceptions about what is and is not a manufacturing strategy. As the 'engine' that provides the power for a manufacturing company to deliver what has been promised by the marketing function, and within the resource limitations suggested by the business strategy, manufacturing strategy should not be subservient to either business or marketing strategies, but should be an equal partner with both. Only if marketing and business strategies are formulated in such a way as to take maximum advantage of manufacturing's strengths and minimize its weaknesses will a company be able to sustain its competitive position. In turn, manufacturing strategy must be in consonance with both marketing and business strategies in terms of attempting to deliver to the customer products with the characteristics and with the resource expenditure that these strategies demand.

FURTHER READING

Buffa, E.S. (1984) *Meeting the Competitive Challenge.* Dow Jones-Irwin, Homewood, Illinois.
Greenhalgh, G.R. (1991) *Manufacturing Strategy.* Addison-Wesley, Sydney.
Hayes, R.H. and Wheelwright, S.S. (1984) *Restoring Our Competitive Edge.* John Wiley & Sons, New York.

Manufacturing performance monitoring

13

13.1 OVERVIEW

In Chapter 11 we learnt how total quality management advocates a process of continual improvement in all organizational activities. To know whether and to what extent we are improving, we must be capable of measuring our performance. In this chapter, we examine the various ways of measuring and monitoring organizational performance. We introduce the concept of control in complex systems, and how the principles of control have been traditionally applied in manufacturing and other organizations in the form of performance measures based primarily on cost. We then examine how these traditional techniques have come in for some severe criticism in recent years, and present some more modern techniques of performance measurement based on both accounting and non-accounting sources of information.

13.2 CHAPTER STRUCTURE

This chapter is divided into four sections:

- performance monitoring in context;
- accounting-based methods of measuring manufacturing performance;
- further criticisms of the traditional accounting approach;
- modern methods of measuring manufacturing performance.

The chapter begins by discussing the cybernetic notion of control and how this relates to manufacturing systems management. In particular, the complementary relationship between planning and control and the role of feedback from the control process to the planning process is emphasized. Desirable characteristics of manufacturing performance measures are discussed.

We then move on to look at traditional accounting methods of measuring manufacturing performance, how these are invariably based on cost, and why they are unsatisfactory for manufacturing companies that are trying to compete on factors other than cost leadership. We also examine the problems that can be associated with local rather than global measures of performance.

Finally, we look at some modern techniques that have been proposed to overcome these limitations. The OPT (Optimized Production Technology) approach discussed in Chapter 6 gives us one technique. Another technique which has appeared very recently is that of activity-based costing which assigns costs to activities, and in which it is recognized that value can be added to the product in ways other than the expenditure of direct labour. Benchmarking is an activity that is rapidly gaining in popularity, and provides a means for companies to compare their own performance with 'international best practice'. Finally we examine a technique which combines financial and non-financial information to monitor performance in areas other than mere cost reduction.

13.3 PERFORMANCE MONITORING IN CONTEXT

Manufacturing companies stay in business by being competitive – that is by offering superior products or the same set of products on more favourable terms than their competitors. In order to ensure that a company achieves a competitive position and that different parts of the organization are pulling their weight in maintaining this position, some form of performance monitoring of both individual units as well as the whole is essential.

Performance monitoring is related to the notion of control in cybernetic systems. For a complex system such as the human body to perform properly, various parameters such as body temperature, blood-sugar level, etc., must be monitored by the autonomic nervous system to ensure they are within acceptable operating limits. If a particular parameter varies outside the normal operating range, some form of corrective action is initiated to restore things back to a state of control. This process is known as **feedback** and is illustrated in Fig. 13.1.

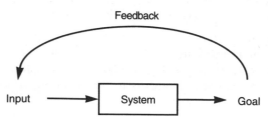

Fig. 13.1 Principle of feedback.

In goal-directed systems such as manufacturing companies, it is essential to be able to control one's progress towards particular goals. This requires regular measurement of the relevant parameters that are regarded to be reliable indicators of the extent of one's success in moving towards or achieving those goals.

We have already had some examples of the notion of control in manufacturing companies in the form of the control of quality of outgoing products, manufacturing processes and incoming raw materials. The monitoring of various parameters that may be regarded as being reasonable measures of these various forms of quality (such as the percentage defects in a batch) will indicate the presence of any quality problems, and steps can then be taken to rectify them.

However, the achievement of the desired level of quality is not the only goal in a manufacturing company. Other goals such as the achievement of a certain production volume, a reduction in production costs or a reduction of customer delivery time may also be important. Other parameters to give a reliable indication of the performance in each area are required. For example, we might monitor the number of customer complaints about poor delivery times and use this as a measure of delivery performance.

Similarly, the number of end products completed each week might be regarded as a measure of production volume performance and so on.

Performance monitoring basically plays a complementary role to production planning in the effective management of a manufacturing organization. The establishment of a particular production plan sets goals for manufacturing in terms of how many of what products of what quality are to be produced by what time. Monitoring of performance in meeting the production plan enables deviations to be detected from the plan in time to take corrective action before it is too late.

It is generally agreed in the literature that a good set of performance measures should have the following characteristics.

- Each performance measure should be quantifiable and specifically relate to at least one of the agreed objectives of the person or unit whose performance is being measured. A change in the value of the performance measure should always be associated with a change in performance in achieving this objective, and vice versa.
- Performance measures should if possible be affected only by changes in actual performance and not by external factors outside the control of the person or unit whose performance is being monitored.

Thus for a particular production line having a critical success factor of product consistency (such as in the confectionery industry, for example, where it may be essential that the consumer of a particular type of chocolate bar should experience exactly the same taste, texture, etc., for every bar purchased), a performance indicator that is a direct measure of such consistency should be set up and regularly monitored. However, although another important objective of the company may be the maximization of sales volume of the products produced on this line, sales volume would not be a fair manufacturing performance measure of the line itself, since it would be likely to be affected by activities of the marketing division that were not directly under the control of manufacturing.

Performance monitoring is often (but does not have to be) associated with the system of **management by objectives (MBO)**. Here the overall goal of the organization is boiled down into a set of quantitative objectives for each organizational sub-unit, each of which is then further broken down into more detailed quantified objectives for sub-sub-units and so on, down to the lowest level of the organization. In theory this break-down is achieved in such a way that the detailed objectives of the sub-units at various levels will all be congruent with the overall goal of the organization. Monitoring of performance of each sub-unit will encourage the achievement of individual sub-objectives, and thus of the overall organizational goal.

The concept of performance indicators and performance monitoring as motivators for influencing behaviour in a way that supports an organization's goals is an important one. If the goal of a particular manufacturing company is to deliver products at minimum cost, then manufacturing costs would obviously be the main performance indicators that would be monitored. The goals of the company would be supported by setting local performance targets in terms of levels of manufacturing cost. The need to achieve these local targets would encourage the manufacturing division to act in an appropriate manner as regards cost control and cost reduction.

The extent to which this type of approach does in fact encourage organizational behaviour which is desirable in terms of achievement of the organization's overall goals is critically dependent on how the sub-goals are set, and what performance indicators are used. Excessive concentration on optimizing the values of local performance measures does not always lead to optimum performance of the whole. A good example of this concerns machine utilization, an often used performance measure in manufacturing companies. Maximization of machine utilization of pre-bottleneck resources may mean an overproduction of items that cannot be moved to the bottleneck process and thus a build-up of work in progress that leads indirectly to increased costs. Thus any system of performance measures must be considered in terms of its behaviour as a whole, with relationships between the individual activities that are monitored being as important as the activities themselves when determining what aspects of the activities need to be monitored.

On the other hand if a certain type of behaviour (such as attention to quality, attention to customer service, etc.) is always regarded as furthering the organization's goals, then performance indicators might be set up to monitor these behaviours independently of what other types of performance measure are used.

Although the notion of continuous improvement which is associated with total quality management has sometimes been seen as being in conflict with the notion of goals and performance measures (because these are usually associated with standards), in reality it is not. A goal could be to achieve a certain degree of improvement in a certain activity, and performance measures will be required to establish whether this improvement is occurring or not. For example, a company may decide to set a target for a 20% improvement in production rate over the next two years. This can easily be implemented in the performance measurement system by setting specific targets for the rate of improvement required in the value of the performance measure from one time period to the next.

13.4 ACCOUNTING-BASED METHODS OF MEASURING MANUFACTURING PERFORMANCE

13.4.1 PRODUCTIVITY AS A BASIS FOR PERFORMANCE

The bottom line measures of a manufacturing company's performance are generally business orientated financial measures of performance such as profit, return on investment or cash flow. Performance in terms of these measures can be increased by trying to maximize the value of goods sold relative to the cost of producing those goods. In this chapter, however, we are not discussing these aggregate measures of business performance, but rather the more detailed measures of specifically manufacturing performance which should be designed to ensure that manufacturing is in fact supporting the business strategy.

In the traditional manufacturing company, the task of maximizing the value of goods sold is generally the function of the sales or marketing division, whilst the job of ensuring that the goods sold are produced at minimum cost is the function of the manufacturing division. Thus the performance measures applied to the manufacturing division have in the past invariably been associated with cost, and the monitoring of these performance measures has been the responsibility of the organization's accounting function.

If manufacturing costs can be progressively decreased for a given level of output (in terms of quantity of units produced in a given time), this has the effect of increasing the overall efficiency of the manufacturing process as measured by the ratio of outputs to inputs. The term **productivity** is generally used to refer to manufacturing efficiency as defined in this way. Formally speaking, productivity (P) is defined by the ratio:

$$P = T_o / T_i \qquad (13.1)$$

where T_o is the total output of the plant in the measuring period, normally expressed as the total number of units produced multiplied by their market value, and T_i is the total cost of the inputs required to produce the output.

Productivity is often used in a manufacturing company as an aggregate measure of performance for the manufacturing division as a whole, generating strong imperatives for the individual functional units within the manufacturing division to contain or reduce their cost. A variety of techniques is available for monitoring and controlling costs, the best known of which is referred to as **standard costing**.

13.4.2 STANDARD COSTING

In the standard costing approach various standards are developed which should be obtained under normal operating conditions. These pertain to such things as labour hours per unit of product, quantities of raw materials used per unit of product, percentage rejects, prices paid for raw materials, machine time per unit of product, machine utilization, etc. When comparing actual costs against standards, any differences are referred to as **variances**. If the actual cost is smaller than the standard the variance is described as **favourable**. If the actual cost is greater than the standard cost, the variance is described as **unfavourable**. Unfavourable variances are examined carefully to determine why the variance occurred and to correct it.

Standards are generally divided into materials standards, labour standards and overhead standards.

Materials standards are divided into material quantity standards and material price standards. Such standards may be established by engineering studies, or by experience. The standard price to be paid for the raw material would be established by the purchasing department. If the quantity of materials used in manufacturing the product exceeds the standard, the difference is called a quantity variance. If the actual price paid for the direct materials differs from the standard price, the difference is called a price variance.

Labour standards are similarly divided into labour efficiency standards and labour rate standards. Labour efficiency standards relate to the amount of time required to manufacture a product and may be established through time and motion studies which establish the most efficient ways of performing each operation. Labour rate standards relate to the wage each employee should receive, which of course may be outside the control of the organization in unionized situations, although in smaller companies it may to some extent be subject to the law of supply and demand.

Both material and labour standards and actual costs can be associated directly with, and assigned to, specific batches of individual products, and often form the basis of product costing. Manufacturing overhead, on the other hand, which consists of rent, depreciation, utilities, etc., is an indirect cost. Overhead costs may be assigned to the costs of individual products in a number of ways, such as in proportion to the direct labour hours used per unit of product or the direct machine hours used per unit of product. The method of overhead allocation based on the number of direct labour hours expended has in the past been by far the most common, and this has resulted in distorted pictures of manufacturing reality, as will be seen in later sections.

Let us now examine the concept of productivity in a little more detail. We can expand the notion of productivity by looking at the inputs (i.e. the denominator of expression 13.1) in terms of individual components.

The inputs required by a manufacturing company in order to function can be divided into the following four types:

- labour;
- raw material;
- energy;
- capital.

Thus the total productivity of a manufacturing company can be expressed in the following form:

$$P = T_o/(L_i + R_i + C_i + E_i)$$

where L_i is the direct labour input (i.e. the cost of labour directly expended on the physical production of the product), R_i the raw materials input (the cost of raw materials used), C_i the capital input (the capital invested in plant and machinery required to produce the product) and E_i the energy input (the cost of running this plant and equipment, including general overhead).

The division of the inputs to a manufacturing organization into different classes has served as a stimulus to define what are termed 'partial' productivities which are calculated as the ratio of the total output to the various 'partial' inputs. Thus:

Labour productivity $P_1 = T_o/L_i$

Raw materials productivity $= T_o/R_i$

$$\text{Capital productivity} = T_o/C_i$$

$$\text{Energy productivity} = T_o/E_i$$

Up to the 1960s most manufacturing was labour intensive (meaning that direct labour costs constituted the major proportion of the cost of producing a product). Raw materials were relatively plentiful and cheap, production machines unsophisticated, and overheads were often regarded as fixed. Hence manufacturing companies were concerned only with labour productivity as the main measure of manufacturing performance. Since the 1960s, however, we have seen trends which have largely invalidated this notion. The cost of both raw materials and energy has increased dramatically, production plant and machinery have increased in sophistication and cost and are performing automatically an increasing number of tasks that were hitherto performed manually. This has meant that direct labour now represents a much smaller proportion of manufacturing cost than it did 30 years ago, as shown in the two typical cost breakdowns shown in Fig. 13.2.

This means in turn that the use of labour productivity as the prime measure of manufacturing performance can give a grossly distorted view of true manufacturing performance. This is augmented by the interrelated nature of partial productivity measures with each other.

As an example of this consider the case of a company that makes a large investment in an expensive form of automation. The result of this investment will very likely be a saving in direct labour costs, and if the company is continuing to base its overall performance measurements on labour productivity, this will rise. However, the total increase in capital and overhead costs resulting from use of the automation may possibly result in the total productivity falling. Thus the use of labour productivity in this case can be misleading.

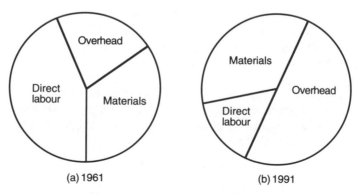

Fig. 13.2 Cost of production.

Manufacturing cost structures of the type shown in Fig. 13.2(b) rather than Fig. 13.2(a) are now the norm. It is, therefore, surprising the number of companies that cling to labour productivity as the prime measure of performance, and are obsessively concerned with controlling and reducing the direct labour hours expended per unit of product when in fact labour represents such a small proportion of the total cost.

13.4.3 OVERHEAD ALLOCATION

The traditional focus on direct labour time and cost as the main determinant of manufacturing performance has other types of distorting effect. In the traditional accounting approach, overhead costs (i.e. those costs not directly attributable to the production of a specific batch of a specific product) are frequently 'absorbed' into the product cost by allocating proportions of the total overhead to individual products in direct proportion to the total direct labour hours consumed in producing each product during the accounting period.

The type of effect that can occur using this method of overhead allocation can be seen by reference to the example depicted in Table 13.1, in which we have two products (assumed to be made on separate dedicated lines) with direct labour and material costs shown, which must share between them a total overhead per period of £180 000.

In the first situation (top half of the table) where the labour times (and hence costs) for both products are the same, the overhead allocation to

Table 13.1 Allocation of overhead

	Product A	Product B
Overhead/period = £180 000		
Production	10 000	10 000
Labour/unit	£1.00	£1.00
Material/unit	£9.00	£9.00
Overhead/unit	£9.00	£9.00
Total cost/unit	£19.00	£19.00
Install automation: Overhead/period = £220 000		
Production	10 000	10 000
Labour/unit	£0.20	£1.00
Material/unit	£9.00	£9.00
Overhead/unit	£3.70	£18.30
Total cost/unit	£12.90	£28.30
Productivity of A:	UP	
Productivity of B:	DOWN	
Total productivity:	DOWN	

each product, assumed taken over a period's production of 10 000 units, works out at £9 per unit, giving a total cost per unit of £19 for each product.

If we now assume that automation is installed on the line producing Product A, reducing the labour cost to 20p per unit, and that the capital and maintenance cost of the automation are classed as general overhead (which as a result increases to £220 000 per period) the resulting cost per unit of product using the same overhead allocation approach is as shown in the lower section of Table 13.1.

The total unit cost of Product A has been reduced to £12.90 whereas the unit cost of Product B (even though no change has been made to its production line) has increased to £28.30 since it is now absorbing a much higher proportion of the overhead. Although the productivity of the line producing Product A has increased, overall productivity has in fact been reduced.

This represents an example of how an emphasis on local rather than global performance measures can result in reduced overall performance. Individual production units may strive to reduce their direct labour hours not because of the real cost reductions involved (which can be relatively insignificant bearing in mind the small proportion direct labour represents of the total) but because it can result in them being burdened with a reduced proportion of the overhead. However, the overhead still has to be borne by somebody, and if the actions taken to reduce the direct labour content actually result in an increase in the general overhead, locally based productivity measures can give a very misleading picture of reality. Effort might be better expended by the company in the above example in trying to reduce the overhead rather than in devising distortionary systems for allocating it.

13.5 FURTHER CRITICISMS OF THE TRADITIONAL ACCOUNTING APPROACH

Traditional accounting measures of manufacturing performance clearly have some severe limitations. The use of productivity (i.e. efficiency) and the associated concentration on cost as fundamental manufacturing performance measures has recently come in for some severe criticism. We have seen an increasing number of companies who have increased their productivity (i.e. manufacturing efficiency) but have declined in profitability, often due to loss of sales. Obviously, although the ratio of total value of goods produced to total inputs may be increased by cost reduction programmes and other efficiency measures, profitability may be simultaneously reduced by lost sales due to poor quality, long delivery times or lack of responsiveness to changes in the market. All these may be side-effects of a focus on cost reduction as the main local objective of the manufacturing division. To systematically analyse these problems it must be remembered that to produce goods at a cost lower than other companies is not the only basis of competing in the marketplace, and indeed attributes other than low prices are becoming increasingly demanded by today's customers.

It was indicated in Chapter 1 of this book that as alternatives to, or in addition to, cost, a manufacturing company may decide to compete on the basis of superior performance in one or more of the following types of characteristic:

- quality;
- delivery;
- flexibility;
- innovation; etc.

A disparity between productivity and profitability can occur in many companies. They may have a sound business strategy at the corporate level in terms of having a clear idea of what their competitive posture should be in relation to the above attributes, but they may fail to translate these business objectives into manufacturing objectives by establishing appropriate measures of manufacturing performance (which in the long run determine actual behaviour). Manufacturing performance measures in the majority of firms are based on the achievement of efficiency (through cost reduction) and thus on productivity, regardless of the business strategy of the firm.

If the latter is to focus on very short delivery times as a basis for competition, but the manufacturing division is driven by objectives and performance measures based solely on cost, the corporate strategy is likely to fail since shopfloor policies which are optimal with respect to reducing local costs may very well not be optimal with respect to reducing delivery times.

Another reason why productivity may be an inappropriate measure of manufacturing performance is that different issues tend to be important at different stages of a product's lifecycle. Most companies will simultaneously be producing different products in different phases of their lifecycles. This indicates not just that some better performance measure needs to be chosen but also that different performance measures need to be applied to the manufacture of different products at different times. For example, most products go through a typical lifecycle in terms of volume of sales as shown in Fig. 13.3. In the early part of the lifecycle, the competitive emphasis is likely to be on the innovative new features of the product. Cost is unlikely to be the prime consideration in determining performance at this stage, and an over-emphasis on cost-cutting could well threaten the appropriate degrees of advancement by experimentation along the technological learning curve associated with the new innovation, and even

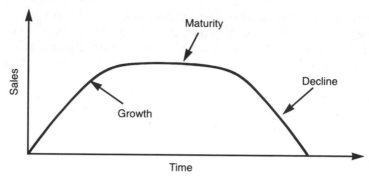

Fig. 13.3 Phases of a product's lifecycle.

discourage innovation of any kind. As a product reaches the phase of maturity, cost-cutting becomes increasingly important so that the firm can consolidate its position against competitors. As the product is phased out, the emphasis might change to product reliability and availability which again require different performance measures for the evaluation of manufacturing effectiveness.

More flexible performance measures would also be needed in situations where different product groups were being manufactured on the same facility for different markets. It might well be that the basis for competition in each market is different, and hence these different groups of products need to be judged against different performance measures.

A further aspect of traditional methods of manufacturing performance measurement is their emphasis on local rather than global measures of performance, and their failure to take into account the fact that optimizing the performance of the whole organization is not necessarily the same as optimizing the performance of the individual parts.

We have already seen an example of this in relation to overhead allocation. As a further example, take the issue of machine utilization which is a common local manufacturing performance measure that might be associated with the individual work centres in a factory. Machines are often expensive and their capital cost is recovered in accounting terms by assuming a fixed depreciation cost per year and distributing this cost as overhead over the individual items produced by the machine in proportion to the time taken per item. This method encourages the work centre supervisor to produce as many items as possible in a given time in order to reduce the cost per item. Work centres are encouraged to go on producing whether their output is needed or not, in order to be able to put in favourable cost variance reports at the end of the accounting period.

Maximization of output would be quite acceptable if the work centre was a bottleneck and market demand was in excess of plant capacity.

However, as we have seen in earlier chapters, output maximization for non-bottleneck work centres simply leads to a needless build-up of inventory and reduces rather than increases overall plant performance because of the unnecessary investment and storage costs associated with this inventory. Thus, in this particular situation, attempts at increasing performance based on local measures certainly do not necessarily increase global performance.

13.6 MODERN METHODS OF MEASURING MANUFACTURING PERFORMANCE

In spite of the criticisms of traditional ways of measuring manufacturing performance, there is as yet no generally accepted method of performance measurement that assesses manufacturing activities in relation to the manufacturing strategy and through this to the business strategy of the company in an entirely satisfactory way. There are nevertheless a number of approaches which have been proposed in the form of solutions to the problem, and which have been adopted to a greater or lesser extent by various sections of manufacturing industry. In the final part of this chapter, we shall examine each of these in turn from a critical perspective.

13.6.1 WORLD CLASS MANUFACTURING PERFORMANCE MEASURES

Maskell (1991) has listed the set of desirable characteristics for what he calls 'world class manufacturing performance measures'. These are listed as follows:

- they should be directly related to strategy;
- they should be primarily non-financial;
- they should vary between locations;
- they should change over time;
- they should be simple and easy to use;
- they should give fast feedback to operators and managers;
- they should foster improvement rather than just monitor.

He goes on to point out that virtually none of the traditional financial measures of performance satisfy any of these criteria.

We will briefly discuss each one of these in turn. Clearly the first point would suggest that if a company were pursuing a competitive strategy of, for example, product variety and design flexibility, the key performance measures would need to be directly related to these areas of performance rather than cost and efficiency (although the latter could of course not be totally neglected). Different measures would, in turn, become pre-eminent if, for example, the company were pursuing a quality-based competitive strategy or a delivery-based competitive strategy.

The second characteristic follows naturally from the first in that detailed shopfloor performance measures which are concerned with competitive strategies not based on being the lowest cost competitor will need to be predominantly non-financial and directly stimulate behaviour on the shop floor which is consistent with the company's strategic objectives. For example, if a company is competing on the basis of superior delivery performance, measures such as the number of orders past due, manufacturing cycle time, or the number of schedule changes per week should be used. These measures would be much more relevant to the company's strategic posture than, for example, unit production costs, attempts to minimize which might encourage long production runs of individual products, leading in turn to delayed product delivery which would be counter to strategic aims.

The third and fourth characteristics suggest that the measures themselves should be flexible and should be allowed to change both between different locations and over time, unlike traditional accounting measures which tend to be 'set in concrete' and applied universally whether they are appropriate to a particular situation or not. Clearly different strategic business units of a company could be selling into different markets requiring different competitive strategies. It should be possible to use different sets of performance measures depending on what the important factors are for that particular unit. Likewise, as a product or product group matures in its lifecycle, it should be possible to change the performance measures appropriately.

Good performance measures should be simple and easy to use, and also provide rapid feedback to those whose performance is being measured. This is rarely true of traditional financial performance measures which are often expressed in the form of complex ratios designed to measure several factors simultaneously, and are often devoid of any tangible meaning and difficult to relate to shopfloor reality. This can also of course be true of non-financial performance measures. For example, some companies measure customer service level using a composite ratio which incorporates several different aspects of customer service such as orders delivered late, orders partially shipped, customer returns, etc., which might have different weighting factors attached to them. However, not only is this difficult to relate to what is actually happening in the customer service area, it can also obscure actual changes in performance. For example, an increase in customer returns can be offset by an increase in customer deliveries, which might leave the ratio the same, even though performance has actually changed in this area. By contrast, simple measures such as the actual number of customer returns as a proportion of those shipped, the number of on-time deliveries as a proportion of orders shipped, etc., are much more directly meaningful to those people who are responsible for trying to improve their performance. If indicators are used which are easy to measure and can be displayed on boards in the factory so that trends can be seen virtually as they occur, it is much more likely that the problems that might be causing poor performance or the particular actions that are leading to good performance can be explicitly recognized and directly associated with changes in the performance measure, thus leading to the possibility of accelerating the learning curve towards behaviour patterns that are consistent with the company's strategic goals. This form of rapid feedback rarely occurs with the traditional financial performance measures which are often only available weeks or months after the events that influenced them.

Finally, good manufacturing performance measures should foster a climate of continuous improvement rather than mere conformance to an 'acceptable' set of standards of performance as do, for example, standard costing systems. Fast feedback of information on performance certainly helps in this regard and helps to focus on key improvement areas. The setting of continually improving performance goals or targets, rather than standards, is another way in which an appropriate organizational climate can be fostered.

Lists of typical performance measures that might be used to gauge performance relevant to different types of competitive posture are shown in Table 13.2. Obviously the type of performance measure on which a

Table 13.2 Performance measures for different competitive strategies

Delivery performance measures:
- Vendor delivery performance
- Production schedule adherence
- Order and schedule changes
- Customer service level
- Lost sales analysis

Flexibility performance measures:
- Number of parts and levels in BOM
- Percentage standard, common and unique parts in BOM
- Number of different processes
- Customer differentiation point
- Output/capacity ratio
- New product launches per year
- Time to market of new product
- Degree of cross training

Quality performance measures
- Incoming defectives
- Process defectives
- Finished product defectives
- Customer returns
- Percentage rework
- Percentage scrap
- Mean time between breakdowns
- BOM and routeing accuracy
- QC and test labour hours

Financial performance measures
- Waste rate
- Inventory turns
- Value-added analysis
- Cost productivity measures
- Overhead efficiencies
- Chequebook accounting
- System complexity

company places most emphasis will depend on which competitive posture it is adopting. This is not of course to suggest that the other performance measures can be neglected. The problem remains that performance measures with the 'desirable' characteristics outlined above are inevitably local in nature, and it is still necessary to find a satisfactory tradeoff between these local measures in order to maximize effectiveness on a global level. Thus whilst laying most emphasis on one set of measures that support the declared strategic aims of the company (e.g. product flexibility), acceptable values of performance must still be achieved in terms of cost, quality and delivery. One possible approach to this problem is to monitor the less critical areas (e.g. cost, quality, delivery) using only a small number of fairly aggregate parameters, whilst performing considerably more detailed monitoring of those measures that indicate performance in relation to the key strategic focus of the company (in this case product flexibility).

Another area of performance companies are starting to monitor these days relates to human and social issues and employee involvement and satisfaction. Simple indicators such as staff turnover rates, number of suggestions per employee, quality circle participation, amount of training time per employee or number of skills per person are all potential indicators of organizational climate which can give valuable information about the effectiveness of change programmes.

The problem of how to integrate local measures of the type described above into some more aggregate measure that cannot only indicate overall manufacturing effectiveness, but also facilitate effectiveness comparisons between different plants (who may themselves be competing in different ways) is a challenging and as yet unsolved problem. One advantage of the traditional measures was that performance reports are based on a well defined and consistent methodology which is likely to be generally understood by people both inside and outside the company, and can facilitate inter-plant comparisons. However, the fact that such methodology has been clearly demonstrated to be largely irrelevant to modern manufacturing's needs should not be overshadowed by the desire to retain the familiar system simply because no better system has yet emerged which has been generally accepted.

13.6.2 THE OPT APPROACH

The OPT (Optimized Production Technology) approach, which we have examined in Chapter 6, tries to address directly the difficult issue of local manufacturing performance measures often being sub-optimal with respect to overall manufacturing performance. The criterion for manufacturing performance recommended by the OPT approach is a global measure based on maximization of the ratio:

(Value of goods sold)/(Total operating costs + Total inventory costs)

through the simultaneous maximization of the numerator and minimization of the two terms in the denominator.

Rather than using individual local criteria for different work stations or cost centres, the OPT approach for maximizing this global performance measure is to follow the nine principles of OPT discussed in Chapter 6. These nine principles are incorporated into the recommended OPT method for developing schedules computed in such a way as to maximize the utilization of the bottleneck resource. OPT thus represents a rather centralized philosophy in which individual performance is assessed more in terms of the ability to operate according to the global OPT schedule rather than in terms of conventional local criteria such as cost minimization.

The OPT global measure of effectiveness is basically a form of productivity measure. However, the substitution of the value of goods sold for the value of goods produced does allow any loss of sales due to quality or delivery problems to be reflected in a declining value of the performance measure. The problem is that OPT does not help us in establishing a direct relationship between the individual terms of this global performance measure and measurable operating parameters that might impact on the firm's ability to compete on the basis of anything other than cost. It becomes very difficult to examine tradeoffs between the different ways in which global performance might be increased by, for example, focusing on improving delivery performance rather than reducing cost. Although the OPT criterion is undoubtedly a good global measure, it is much too aggregated to be of any direct use in influencing detailed operational policies on the shop floor. Guidance on operational policies in OPT comes not from performance measures applied to individual work centres, but through use of the OPT system itself. The OPT methodology provides some guidance through the recommended application of the nine OPT principles, but none of these explicitly address such issues as flexibility, quality or innovation, the emphasis being basically on schedule reliability and cost.

An additional problem with the OPT criterion is that it is not strictly speaking a measure of manufacturing performance since it can be influenced by marketing and sales policies that are not under the control of the manufacturing director. Good manufacturing performance measures should be restricted to measuring only those factors that are under manufacturing's direct control.

13.6.3 ACTIVITY-BASED COSTING

A new method of cost accounting is increasingly finding favour in manufacturing industry that overcomes some of the limitations with traditional cost accounting systems that we outlined earlier. This new method is called **activity-based costing (ABC)** or alternatively activity-based management. As its name implies, activity-based costing is concerned with the allocation of costs to products through the individual activities involved in producing the product, rather than merely through some simple proportionality factor such as direct labour hours as is done in the traditional system. Essentially ABC is a relatively sophisticated technique for overhead allocation which tries to assess in a fairer and more realistic way what proportion of different classes of overhead should be allocated to what products, thereby trying to remove as many costs as possible from the 'general overhead' category to the 'direct product cost' category.

In traditional costing systems, all costs which are not classified as materials or direct labour are lumped together as overhead and are allocated to (or absorbed by) individual products, usually according to direct labour hours used. As we have seen earlier, this can lead to the phenomenon of, for example, an obsession with the reduction of direct labour content merely because this will reduce the overhead burden allocated. In reality the total overhead burden itself still remains, and a higher proportion of it will be allocated to areas which do not reduce their direct labour content, regardless of whether a reduction in direct labour is in fact supportive of the company's competitive strategy. This can of course give a grossly distorted picture of what activities will in fact really benefit the organization as a whole and what will merely be optimal to localized areas.

In the activity-based costing approach, products (or more specifically the timely production and shipments of the right products to the right customers at the right time) are regarded as consumers of 'activities' (such as product design, negotiating with suppliers, machine set-up and maintenance, loading of pallets on trucks, etc.) which are traditionally regarded as 'overhead'. In turn each activity is regarded as a consumer of resources (such as labour, plant, machinery, consumables, etc.) which in turn incur measurable costs. This structure is shown schematically in Fig. 13.4. Activity-based costing essentially develops what might be regarded as 'bills of resources' for individual products through an assessment of how much of what types of activity are involved in the production and shipment of that product. Similar individual activities are grouped into activity centres (sometimes termed **cost 'pools'**) and key cost performance indicators (e.g. the number of batches processed on a given machine in a given time) are developed for each centre. These performance indicators are known as **cost drivers**. Individual cost drivers can be specifically related to individual products, and can serve as the link between activity and product which actually forms the basis for detailed cost allocation. Cost drivers can be monitored either to ensure they remain in a state of control (within

Products consume **activities**

Activities consume **resources**

Resources consume **costs**

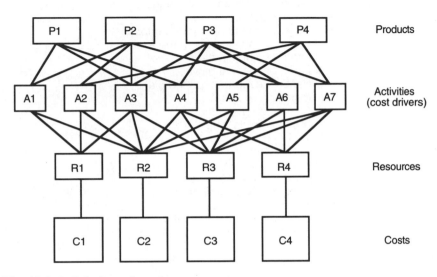

Fig. 13.4 Activity-based costing.

acceptable limits) or to check on the effectiveness of improvement pro-grammes in reducing them. Some typical manufacturing cost drivers are shown in Table 13.3.

As an example, a particular company might have a large number of engineering changes which need to be introduced, processed and con-trolled. If the costs associated with these activities can be aggregated into a single cost pool (which might be termed the 'engineering change cost pool') then the cost associated with a single engineering change can be calculated by division of the total costs accumulated per period in this pool by the total number of engineering changes per period. The number of engineering changes per period per product then serves as the 'cost driver' which is used to assign engineering change costs to individual products.

Activity-based costing provides much more meaningful information on real product costs, on the difference between value and non-value adding activities, and on issues of strategic importance to the business. It can actually form the basis of a tailor-made costing system which can serve strategic needs without the distortions of traditional costing systems.

Table 13.3 Typical ABC cost drivers

- Number of production batches
- Number of goods-received batches
- Number of purchase orders
- Number of customer orders
- Number of suppliers
- Number of engineering changes
- Number of component parts
- Number of component part numbers
- Number of unique parts in the assembly
- Number of steps in the routeing
- Number of material moves
- Distance moved through the plant
- Number of set-ups
- Total change over time
- Production cycle time
- Number of rejects
- Number of returns
- Number of line stops
- Number of cases shipped
- Weight of product shipped
- Number of trucks loaded
- Number of tools issued to the shop floor

13.6.4 BENCHMARKING

Benchmarking is an activity which is rapidly gaining popularity as a means of a company measuring its own performance in certain key activities against the performance of other companies who are acknowledged leaders in the field. Of most relevance to manufacturing management is **process benchmarking** in which companies are chosen with similar generic types of process for the purposes of comparison of performance in specific areas which are regarded as key to the success of the business. It is not necessary for the company chosen as a 'benchmarking' partner to manufacture the same products, or even to be in the same industry. For example, a small batch manufacturing company might compare certain aspects of its process performance such as process cycle times, defect rates, in-process inventories, average product lead time, mean time to develop a new product, etc., with other small batch manufacturing companies who are generally regarded as high performers in these measures, but make totally different products. Indeed, it is often more appropriate if the company whose performance is chosen to be benchmarked is not a direct competitor, as it is then more likely to reveal information that will indicate its sources of high performance. The performance of the reference company is then taken as a 'benchmark' which provides an improvement goal towards which to aim.

Some very well known companies such as Xerox and Hewlett-Packard actually make their current performance levels in certain key measures available in the public domain. Information such as this serves to define what has become known as **international best practice** and provides a clearly definable performance goal for all companies to attempt to reach. Other high performing companies must be approached with a benchmarking proposal which normally leads to the submission to the benchmarked company of a detailed questionnaire on various aspects of their activities and performance, with a follow-up visit by key personnel of the benchmarking company to obtain further, more detailed information.

Benchmarking can be very general (i.e. directed towards the most generalizable aspects of a manufacturing company's activities, and thus equally applicable to any industry), or highly specific and related to the performance of specialized processes that are quite individual to particular industries or sectors of industries. The process of benchmarking involves deciding what aspects of one's activities one wishes to compare with another company and with which company to make the comparison. Activities to be benchmarked should normally be those that are strategically important (e.g. identified as key success factors for the business). The company chosen for comparison would normally be one that had a proven record of performance in the field, but valuable information can also be obtained by performing the exercise with a company in the local vicinity, if only to get some slightly more objective picture of one's own performance in relation to others. Benchmarking can also provide a valuable way of determining how other companies in the same industry have organized their value chains to pursue their own forms of competitive advantage, and thus to identify potential opportunities for competitive advantage for one's own company.

13.6.5 SYSTEMATIC PERFORMANCE MEASUREMENT ANALYSIS

Some organizations have implemented advanced information systems which depart from the traditional cost accounting driven measures of manufacturing performance, and explicitly recognize that different levels of the organization require different types of performance information. Whatever the level, the characteristics of these information systems may be summarized as follows:

- external financial reporting requirements do not dominate the management information system;
- performance is measured using both financial and non-financial factors;
- forward vision is provided by the measurement of key drivers of performance, often non-financial factors;

- customer service requirements, industry key success factors, key elements of the business strategy and key financial factors are translated into functional requirements at all levels.

The output from the information system is primarily in the form of graphs and tables whose purpose is to act as measures to drive behaviour towards improving value to shareholders.

This approach requires a deep understanding of the business and the drivers of performance and recognizes the important place of the owners (shareholders). Information systems of this type encourage behaviour that is appropriate for the organization, its competitive position in the industry and the direction the business is taking. It allows senior managers an understanding of the important issues at lower levels and at the same time links the activities of employees and work teams to the financial performance measures. Organizations which have information systems like this find that managers have more time to actually manage, as opposed to just finding out what is going on. A further benefit is the knowledge that individuals and teams are focused on factors and results which impact on all important areas of performance, not simply those which may be measured by the traditional accounting system.

13.7 CONCLUSION

Manufacturing performance monitoring of some form is essential for any orderly progression of a manufacturing company in the direction of its chosen goals, in that it provides feedback for corrective action, and motivates behaviour which is consistent with goals. Unfortunately, traditional methods of measuring manufacturing performance, based primarily on cost, often fall far short of adequately achieving these purposes. New methods of manufacturing performance are starting to be introduced which overcome these limitations, but most of these are still in their infancy. Considerably more research needs to be done in this area before we are likely to see any generally accepted standards of manufacturing performance measurement.

REFERENCE

Maskell, B.H. (1991) *Performance Measures for World Class Manufacturing*. Productivity Press, Cambridge, Mass.

FURTHER READING

Foster, G. and Horngren, C.T. (1987) JIT: cost accounting and cost management issues. *Management Accounting*, June, pp. 19–25.

Richardson, P.R. and Gordon, R.M. (1980) Measuring total manufacturing performance. *Sloan Management Review*, Winter, pp. 47–58.

Index